QA 76.73 .V77 K38 1989

Kavanagh, Paul.

VS COBOL II for
COBOL programmers

$39.95

DATE			

VS COBOL II for COBOL Programmers

VS COBOL II for COBOL Programmers

Paul Kavanagh

Intertext Publications
McGraw-Hill Book Company

New York St. Louis San Francisco Auckland Bogotá
Hamburg London Madrid Mexico Milan Montreal
New Delhi Panama Paris São Paulo
Singapore Sidney Tokyo Toronto

Library of Congress Catalog Card Number 89-83756

10 9 8 7 6 5 4 3 2 1

ISBN 0-07-033571-0

Intertext Publications/Multiscience Press, Inc.
One Lincoln Plaza
New York, NY 10023

McGraw-Hill Book Company
1221 Avenue of the Americas
New York, NY 10020

Composed by Context, Inc.

This book is dedicated to all the people who have helped to make me a better programmer by their example or by the opportunities they gave me:

Jim Belcher
Ray Boguslavski
Jerry Cohen
Sheldon Dansiger
John Delaney
Carl Holz
Mark Kaplinsky
Brian Lennon
Pauli Overdorff
Terry Taylor,

. . . to the people who have helped me and encouraged me in this effort, and reviewed the book:

Jim Foley
Sheila Neale
Felix Rubinchik
Natalia Trifonov,

. . . to editor Jay Ranade, and Alan Rose at Intertext Publications, and to the authors of really great books on programming, particularly Brian Kernighan.

. . . to my brothers, Matt and John, and my parents, John and Dinah Kavanagh.

. . . and most of all, to Karen and Danny Kavanagh for their support and for all the time I spent working instead of with them.

The book was written on my home computers, a 10MHz 80286 Everex with a Canon Laser printer and a Toshiba 1000 laptop, using MKS VI and WordPerfect 5.0 for word processing, Lotus Freelance Plus for graphics. Programs were developed on the micros using Microsoft COBOL 3.0 (developed by Micro Focus) and tested with VS COBOL 1.1 and 2.0 under MVS on an IBM 3090 Model 400.

Contents

Preface

This book is intended for programmers, designers, analysts, and their managers in IBM COBOL installations. It assumes a working knowledge of COBOL, and makes no attempt to teach basic programming concepts. VS COBOL II is IBM's strategic COBOL. It is a key language in their two important system families, SAA and AIX. If you are working in COBOL in an IBM environment, you will need to know all the features covered in this book.

The Style and Structure Of This Book

The style of this book has deliberately been kept simple. I know well that in our business there are always new developments to learn and great demands on our time. I have worked to make this book easy and pleasant to read. For the most part, rules and advice are illustrated with real-life examples.

The book has been structured in such a way that it may be used as a self-teaching guide. Chapters and sections are structured so that the book can be picked up and put down at frequent intervals. You can also use it as a textbook for a seminar on the subject. I have done this several times.

Why This Book Is Complete

This book specifically discusses IBM VS COBOL II, not the 1985 ANSI standard, which is different. It includes all the changes from OS/VS COBOL to the current VS COBOL II, including Release 3. It is important that Release 3, which complies with SAA and ANSI 1985, is included. It includes many examples, including CICS, VSAM, and internal sort programs. Complete reference materials are given in the Appendices.

What Is Included

The first chapter gives a brief history of COBOL, an overview of the changes introduced with VS COBOL, and reasons for them. Chapters 2 through 4 cover changes in the COBOL programming language to support structured programming. Chapters 5 through 9 cover the other changes in program coding, including pointers and international language support. Chapters 10 through 13 are on the environmental interfaces, such as CICS and MVS/XA. Chapters 14 through 16 are on debugging, which is greatly improved. Chapters 17 through 19 are on compiler-directing statements, performance issues, and conversion from OS/VS COBOL respectively. The final chapter covers the changes introduced in Release 3.

Operating System Environment

MVS, VM, and DOS/VSE are the only operating systems supported by the VS COBOL II compiler. This book applies to all three, although Chapter 13 is specific to MVS, and there is some bias toward MVS in Chapters 10 and 12. If you are working in OS/2, OS/400, or AIX, this book may still be useful. Your COBOL language is essentially the same, although environmental features such as debugging and VSAM file support will be different.

There have been four versions of this compiler; 1.0, 1.1, 2.0, and 3.0. This book details the differences between versions. The bulk of the examples in the book, other than the final chapter, are chosen to compile and run under any release of the compiler.

Summary

VS COBOL II contains many changes from OS/VS COBOL. To take advantage of the structured programming improvements, you must stand back and rethink the approach to program structure. This book tries to provide enough examples to allow this. Other changes will cause problems in converting older programs. Examples are given for these issues, too. After reading this book you will know all the new and changed features of VS COBOL II, and how to use them effectively.

— Paul Kavanagh

1

Introduction to VS COBOL II

VS COBOL II is the new IBM version of the COBOL language. With the introduction of Release 3, VS COBOL II meets the industry-standard ANSI 1985 specification and conforms to SAA, the IBM blueprint for the future of software. Over the next few years, all IBM COBOL programmers will be converting to this product. In this chapter I discuss the reasons for its introduction, the changes made since its first release, and its relationship to other versions of COBOL. The major new features are briefly introduced here to be discussed in detail later.

1.1   WHY VS COBOL II?

The COBOL language has been a survivor in a rapidly changing industry. At the time of its introduction in 1959, only a few thousand computers were in use, mostly in governments or universities. Since then, several generations of hardware have come and gone. Transistors, integrated circuits, and large-scale integration have been introduced. User input has changed from the batching of punched cards and collection of boxes of line printer output to immediate interaction using color graphics terminals and laser printers. There are now many millions of computers, mostly on desktops and nearly all more powerful than any that existed when the language was invented.

1.1.1 Replacements for COBOL

COBOL is one of the oldest computer languages: Of those still in use, only FORTRAN and LISP are older. A great number of new programming languages have been introduced in the last 30 years. Many have been specialist languages, aimed at niches that do not compete with COBOL, for instance, languages for scientific, statistical, simulation, or embedded systems programming. Others have been designed as languages for business functions or as general-purpose programming tools, and their proponents have billed them as improvements on and replacements for COBOL in all or some of its uses. RPG II/III is an example of a business language, and PL/I of a general-purpose language, which have failed to supplant COBOL. There has been speculation that "fourth-generation" languages will replace COBOL in many situations, and most recently microcomputer-based spreadsheet and database languages have proliferated.

However, up to 80% of the world's code inventory is in COBOL, and it is still the language used by most professional programmers. This alone would be sufficient to maintain the language's importance into the next century even if COBOL development were to cease tomorrow. In reality, however, it remains the language of choice for substantial business programming jobs. Many of the replacements have proved unsuitable for large projects. Others have had insufficient advantage to justify overturning the existing standard.

1.1.2 Upgrades to Languages

All working languages are updated periodically. FORTRAN, for instance, underwent a major revision with the 1977 standard, and ALGOL in 1968. LISP has evolved continuously since its introduction. C is acquiring an ANSI standard and is possibly evolving into an enhanced language, C++. Pascal has metamorphosed into Modula-2.

1.2 THE ANSI 1985 STANDARD

COBOL has remained very stable in the 30 years since its introduction. The X3.23 committee of the American National Standards Institute updates the language standard periodically. This body introduced new standards in 1968 and 1974, which caused very little disturbance. The latest revision is ANSI X3.23-1985, introduced in 1985. This has introduced greater changes in the language syntax than the previous updates, but considerable pains were taken to preserve compatibility with programs written to previous standards. The changes do allow COBOL to incorporate ideas on structured programming which have been developed since its introduction.

The 1985 standard took a long time to complete. There had been earlier attempts to agree on a 1980 standard, which led nowhere. It is a very difficult job to reach agreement among all the vendors and users of COBOL, when any change can have very expensive consequences.

IBM has always tracked the ANSI standard for marketing reasons, although IBM COBOL also contains significant extensions to the standard. The government and many major clients require compliance with the standard. The IBM OS/VS COBOL compiler (the COBOL compiler available before VS COBOL II) was based on the 1974 ANSI standard, as the earlier IBM ANS COBOL product had been based on the 1968 ANSI standard. The changes made for the 1985 standard are also substantial improvements. All things considered, there was clearly a need for IBM to develop a new compiler based on the 1985 standard.

1.3 IBM DIRECTIONS AND SAA

Since the initial launch of the VS COBOL II compiler, IBM has announced Systems Application Architecture (SAA). This set of specifications is intended to tie together several separate lines of development and create a platform for the development of applications which can run across all IBM's major product lines. SAA is still at an early stage in its life cycle. Application development products have been announced, mostly for the AS/400 and PS/2, but the applications that build on this, beginning with Office Vision, are still to come. At present, SAA serves as a guideline for software developers and other users of IBM computers. Third-party products which conform to SAA are beginning to be announced. Software products which support SAA have a considerably more secure future than those which have been omitted.

For a product such as a programming language to be included in SAA, it must be supported on all of IBM's SAA environments, that is, MVS and VM on the System/370, OS/400 on the AS/400, and OS/2 on the PS/2. The three traditional programming languages supported

in the initial announcements and documented in the initial literature
were:

FORTRAN (ANSI 1977)
C (ANSI Standard)
COBOL (ANSI 1985)

Since the first announcements, IBM has added RPG III to the architecture, and it has since suggested that PL/I will be included also,
but in a limited sense. Not all of the supported languages are available now in all environments. C is only available as a fully supported
IBM product for OS/2, for instance. COBOL is available on all three
platforms.

IBM COBOL compilers supported under SAA are:

System/370 MVS and VM	VS COBOL II
AS/400	AS/400 COBOL
OS/2	IBM COBOL/2

Any installation that is a user of IBM COBOL will want to be
aware of the SAA specifications when making strategic decisions.
There are clear advantages to the ability to develop applications
which can be ported to different kinds of hardware, with very different prices and performance. For example, development on microcomputers is usually much more productive. Delivery of applications in a
distributed environment offers advantages in responsiveness and
cost. Many users need to port systems because of growth or downsiz-
ing.

1.4 ARCHITECTURAL LIMITS

In the early 1980s, IBM introduced MVS/XA, which was the Extended Architecture version of MVS. This was a very important enhancement to IBM's flagship operating system. It was named after
the biggest single improvement it delivered, which was an extension
of addressability beyond the limit of previous versions of OS/VS.

Before the introduction of MVS/XA, there were two architectural
limits that proved to be serious problems to large mainframe users.
These were the limits on real storage per processor and on virtual
storage per task. MVS/370, the previous version of the operating
system, restricted IBM mainframe computers to the use of 16

megabytes of memory. The programs that ran on them were similarly restricted to 16 megabytes of virtual memory.

1.4.1 Real Storage

There is a limit on the total real storage available to the machine of 16 megabytes (later increased to 32 megabytes) under MVS/370. A processor can only address this limited amount of memory. The result of this is to constrain the amount of virtual storage a system can have without excessive paging, since applications access all the virtual storage through the same real storage "window." This limit is immediately lifted with the installation of MVS/XA.

1.4.2 Virtual Storage

There is a limit on virtual storage in a single address space to 16 megabytes. This is most often a problem in CICS shops. Most batch, TSO, or IMS/DC programs were able to run satisfactorily within a 16 Mb address space. However, all the programs in one CICS region run in that single address space. They must all fit in with the operating system and CICS code, leaving a space of about 5 or 6 megabytes for all the application programs and work areas. This problem, which is known as Virtual Storage Constraint, has been a fact of life for CICS shops for some time.

With the introduction of MVS/XA, IBM introduced 31-bit addressing, allowing programs to reach up to two billion bytes of storage. Initially, only programs written in Assembly language could take advantage of the new architecture. CICS is written in assembly language, and over time IBM has rewritten parts of the CICS code to move them above the line. Still, the bulk of most installation's applications are in high-level languages such as COBOL and PL/I, and the existing IBM higher-level language compilers continued to be constrained by the 24-bit addressing limit to stay within 16 megabytes. This meant there was pressure from COBOL and PL/I users for a rewrite of the IBM compilers to support the new extended architecture as soon as possible. The COBOL compiler that has this support is VS COBOL II. Any shop which plans to take advantage of extended addressing in its COBOL programs will have to convert to COBOL II, and this has been the most common reason for making the transition up to now.

1.5   THE INTRODUCTION OF VS COBOL II

The convergence of the trends described above (MVS/XA, the ANSI 1985 standard, and SAA) led to the announcement of the IBM product VS COBOL II. This was originally introduced as an ANSI 1974 compiler with extensions, because the compiler predated the completion of the 1985 standard. IBM added as many features from the incomplete standard as they could at the time.

IBM needed the new compiler because of features like the XA support, which was critical to some large customers, and the CICS enhancements. There is some reason to think that IBM rushed the initial release. The first versions of the product (1.0, 1.1) were missing some features essential to many users, such as exponentiation and floating-point arithmetic, and some that were desired for backward compatibility, such as TALLY. Release 2.0 includes all these, but still does not have all the ANSI features. With the introduction of Release 3.0 at the end of 1988, VS COBOL II fully conforms to the ANSI 85 standard. Among the ANSI 85 enhancements now included are nested programs, reference modifications, and seven-dimensional tables. This book explains the features of all releases, including Release 3.0. New features in Release 3.0 are specifically discussed in Chapter 20.

VS COBOL II has been available to major users for years now and is a mature product which has proven to be reliable and fast. IBM states that OS COBOL has been functionally stabilized. This means that they plan no major enhancements to the OS/VS compiler. Over the next few years, VS COBOL II will become the standard COBOL at all IBM sites.

1.6   MAJOR DIFFERENCES

In the rest of this book, the language accepted by the IBM VS COBOL II compiler product will be referred to as COBOL II and the language accepted by the OS/VS COBOL compiler will be referred to as OS COBOL.

The major differences introduced with COBOL II are:

- new programming features, such as structured programming and pointers
- support for MVS/XA and MVS/ESA
- enhancements to subsystem interfaces, such as CICS, VSAM, and SORT

- changes to methods of program debugging
- removal of obsolete and nonstandard features

The rest of this chapter summarizes these differences, which are then explained in detail in the rest of the book.

1.6.1 Structured Programming

COBOL II has been extended to support the generally recognized structured program control structures. These structures are discussed in Chapters 2 through 4. Use of these structures makes COBOL II programs look rather different from older COBOL, and more like other popular languages such as PL/I, C, and Pascal. Once learned, they make for more logical and maintainable code.

The addition of explicit scope terminators (such as END-IF) to COBOL allows the natural expression of programs with nested statements. This makes them easier to maintain and more readable. In addition, these terminators remove the need for periods except on the last line of a paragraph. Missing or extraneous periods can produce bugs which are hard to find on a listing.

The PERFORM statement can now be coded in-line; this change alone has a big change on the structure of programs. It is no longer necessary to break up a program into arbitrary paragraphs to express loops. Instead, the paragraph structure can be chosen to reflect the natural structure of the problem.

The EVALUATE statement gives the language a case structure like the PL/I SELECT and C SWITCH.

Listings 1-1 and 1-2 show examples of the same program written in OS COBOL and COBOL II.

1.6.2 Comparison of COBOL II to Other Languages

Listing 1-3 shows a simplified skeleton control structure of the program of Listing 1-1 written in COBOL II, PL/I, and C. It is noticeable that, whereas each language has its own keywords, the programs now have very similar structures. The same structured programming principles underly them all. For example, it would be feasible to copy algorithms line-for-line from other languages, which is particularly convenient since books on algorithms are not generally written in COBOL.

```
000100 IDENTIFICATION DIVISION.
000200 PROGRAM-ID.    MONEY.
000300*** MONEY PROCESSING ***
000400*      EDIT SCREEN INPUT IN THE FORM BBBDDDDDD.CCBBBB
000500*      (DOLLAR/CENT/BLANK) TO INTERNAL DECIMAL.
000500*      EXAMPLES: 1500.00    1500    25.1     25000.50
000600*      THIS WILL TRUNCATE NUMBERS > 999999.
000700*      AN EMBEDDED SPACE IS TREATED AS A DECIMAL POINT
000700*      IF THAT HASNT ALREADY OCCURRED, ELSE AS ZERO.
000800*      EXAMPLES: 25 90   ---> 25.90   25. 4  ---> 25.04
000900 ENVIRONMENT DIVISION.
001000
001100 DATA DIVISION.
001200 WORKING-STORAGE SECTION.
001300 01  DEC  PIC 99 COMP-0.
001400 01  LOSE PIC 99 COMP-0.
001500 01  W-MONEY.
001600     02  DL PIC X OCCURS 6  INDEXED BY DL-IX.
001700     02  CT PIC X OCCURS 2  INDEXED BY CT-IX.
001800 01  W-MONEY-9 REDEFINES W-MONEY PIC 9(6)V99.
001900 01  DEC-FOUND-SW    PIC X.
002000     88 DEC-FOUND          VALUE '1'.
002100     88 DEC-NOT-FOUND      VALUE '0'.
002200 LINKAGE SECTION.
002300 01  LS-MONEY-IN.
002400     02  INPUT-FIELD PIC X OCCURS 10 INDEXED BY IP-IX.
002500 01  LS-MONEY-OUT      PIC 9(6)V99 COMP-3.
002600 01  LS-RETURN         PIC X(02).
002700
002800 PROCEDURE DIVISION USING LS-MONEY-IN,
002900                          LS-MONEY-OUT,
003000                          LS-RETURN.
003100
003200 P000-MAIN.
003300* -- '00' REPRESENTS SUCCESSFUL COMPLETION
003400     MOVE '00' TO LS-RETURN
003500
003600     SET DL-IX TO 6
003700     SET CT-IX TO 1
003800     MOVE ZEROES TO W-MONEY
003900     SET DEC-NOT-FOUND TO TRUE
004000     INSPECT LS-MONEY-IN REPLACING LEADING SPACES BY ZEROES
004100*
004200* -- EXAMINE THE INPUT FIELD LOOKING FOR:
004300* -- NO MORE THAN ONE DECIMAL POINT (ERROR 10)
004300* -- SPACES ARE TREATED AS ZEROES
004500* -- OTHER NON-NUMERIC CHARACTER IS AN ERROR (30)
004600* -- FRACTIONAL DIGITS ARE MAPPED TO THE OUTPUT AREA.
004700*
```

Listing 1-1 Money Program in VS COBOL II. (Continued)

```
004800        PERFORM VARYING IP-IX FROM 1 BY 1
004900        UNTIL IP-IX > 10 OR LS-RETURN NOT = '00'
005000           EVALUATE TRUE
005100           WHEN INPUT-FIELD(IP-IX) = '.'
005200             IF DEC-FOUND
005300                 MOVE '10' TO LS-RETURN
005400             ELSE
005500                 SET DEC-FOUND TO TRUE
005600                 SET DEC TO IP-IX
005700             END-IF
005800           WHEN INPUT-FIELD(IP-IX) = SPACE
005900           WHEN INPUT-FIELD(IP-IX) = LOW-VALUES
006000             IF DEC-FOUND

006100                 MOVE '0' TO INPUT-FIELD (IP-IX)
006200             ELSE
006300                 SET DEC-FOUND TO TRUE
006400                 MOVE '.' TO INPUT-FIELD (IP-IX)
006500                 SET DEC TO IP-IX
006600             END-IF
006700           WHEN INPUT-FIELD (IP-IX) NUMERIC
006800            AND DEC-FOUND
006900            AND CT-IX NOT > 2
007000                 MOVE INPUT-FIELD (IP-IX) TO CT (CT-IX)
007100                 SET CT-IX UP BY 1
007200           WHEN INPUT-FIELD (IP-IX) NOT NUMERIC
007300                 MOVE '30' TO LS-RETURN
007400           END-EVALUATE
007500        END-PERFORM
007600*
007700* -- IF PREVIOUS ROUTINE SUCCEEDED
007800* --    MOVE THE DOLLAR DIGITS TO OUTPUT AREA.
007900 MOVE-DOLLARS.
008000        IF LS-RETURN = '00'
008100           COMPUTE LOSE = DEC - 1
008200           PERFORM VARYING IP-IX FROM LOSE BY -1
008300           UNTIL DL-IX < 1
008400             IF IP-IX > 0
008500                 MOVE INPUT-FIELD (IP-IX) TO DL (DL-IX)
008600             ELSE
008700                 MOVE ZERO TO DL (DL-IX)
008800             END-IF
008900             SET DL-IX DOWN BY 1
```

Listing 1-1   Money Program in VS COBOL II. (Continued)

```
009000        END-PERFORM
009100        MOVE W-MONEY-9 TO LS-MONEY-OUT
009200        END-IF
009300
009400        GOBACK.
```

Listing 1-1   Money Program in VS COBOL II.

1.6.3   Further Enhancements

A new IBM extension allows COBOL II programs to manipulate pointers and addresses explicitly, so that data structures such as linked lists can be constructed and passed around between programs. Another extension lets programs access a special register containing the length of data items. Both of these features make it easier to code CICS programs, in particular, because in CICS programs, lengths and addresses are regularly passed between programs and the CICS routines. There are other improvements for CICS programmers, such as the lifting of restrictions on the use of statements like STRING and INSPECT in CICS programs.

COBOL II supports extended graphic character sets. The language can now handle characters such as Japanese Kanji in strings and comparisons. In fact, whole programs can be written in Asian languages except for the COBOL reserved words.

The CALL statement has a new option, BY CONTENT, which protects the contents of the variable in the calling program by passing a copy. This makes it possible to code literals in the CALL statement instead of in working storage, which can make some programs, particularly DL/I, easier to read.

The interfaces with other strategic IBM products have been improved. An extended VSAM return code is now available, which gives an additional 6 bytes of information. An improved sort program interface is introduced, with a performance option for simple cases.

1.6.4   Debugging Enhancements

Debugging has changed considerably with the new product. Many programmers will be surprised at the disappearance of familiar features like READY TRACE, EXHIBIT, and the FLOW compiler option. In their place, IBM has bundled with the compiler a symbolic

```
IDENTIFICATION DIVISION.
PROGRAM-ID.     OLDMONEY.
ENVIRONMENT DIVISION.


DATA DIVISION.
WORKING-STORAGE SECTION.
01  W-TRUE  PIC X VALUE '1'.
01  W-FALSE PIC X VALUE ZERO.
01  DEC     PIC 99 COMP-0.
01  LOSE    PIC 99 COMP-0.
01  W-MONEY.
    02  DL PIC X OCCURS 6  INDEXED BY DL-IX.
    02  CT PIC X OCCURS 2  INDEXED BY CT-IX.
01  W-MONEY-9 REDEFINES W-MONEY PIC 9(6)V99.
01  DEC-FOUND PIC X.
LINKAGE SECTION.
01  LS-MONEY-IN.
    02  INPUT-FIELD PIC X OCCURS 10 INDEXED BY IP-IX.
01  LS-MONEY-OUT    PIC 9(6)V99 COMP-3.
01  LS-RETURN       PIC X(02).


PROCEDURE DIVISION USING LS-MONEY-IN,
                        LS-MONEY-OUT,
                        LS-RETURN.


P000-MAIN.
    MOVE '00' TO LS-RETURN.

    SET DL-IX TO 6.
    SET CT-IX TO 1.
    MOVE ZEROES TO W-MONEY.
    MOVE W-FALSE TO DEC-FOUND.
    INSPECT LS-MONEY-IN
    REPLACING LEADING SPACES BY ZEROES.

    PERFORM ME-SCAN-IN
    VARYING IP-IX FROM 1 BY 1
        UNTIL IP-IX > 10
        OR LS-RETURN NOT = '00'.

    IF LS-RETURN = '00'
        COMPUTE LOSE = DEC - 1
        PERFORM ME-GET-DOLLARS
        VARYING IP-IX FROM LOSE BY -1
            UNTIL DL-IX < 1
        MOVE W-MONEY-9 TO LS-MONEY-OUT.

    EXIT PROGRAM.
```

Listing 1-2   Money Program in OS/VS COBOL. (Continued)

```
ME-SCAN-IN.
    IF  INPUT-FIELD (IP-IX) = '.'
        IF  DEC-FOUND = W-TRUE
            MOVE '10' TO LS-RETURN
        ELSE
            MOVE W-TRUE TO DEC-FOUND
            SET DEC TO IP-IX
    ELSE
    IF  INPUT-FIELD (IP-IX) = SPACE OR LOW-VALUES
        IF  DEC-FOUND = W-TRUE
            MOVE '0' TO INPUT-FIELD (IP-IX)
        ELSE
            MOVE W-TRUE TO DEC-FOUND

            MOVE '.' TO INPUT-FIELD (IP-IX)
            SET DEC TO IP-IX
    ELSE
    IF  INPUT-FIELD (IP-IX) NUMERIC
    AND DEC-FOUND = W-TRUE
    AND CT-IX NOT > 2
        MOVE INPUT-FIELD (IP-IX) TO CT (CT-IX)
        SET CT-IX UP BY 1
    ELSE
    IF  INPUT-FIELD (IP-IX) NOT NUMERIC
        MOVE '30' TO LS-RETURN.


ME-GET-DOLLARS.
    IF IP-IX > 0
        MOVE INPUT-FIELD (IP-IX) TO DL (DL-IX)
    ELSE
        MOVE ZERO TO DL (DL-IX).


    SET DL-IX DOWN BY 1.
```

Listing 1-2   Money Program in OS/VS COBOL.

debugger called COBTEST. If you have used the previous product
TESTCOB before, this will be familiar to you; but it has now been
extended to support split-screen operation under ISPF, and to run in
a batch mode under CICS. Using COBTEST with ISPF, a programmer can set breakpoints and view the execution of code in one window while viewing source code in another.

Listing 1-4 shows a short example of an interaction with the debugger to test the program in Listing 1-1. This example, which is

```
COBOL:
        ...
        PERFORM VARYING ... UNTIL ...
            EVALUATE ...
            WHEN ...
                IF ...
                ............
                ELSE
                ............
                END-IF
            WHEN ...
            WHEN ...
            ...
                    END-EVALUATE
        END-PERFORM

        IF ...
            PERFORM VARYING ... UNTIL ...
                IF ...
                ...
                END-IF
            ...
            END-PERFORM
            ...
        END-IF
```

```
C:
    ...
    for (...; ...; ...) {
        switch ... {
        case ...:
            if (...) {
                ...
            }
            else {
                ...
            }
        case ...:
        case ...:
            ...
        }
    }

    if (...) {
        for (...; ...; ...) {
            if (...) {
                ...
            }
```

Listing 1-3   Money Program Skeleton In Three Structured Languages.
(Continued)

```
         ...
      }
         ...
   }

PL/I:
      ...
   DO ... WHILE (...);
      SELECT ...
      WHEN ...:
         IF ... THEN DO
            ............
         END
         ELSE DO

            ............
         END
      WHEN ...:
      WHEN ...:
         ...
            END
   END

   IF ... THEN DO
      DO ... WHILE (...);
         IF ... THEN DO
            ............
         END
         ...
      END
      ...
   END
```

Listing 1-3   Money Program Skeleton In Three Structured Languages.

kept very simple, shows the programmer initiating the debugger on
the program. The program stops at the first executable statement
(3300) and issues the COBTEST prompt. The programmer can enter
breakpoints, examine variables, and control execution at this prompt.
In this case, she requests a trace and a breakpoint at 9100 and restarts the program. When the program reaches the breakpoint, it
stops and issues the COBTEST prompt again. She lists the value of
the field W-MONEY, then issues RUN to let the program run to
completion and QUIT to exit the debugger.

Debugger Output	*Programmer Input*
	cobtest money
MONEY.003300.1	
COBTEST	trace name
COBTEST	at 9100
COBTEST	go
TRACING	
007900 MOVE-DOLLARS	
AT 9100.1	
COBTEST	list w-money
001500 01 W-MONEY AN	
000450 00	
COBTEST	run
PROGRAM UNDER COBTEST ENDED NORMALLY	quit

Listing 1-4   Example of COBTEST Dialog.

Unlike its predecessor, the COBTEST debugger comes with the compiler and works in all supported environments. Since it can hence be assumed to be available to all COBOL II programmers, IBM was able to remove the debugging code, such as TRACE, FLOW, and EXHIBIT from the COBOL II compiler.

For situations where an interactive debugger is not appropriate, such as the debugging of production problems, a new formatted dump is provided. This lists all the variables in the program with their values. Listing 1-5 shows an example of the way a small record looks in a formatted dump.

1.6.5   Missing Features

IBM has also taken advantage of the opportunity given while rewriting the compiler to drop support for some features that they no longer wish to support for various reasons, for instance those which:

```
Source Code:


001240 01  W-RECORD.
001250 01  FILLER REDEFINES W-RECORD.
001260     02  WR-CHAR          PIC X(06).
001270     02  WR-NUM           PIC 9(4)V99.
001280     02  WR-PACKED        PIC S9(5) COMP-3.


Dump Format:


001240 01  RECORD-1            AN
                    BEAMON4032.00


001250 01  FILLER              AN-GR


001260 02  WR-CHAR             AN              BEAMON


001270 02  WR-NUM              ND              4032.00


001280 02  WR-PACKED           NP-S                +5
```

Figure 1-5   Example of Data Display in a Formatted Dump.

- support obsolete products, such as ISAM and BDAM (which have been replaced by VSAM)
- are not in the ANSI standard, such as the IBM extensions TRANS-FORM and POSITIONING
- are optional in the ANSI standard, such as Report Writer and Communications

These features of OS COBOL which have been dropped will give programmers converting existing code most of their headaches. Very few people used the Communications module and POSITIONING is easily replaced by ADVANCING, but other features are not so easy to forget. The TRANSFORM verb is both commonly used and non-trivial to replace, for instance. In CICS programs, all BLL cell references must be replaced. Several migration aids are available from IBM, and conversion is easy for most programs, but a sizable minority of programs need manual translation.

Early versions of the VS COBOL II compiler (Releases 1.0 and 1.1) were missing several important features, such as floating-point data types (COMP-1, COMP-2), exponentiation (**), TALLY, and the sort special registers, but these were restored in Release 2.

Possibly other features, such as the report writer, will also return in time, either to meet the ANSI 1985 standard or in response to user pressure.

1.6.6 Changes to Storage Constraints

The limits imposed by the compiler are expanded greatly in COBOL II. These limits are covered in Chapter 13, but examples are that the size of the data division is increased from one to 128 megabytes. The maximum size of an elementary item goes from 32K bytes to 16 megabytes.

1.6.7 Reentrant Code

Under MVS, OS COBOL allowed library routines to be shared; that is, two programs could execute the routine at the same time. Under OS COBOL, application programs themselves were not shared except when in a single region under CICS. With COBOL II, programs can be shared. If you compile a program as reentrant, it can be placed in the MVS Link Pack Area or Extended Link Pack Area. Then all requests for the program, even if they are from different CICS regions or batch jobs, will execute from the same copy of code. This gives a saving in memory use, because there are no replicated copies of programs in memory and in loads from program libraries.

1.7 FUTURE ENHANCEMENTS EXPECTED

With Release 3.0, the IBM VS COBOL II product has converged with the ANSI 1985 standard and with IBM SAA COBOL. The language is now consistent and stable across a range of different computer platforms available from IBM and other vendors.

Over its 30-year history, the future of COBOL has periodically appeared clouded by the possibility of improved languages, but it has survived stronger than ever. The threats posed to its predominance in the business community by the introduction of PL/I and RPG have faded, and the fourth-generation languages, some of which are gray-haired themselves now, have yet to establish themselves outside specialized niches. Indeed, as the industry looks more and more to embrace standards, the proprietary fourth-generation solutions may be less likely to succeed. COBOL was and is the original industry standard. Code generators and CASE tools are increasing in popularity. Such tools generally output code in the standard languages COBOL and C, so that it can be targeted to a wide range of hardware. The structured improvements to COBOL make it much more suitable for generation from and interaction with design tools, whether automated or manual.

In the longer run, we can expect to see more of the useful features of other programming languages come over to COBOL. Chapter 20 summarizes the changes that were introduced to give full compliance with the ANSI standard. All of the following features are being incorporated by the ANSI committee into the next standard (for the early 1990s):

- 60-character data and procedure names
- bit fields
- intrinsic functions
- user-defined functions
- comments on the same line as code (introduced by *>)
- free-form source code (no Area A and B)

The function capability will allow COBOL programmers to access libraries of functions as in PL/I and C, for instance for mathematics, string handling, statistics, and graphics. There is no reason that the language, fortified by suitable upgrades such as these, should not continue for another 30 years.

2

Scope Terminators

COBOL II introduces the idea of scope terminators on conditional statements. A scope terminator is a word which defines the end of an IF or other conditional statement. This chapter covers the use of all these, starting with the new END-IF option on the IF statement. With OS COBOL, there were several logical problems dealing with periods in nested IFs; the use of scope terminators tidies these up. The overall effect of scope terminators is to make programs more consistent, so that they are easier to read and maintain.

2.1 CONDITIONAL STATEMENTS

2.1.1 Definition of a Conditional Statement

A conditional statement contains a condition whose truth value will be determined at the time of execution, a series of statements that are executed when the condition is true, and optionally a series of statements that are executed when it is false. The condition can be simple or arbitrarily complex.

IF is a conditional statement, of course. SEARCH, EVALUATE (a new statement in COBOL II which is covered in Chapter 3), and PERFORM (whose enhancements are covered in Chapter 4) are also

Table 2-1   COBOL Verbs with Conditional Features.

```
Control Statements
  EVALUATE  ...    WHEN
  IF        ...    THEN, ELSE
  PERFORM   ...    UNTIL, TIMES
  SEARCH    ...    AT END, WHEN
```

Arithmetic Statements	Optional Conditional Clauses
ADD ...	ON SIZE ERROR
COMPUTE ...	ON SIZE ERROR
DIVIDE ...	ON SIZE ERROR
MULTIPLY ...	ON SIZE ERROR
SUBTRACT ...	ON SIZE ERROR

I/O Statements	Optional Conditional Clauses
DELETE ...	INVALID KEY
READ ...	AT END, INVALID KEY
RETURN ...	AT END
REWRITE ...	INVALID KEY
START ...	INVALID KEY
WRITE ...	INVALID KEY, END-OF-PAGE

Miscellaneous Statements	Optional Conditional Clauses
CALL ...	ON OVERFLOW
STRING ...	ON OVERFLOW
UNSTRING ...	ON OVERFLOW

conditional statements. There are many other COBOL verbs which contain conditional features in some circumstances. For example, the READ statement can contain the conditional clause AT END. Table 2-1 lists all the COBOL verbs that may be conditional.

2.1.2   The Scope of a Statement

The scope of a conditional statement is the range of executable statements over which it extends. In OS COBOL, the scope of an IF extends over all the following statements until the next period or the matching ELSE statement. The scope of an ELSE extends to the next period. Listing 2-1 illustrates scope in OS COBOL.

```
PROCEDURE DIVISION.

    IF EXPOSURE-LEVEL > EXP-LIMIT
        SET STOP-PURCHASE TO TRUE
        PERFORM RAISE-ALARM
        PERFORM PRIORITIZE-SELLS.

    IF EXPOSURE-LEVEL > EXP-LIMIT
        SET STOP-PURCHASE TO TRUE
        PERFORM RAISE-ALARM
        PERFORM PRIORITIZE-SELLS
    ELSE
        SET OK-PURCHASE TO TRUE
        PERFORM FINALIZE-TRADE.
```

Listing 2-1   Scope of OS COBOL IF Statements.

2.1.3   Scope Termination in OS COBOL

A scope terminator is a language element which ends the scope of a conditional statement. In OS COBOL, the scope terminators are the period (.) and ELSE.

2.1.4   Scope Termination in Other Languages

The use of the period to terminate scope is an idea unique to COBOL among popular high-level languages. It is not without problems. It is generally the custom in other programming languages (including PL/I, C, Pascal, ALGOL, MODULA-2, and ADA) to implicitly end the scope of a conditional statement such as an IF or the equivalent of a PERFORM after one executable statement. They use block begin/end markers—DO,END for PL/I and {,} for PL/I and C, for instance—to put multiple statements under the scope of a condition.

Listing 2-2 shows the use of these block markers in two other programming languages to code a problem which is awkward to handle in OS COBOL. The problem is expressed first in pseudo-code.

```
Description:
        If something must be displayed on the screen,
                determine whether to display message 1 or
        message 2 (which is in two parts)
                then clear the work areas used
PL/I:
                IF DISPLAY_SOMETHING THEN DO;
                        IF MUST_DISPLAY_1 THEN
                                CALL DISPLAY_1;
                        ELSE DO;
                                CALL DISPLAY_2A;
                                CALL DISPLAY_2B;
                        END;
                        CALL FREE_AREAS;
                END;


C:

                If (display_something) {
                        if (must_display_1)
                                display_1();
                        else    {
                                display_2A();
                                display_2B();
                        }
                        free_areas();
                }
```

Listing 2-2   IF Statements and Scope Termination in Other Languages.

2.1.5   Problems with Nested Statements

In OS COBOL, the presence of conditional statements leads to problems with nested statements. The problem with the period is that it is too powerful; it terminates everything. You cannot use the period to terminate any statement nested in an IF without terminating the IF as well. Listing 2-3 shows three examples of OS COBOL program fragments with problems caused by scope termination issues in nested code. The examples include ON SIZE ERROR, INVALID KEY, and IF, but in each case the problem is the same. The conditional statement cannot be terminated without using a period, which ends the outer statement as well.

Listing 2-4, on the other hand, shows OS COBOL program fragments which correct the errors by reorganizing the code. In these

```
DATA DIVISION.
.....
PROCEDURE DIVISION.
* -- ALL OF THE FOLLOWING OS COBOL EXAMPLES CONTAIN BUGS
* -- AS INDICATED BY THE INCORRECT INDENTATION.
EXAMPLE-1.
************** -- ON SIZE ERROR
* THE ADVICE SHOULD ALWAYS BE PRINTED, BUT IS PRINTED ONLY
* ON SIZE ERROR HERE
            IF TEMP-EMPLOYEE
                PERFORM 1000-TEMP-PROCESS
                COMPUTE TAX-DEDUCT = T-RATE * HRS-WORKED
                ON SIZE ERROR
                    DISPLAY 'SIZE ERROR'
                PERFORM 2000-PRINT-ADVICE.

EXAMPLE-2.
************** -- IF
* FREE-AREAS SHOULD ALWAYS BE DONE, BUT IS DONE HERE
* ONLY FOR DISPLAY-2
            IF DISPLAY-SOMETHING
                IF DISPLAY-1
                    PERFORM DISPLAY-1
                ELSE
                    PERFORM DISPLAY-2
                PERFORM FREE-AREAS.

EXAMPLE-3.
************** -- READ
* THE CONTRACT-RECORD SHOULD BE READ ALWAYS. HERE IT IS
* READ ONLY WHEN THE FIRST READ FAILS.
            IF FIRST-TIME-IN-PROGRAM
                READ COMMODITY-RECORD
                AT END
                    DISPLAY 'NO COMMODITY RECORD'
                    PERFORM ERROR-ROUTINE
                READ CONTRACT-RECORD
                AT END
                    DISPLAY 'NO CONTRACT RECORD'
                    PERFORM ERROR-ROUTINE.
            PERFORM FREE-AREAS.
```

Listing 2-3   OS COBOL Bugs Caused By Problems with Scope Termination.

examples, it is necessary to repeat the test, repeat part of the code body, or move code out of the IF statement into a separate paragraph. All these corrections lead to programs that are less intuitive and less like the specification, which can cause bugs.

```
     DATA DIVISION.
     .....
     PROCEDURE DIVISION.
     * -- ALL OF THE FOLLOWING OS COBOL EXAMPLES SHOW THREE
     * -- UGLY WAYS TO AVOID SCOPE TERMINATION PROBLEMS.
     EXAMPLE-1.
     ************** -- ON SIZE ERROR
     * REPEAT THE TEST
           IF TEMP-EMPLOYEE
               PERFORM 1000-TEMP-PROCESS
               COMPUTE TAX-DEDUCT = T-RATE * HRS-WORKED
               ON SIZE ERROR
                   DISPLAY 'SIZE ERROR'.

           IF TEMP-EMPLOYEE
               PERFORM 2000-PRINT-ADVICE.
     EXAMPLE-2.
     ************** -- IF
     * REPEAT THE LAST PIECE OF CODE UNDER THE IF AND ELSE
           IF DISPLAY-SOMETHING
               IF DISPLAY-1
                   PERFORM DISPLAY-1
                   PERFORM FREE-AREAS
               ELSE
                   PERFORM DISPLAY-2
                   PERFORM FREE-AREAS.
     EXAMPLE-3.
     ************** -- READ
     * TAKE IT OUT OF THE IF AND MAKE IT A SUB-ROUTINE
           IF FIRST-TIME-IN-PROGRAM
               PERFORM READ-RECORDS
               PERFORM FREE-AREAS.
     READ-RECORDS.
           READ COMMODITY-RECORD
           AT END
               DISPLAY 'NO COMMODITY RECORD'
               PERFORM ERROR-ROUTINE.
           READ CONTRACT-RECORD
           AT END
               DISPLAY 'NO CONTRACT RECORD'
               PERFORM ERROR-ROUTINE.
```

Listing 2-4   OS COBOL Avoiding Problems with Scope Termination.

2.2   SCOPE TERMINATION IN COBOL II

Table 2-2 lists all the scope terminators in COBOL II. This table should be compared to Table 2-1; there is a scope terminator for each conditional statement. The period and ELSE function exactly as

Table 2-2   COBOL II Scope Terminators.

```
        .       (period)
      ELSE

      Control Statements
        END-EVALUATE ...
        END-IF       ...
        END-PERFORM  ...
        END-SEARCH   ...


      Arithmetic Statements
        END-ADD      ...
        END-COMPUTE  ...
        END-DIVIDE   ...
        END-MULTIPLY ...
        END-SUBTRACT ...


      I/O Statements
        END-DELETE   ...
        END-READ     ...
        END-RETURN   ...
        END-REWRITE  ...
        END-START    ...
        END-WRITE    ...


      Miscellaneous Statements
        END-CALL     ...
        END-STRING   ...
        END-UNSTRING ...
```

before; the other terminators end the scope of the immediately pre-ceding matching statement. Examples of the use of all these follow.

2.3   THE END-IF STATEMENT

As a specific example of scope termination, we will consider the new END-IF option which terminates the IF statement. On an individual IF statement which is not nested, this has the same effect as a pe-riod, as the examples in Listing 2-5 illustrate (although the END-IF word is easier to see in a listing than a period).

```
DATA DIVISION.
.....
PROCEDURE DIVISION.
    IF DISPLAY-SOMETHING
        PERFORM DISPLAY-1.

    IF DISPLAY-SOMETHING
        PERFORM DISPLAY-1
    ELSE
        PERFORM DISPLAY-2.

    IF DISPLAY-SOMETHING
        PERFORM DISPLAY-1
    END-IF

    IF DISPLAY-SOMETHING
        PERFORM DISPLAY-1
    ELSE
        PERFORM DISPLAY-2
    END-IF
....
```

Listing 2-5   COBOL II Examples of END-IF.

2.3.1   END-IF in Nested IF Statements

END-IF differs from the period when used in nested statements. Unlike the period, an END-IF only terminates the immediately preceding IF statement. In Listing 2-6, the first example uses a period to terminate two IF statements which are nested. The second example uses two END-IFs to do the same thing more explicitly. The third example terminates the inner IF statement and executes a further statement before ending the outer one.

2.4   SCOPE TERMINATORS AND NESTING

Listing 2-7 shows the same program fragments as Listing 2-3, corrected with the use of COBOL II scope terminators. In each case, the scope terminator ends the scope of its corresponding conditional statement, allowing the code to function as intended.

```
DATA DIVISION.
.....
PROCEDURE DIVISION.
* -- HERE THE PERIOD ENDS BOTH IF STATEMENTS
      IF DISPLAY-SOMETHING
          IF MUST-DISPLAY-1
              PERFORM DISPLAY-1
          ELSE
              PERFORM DISPLAY-2.
      PERFORM FREE-AREAS

* -- HERE END-IFS END BOTH IF STATEMENTS
      IF DISPLAY-SOMETHING
          IF MUST-DISPLAY-1
              PERFORM DISPLAY-1
          ELSE
              PERFORM DISPLAY-2
          END-IF
      END-IF
      PERFORM FREE-AREAS

*-- HERE AN END-IF TERMINATES ONE IF STATEMENT
      IF DISPLAY-SOMETHING
          IF MUST-DISPLAY-1
              PERFORM DISPLAY-1
          ELSE
              PERFORM DISPLAY-2
          END-IF
          PERFORM FREE-AREAS
      END-IF.
```

Listing 2-6   COBOL II Example of END-IF with Nested IFs.

2.4.1   Previous Recommendations Against Nested IFs

Some experts have recommended against the use of nested conditions in COBOL programs because of the problems discussed above. These writers have not generally opposed nested IFs in other languages, such as PL/I and C. It was the problems of scope termination in COBOL that they were objecting to. The addition of scope terminators is a major reason that nested IFs are used more in COBOL II than previously. If you previously avoided them, or your place of work had a standard which ruled them out, you should rethink this position now since the problem has been resolved.

```
DATA DIVISION.
. . . . .
PROCEDURE DIVISION.
* -- ALL OF THE FOLLOWING EXAMPLES USE COBOL II
* -- SCOPE TERMINATORS
EXAMPLE-1.
*************** -- ON SIZE ERROR
    IF TEMP-EMPLOYEE
        PERFORM 1000-TEMP-PROCESS
        COMPUTE TAX-DEDUCT = T-RATE * HRS-WORKED
        ON SIZE ERROR
            DISPLAY 'SIZE ERROR'
        END-COMPUTE
        PERFORM 2000-PRINT-ADVICE.

EXAMPLE-2.
*************** -- IF
    IF DISPLAY-SOMETHING
        IF DISPLAY-1
            PERFORM DISPLAY-1
        ELSE
            PERFORM DISPLAY-2
        END-IF
        PERFORM FREE-AREAS.

EXAMPLE-3.
*************** -- READ
    IF FIRST-TIME-IN-PROGRAM
        READ COMMODITY-RECORD
        AT END
            DISPLAY 'NO COMMODITY RECORD'
            PERFORM ERROR-ROUTINE
        END-READ
        READ CONTRACT-RECORD
        AT END
            DISPLAY 'NO CONTRACT RECORD'
            PERFORM ERROR-ROUTINE.

        PERFORM FREE-AREAS.
```

Listing 2-7   COBOL II with Scope Termination.

2.4.2   When Not to Use Scope Terminators in COBOL II

COBOL II introduces a scope terminator for every conditional statement. They are all optional, in the sense that the conditional statements can be coded without them. In particular, it is always possible to take OS COBOL code and compile it under COBOL II without adding scope terminators. A lot of effort went into assuring that this would be so, for good reason. It would generally be best to leave blocks of coded and tested old COBOL code alone, rather than going back and reworking them to the new style, possibly introducing errors.

It will be several years before all possible COBOL environments support the ANSI 1985 and VS COBOL II enhancements, so another reason for avoiding the new scope terminators could be concerns about portability to other systems. Authors of portable software packages generally have to shun new features until they are available everywhere.

On the other hand, if you are using any of the new features (such as in-line PERFORMs, covered in Chapter 4), you will want to use scope terminators, because they allow you to code conditional statements freely nested within other statements. In fact, you will have to use them because they are mandatory in some nested situations, as described below.

2.4.3   When Scope Terminators Are Mandatory

Scope terminators are mandatory on in-line PERFORM and EVALUATE statements and within the scope of these statements. The reason that other statements, such as IF statements, do not require scope terminators is because of the need for compatibility with OS COBOL. Compatibility with old programs is not an issue inside the scope of an in-line PERFORM or EVALUATE statement, since these statements were not available in OS COBOL. In Listing 2-8, the first paragraph does not compile because of a missing scope terminator.

2.4.4   Recommended Use of Scope Terminators

Use of scope terminators, other than the cases mentioned above, is a stylistic issue. This book recommends using scope terminators on all IF and SEARCH statements. This means that all program control statements (IF, SEARCH, EVALUATE, PERFORM) end consistently. I recommend using scope terminators on other statements (arithmetic, I/O, and miscellaneous) only when they are required because the

```
*  -- END-IF is mandatory , so this is an error
            PERFORM VARYING C-IX FROM 1 BY 1
            UNTIL C-IX > 10
               IF DISPLAY-1
                   PERFORM DISPLAY-1
               ELSE
                   PERFORM DISPLAY-2
            END-PERFORM


*  -- this is O.K.
            PERFORM VARYING C-IX FROM 1 BY 1
            UNTIL C-IX > 10
               IF DISPLAY-1
                   PERFORM DISPLAY-1
               ELSE
                   PERFORM DISPLAY-2
               END-IF
            END-PERFORM
```

Listing 2-8   Mandatory END-IF.

statement has a conditional form. I also recommend that you use periods only to end paragraphs, when they are required. This policy avoids a gratuitous coding burden and ensures that any code can be moved in and out of nested conditional statements without alteration.

Examples of all the scope terminators are given in Listings 2-9 through 2-13. END-PERFORM and END-EVALUATE will be covered in further detail in following chapters.

2.5   THE EFFECT ON MAINTENANCE

Program maintenance can now be simplified by the use of scope terminators. A particular advantage is that when you introduce changes, it is not necessary to restructure existing code. In OS COBOL, if you added an IF statement to an existing block of code, it

```
IF FUNDS-TYPE = 'S'
    MOVE DATE-TODAY TO FUNDS-AVAILABLE-DATE.

IF FUNDS-TYPE = 'S'
    MOVE DATE-TODAY TO FUNDS-AVAILABLE-DATE
ELSE
    MOVE DATE-TOMORROW TO FUNDS-AVAILABLE-DATE.
```

Listing 2-9   Period as a COBOL II Scope Terminator.

---

might need rewriting because of these problems. In COBOL II, there should be no need to reorganize the code. Below are some examples of these restructuring problems and the ways in which they can be cleaned up by use of scope terminators.

```
EVALUATE FUNDS-TYPE
WHEN 'S'
    MOVE DATE-TODAY TO FUNDS-AVAILABLE-DATE
WHEN OTHER
    MOVE DATE-TOMORROW TO FUNDS-AVAILABLE-DATE.
END-EVALUATE

IF FUNDS-TYPE = 'S'
    MOVE DATE-TODAY TO FUNDS-AVAILABLE-DATE
END-IF

PERFORM VARYING I FROM 1 BY 1 UNTIL I > 10
    MOVE 1 TO ELEMENT (I)
END-PERFORM

SEARCH ELEMENT
WHEN ELEMENT (I) = TARGET-FIELD
    MOVE ELEMENT (I) TO WORK-AREA
AT END
    SET ELEMENT-NOT-FOUND TO TRUE
END-SEARCH
```

Listing 2-10   Control Statement Scope Terminators.

```
ADD MONTHLY-TOTAL (MONTH) TO ANNUAL-TOTAL
ON SIZE ERROR
     PERFORM GLOBAL-ERROR-PROC
END-ADD

COMPUTE VOLUME-1 = HEIGHT-1 * WIDTH-1 * LENGTH-1
ON SIZE ERROR
     PERFORM GLOBAL-ERROR-PROC
END-COMPUTE

DIVIDE PARTIES-SHARING INTO RESOURCE-AVAILABLE
ON SIZE ERROR
     PERFORM GLOBAL-ERROR-PROC
END-DIVIDE

MULTIPLY FOREIGN-CURRENCY-RATE BY EXCHANGE-FACTOR
ON SIZE ERROR
     PERFORM GLOBAL-ERROR-PROC
END-MULTIPLY ...

SUBTRACT TAX-OWED FROM GROSS-INCOME GIVING AMOUNT-OF-CHECK
ON SIZE ERROR
     PERFORM GLOBAL-ERROR-PROC
   END-SUBTRACT
```

Listing 2-11   Arithmetic Statement Scope Terminators.

2.5.1   Maintenance Example with OS COBOL

Listings 2-14 through 2-17 show a piece of OS COBOL code in the course of being changed by a maintenance programmer. The original code is in Listing 2-14. In this example, this block of code has to be made dependent on the condition MASTER-NEEDS-UPDATING. In Listing 2-15, you add the IF statement and indent the code. In Listing 2-16, you remove every period but the last.

The meaning of this piece of code is now changed; the indentation has been changed to show this. You now have to decide how to restructure this to make it work the way it used to. Listing 2-17 shows

```
DELETE MASTER-FILE
INVALID KEY
     PERFORM NO-MASTER-FOUND
END-DELETE

READ MASTER-FILE
AT END
     SET EOF-MF TO TRUE
END-READ

RETURN SORT-FILE
AT END
     SET EOF-SORT TO TRUE
END-RETURN

REWRITE MASTER-RECORD
INVALID KEY
     PERFORM NO-MASTER-FOUND
END-REWRITE

START MASTER-FILE KEY = SEARCH-KEY
INVALID KEY
     PERFORM NO-MASTER-FOUND
END-START

WRITE MASTER-RECORD
INVALID KEY
     PERFORM MASTER_INSERT_FAILURE
END-WRITE
```

Listing 2-12   I/O Statement Scope Terminators.

two examples of this. For instance, you could reorder some statements (1) or pull out a new paragraph and perform it (2).

2.5.2   Maintenance Example with COBOL II

In contrast, Listings 2-18 through 2-19 show a similar series using COBOL II. Listing 2-18 shows the original piece of COBOL II code.

```
CALL 'SUBPGM' USING ARG-1 ARG-2
ON OVERFLOW
    PERFORM OUT-OF-MEMORY-PROC
END-CALL

STRING FIRST-NAME  DELIMITED BY SPACE,
       MIDDLE-NAME DELIMITED BY SPACE,
       LAST-NAME   DELIMITED BY SPACE
INTO NAME-OUTPUT
ON OVERFLOW
    MOVE LAST-NAME TO NAME-OUTPUT
END-STRING

UNSTRING NAME-INPUT
INTO   FIRST-NAME  DELIMITED BY ALL SPACE,
       MIDDLE-NAME DELIMITED BY SPACE,
       LAST-NAME   DELIMITED BY SPACE
ON OVERFLOW
    SET NAME-OVERFLOWED TO TRUE
END-UNSTRING
```

Listing 2-13   Miscellaneous Statement Scope Terminators.

Listing 2-19 shows this made conditional by adding the IF statement with END-IF and indenting the code. It should be clear that this sequence is much simpler than the preceding one, and that this type of maintenance is easier with COBOL II than with OS COBOL.

2.5.3   Another Maintenance Example: OS COBOL

The next example in Listings 2-20 through 2-23 uses nested IFs. The initial code is in Listing 2-20. In Listing 2-21, this is changed so that the screen displayed depends on a variable. The nesting has been

```
SET RECORD-UPDATED TO TRUE.
REWRITE MASTER-FILE
INVALID KEY
    PERFORM FILE-ERROR.
ADD 1 TO RECORDS-PROCESSED.
MOVE RECORD-KEY TO HOLD-KEY.
ADD RECORD-AMOUNT TO TOTAL-AMOUNT.
```

Listing 2-14   OS COBOL Maintenance Example 1.

```
IF MASTER-NEEDS-UPDATING
    SET RECORD-UPDATED TO TRUE.
    REWRITE MASTER-FILE
    INVALID KEY
        PERFORM FILE-ERROR.
    ADD 1 TO RECORDS-PROCESSED.
    MOVE RECORD-KEY TO HOLD-KEY.
    ADD RECORD-AMOUNT TO TOTAL-AMOUNT.
```

Listing 2-15   OS COBOL Maintenance Example 2.

```
IF MASTER-NEEDS-UPDATING
    SET RECORD-UPDATED TO TRUE
    REWRITE MASTER-FILE
    INVALID KEY
        PERFORM FILE-ERROR
        ADD 1 TO RECORDS-PROCESSED
        MOVE RECORD-KEY TO HOLD-KEY
        ADD RECORD-AMOUNT TO TOTAL-AMOUNT.
```

Listing 2-16   OS COBOL Maintenance Example 3.

```
(1)
    IF MASTER-NEEDS-UPDATING
        SET RECORD-UPDATED TO TRUE
        ADD 1 TO RECORDS-PROCESSED
        MOVE RECORD-KEY TO HOLD-KEY
        ADD RECORD-AMOUNT TO TOTAL-AMOUNT
        REWRITE MASTER-FILE
        INVALID KEY
            PERFORM FILE-ERROR.

(2)
    IF MASTER-NEEDS-UPDATING
        SET RECORD-UPDATED TO TRUE
        ADD 1 TO RECORDS-PROCESSED
        PERFORM REWRITE-MASTER
        ADD 1 TO RECORDS-PROCESSED
        MOVE RECORD-KEY TO HOLD-KEY
        ADD RECORD-AMOUNT TO TOTAL-AMOUNT.

REWRITE-MASTER.
    REWRITE MASTER-FILE
    INVALID KEY
        PERFORM FILE-ERROR.
```

Listing 2-17   OS COBOL Maintenance Example 4.

```
      SET RECORD-UPDATED TO TRUE
      REWRITE MASTER-FILE
      INVALID KEY
           PERFORM FILE-ERROR
      END-REWRITE
      ADD 1 TO RECORDS-PROCESSED
      MOVE RECORD-KEY TO HOLD-KEY
      ADD RECORD-AMOUNT TO TOTAL-AMOUNT
```

Listing 2-18   COBOL II Maintenance Example 1.

```
  IF MASTER-NEEDS-UPDATING
      SET RECORD-UPDATED TO TRUE
      REWRITE MASTER-FILE
      INVALID KEY
           PERFORM FILE-ERROR
      END-REWRITE
      ADD 1 TO RECORDS-PROCESSED
      MOVE RECORD-KEY TO HOLD-KEY
      ADD RECORD-AMOUNT TO TOTAL-AMOUNT
  END-IF
```

Listing 2-19   COBOL II Maintenance Example 2.

```
  IF MODE-IS-DISPLAY
      PERFORM 1000-READ-TRADES
      PERFORM 2000-CALCULATE-RISK
      PERFORM 3000-DISPLAY-SCREEN-A
      PERFORM 4000-PROCESS-RESPONSE.
```

Listing 2-20   Second OS COBOL Maintenance 1.

```
  IF MODE-IS-DISPLAY
      PERFORM 1000-READ-TRADES
      PERFORM 2000-CALCULATE-RISK
      IF SCREEN-A
           PERFORM 3000-DISPLAY-SCREEN-A
      ELSE
           PERFORM 3000-DISPLAY-SCREEN-B
           PERFORM 4000-PROCESS-RESPONSE.
```

Listing 2-21   Second OS COBOL Maintenance 2.

```
IF MODE-IS-DISPLAY
    PERFORM 1000-READ-TRADES
    PERFORM 2000-CALCULATE-RISK
    IF SCREEN-A
        PERFORM 3000-DISPLAY-SCREEN-A
        PERFORM 4000-PROCESS-RESPONSE
    ELSE
        PERFORM 3000-DISPLAY-SCREEN-B
        PERFORM 4000-PROCESS-RESPONSE.
```

Listing 2-22   Second OS COBOL Maintenance 3.

altered to reflect the change in meaning. It is not possible this time to move 4000- above 3000- (and process the response before the screen is displayed). It will be necessary to repeat the final perform statement.

Now suppose this has to be changed so that the calculation depends on a variable also. There are several ways to do this. Unfortunately, you have to sit and think which way to do it when it ought to be a trivial change. Listing 2-23 shows one way.

```
IF MODE-IS-DISPLAY
    PERFORM 1000-READ-TRADES
    IF CALC-A
        PERFORM 2000-CALCULATE-RISK-A
        PERFORM REST-OF-STUFF
    ELSE
        PERFORM 2000-CALCULATE-RISK-B
        PERFORM REST-OF-STUFF.

REST-OF-STUFF.
    IF SCREEN-A
        PERFORM 3000-DISPLAY-SCREEN-A
    ELSE
        PERFORM 3000-DISPLAY-SCREEN-B.

    PERFORM 4000-PROCESS-RESPONSE.
```

Listing 2-23   Second OS COBOL Maintenance 4.

```
IF MODE-IS-DISPLAY
    PERFORM 1000-READ-TRADES
    IF CALC-A
        PERFORM 2000-CALCULATE-RISK-A
    ELSE
        PERFORM 2000-CALCULATE-RISK-B
    END-IF
    IF SCREEN-A
        PERFORM 3000-DISPLAY-SCREEN-A
    ELSE
        PERFORM 3000-DISPLAY-SCREEN-B
    END-IF
    PERFORM 4000-PROCESS-RESPONSE
END-IF
```

Listing 2-24   Second COBOL II Maintenance.

2.5.4   Second Maintenance Example Using COBOL II

Listing 2-24 shows maintenance to the same fragment of code as above, but written in COBOL II. Each change was a straightforward local change to the line it affects. There was no restructuring to do.

2.6   CONCLUSION: THE EFFECT ON PROGRAM STRUCTURE

Using scope terminators, programs can be written in a more natural manner. Control statements can be nested to reflect the problem. To make the language do what you want, it is no longer necessary to use artifices such as shuffling the order of statements within the scope of a conditional statement, introducing arbitrary paragraphs to reduce nesting, and putting duplicate lines of code on each path of a conditional statement.

3

The PERFORM Statement

COBOL II introduces several changes to the PERFORM statement. In this chapter, all these changes are covered with examples. All the enhancements are optional: any PERFORM statements that worked in OS COBOL will continue to work, and there is no need to change any existing programs or the way you write new programs unless you want to. However, the change in the PERFORM statement, like the scope terminator, can make a big improvement in the appearance of program code.

An in-line PERFORM statement is now available. The statements of the PERFORM body can be coded in-line (right after the PERFORM statement). You generally use this for loops, so you can see what is being performed on the same page as the conditions for its invocation.

The UNTIL test of the PERFORM statement can be specified as being either before or after the statements of the loop body at the option of the programmer. Using PERFORM WITH TEST AFTER, you can guarantee that the body will be executed at least once.

3.1 THE TWO TYPES OF PERFORM

The PERFORM statement in COBOL is used to express two quite different constructs: the subroutine and the loop. In other programming languages, the two concepts represented by the PERFORM

Customer Report Structure Chart

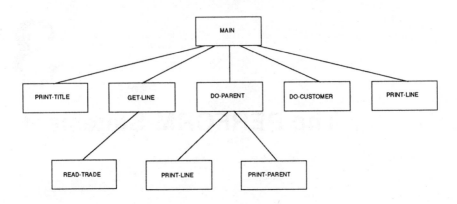

Figure 3-1   Design of Small Report Program.

statement are generally two different statements. In PL/I, for instance, a subroutine is coded with a CALL and a loop with a DO statement.

A subroutine is a piece of code which is separate from the main routine which called it. Such a routine is separated either because it is a self-contained function or because it is a group of statements executed in several different places, which is separated out in order to be coded once. In the first case, these routines are generally recognized in the design phase, and may well be drawn on a structure chart or action diagram. Figure 3-1 shows a design for a small report program, represented as a structure chart. Listing 3-1 shows an outline COBOL program which follows this structure.

A loop consists of a body of code and a set of conditions controlling the execution of that body from zero to many times. It is typified by the use of PERFORM . . . VARYING or PERFORM . . . TIMES, or, of course, it can be built using GO TO, IF, and paragraph names. It is not normally indicated on a structure chart or action diagram as a separate routine. In OS COBOL, there was a problem caused by the need to make any code in a PERFORM loop a separate subroutine. This issue resulted in the development of several schools of thought on coding loops.

One possibility is to use PERFORM to specify all loops. This has the advantage of consistency. All loops are recognizable because they are treated in a standard manner. The disadvantage is that the

```
      IDENTIFICATION DIVISION.
      ENVIRONMENT DIVISION.
      DATA DIVISION.
      PROCEDURE DIVISION.
      MAIN.
              PERFORM PRINT-TITLE
*--           UNTIL END-OF-FILE:
                  PERFORM GET-LINE
*--               IF PARENT NOT = LAST PARENT
                      PERFORM DO-PARENT
                  PERFORM DO-CUSTOMER

              PERFORM DO-PARENT
              PERFORM PRINT-LINE
              GOBACK.

      DO-CUSTOMER.
*--     SAVE CUSTOMER LINE IN BUFFER
              ACCUMULATE TO PARENT LINE
              ...

      DO-PARENT.
*--     ACCUMULATE TO TOTAL LINE
*--     DO FOR EACH LINE IN BUFFER
*--           LOOK FOR EXCEPTION

*--     IF FOUND EXCEPTION
*--           DO FOR EACH LINE IN BUFFER
                  PERFORM PRINT-LINE
              PERFORM PRINT-PARENT

*--     CLEAR BUFFER

      PRINT-PARENT.
              ...

      PRINT-LINE.
              ...

      PRINT-TITLE.
              ...
      GET-LINE.
*--           BUILDS CUSTOMER LINE FROM DETAIL TRADE RECORDS
              ...
              PERFORM READ-TRADE

      READ-TRADE.
              ...
```

Listing 3-1   Customer Report Skeleton Program.

```
DO-PARENT SECTION.
*--  ACCUMULATE TO TOTAL LINE
        PERFORM FIND-EXC
        VARYING BUF-IX FROM 1 BY 1
        UNTIL BUF-IX > BUF-SIZE
        OR EXCEPTION-FOUND.

        IF EXCEPTION-FOUND
            PERFORM PR-BUF
            VARYING BUF-IX FROM 1 BY 1
            UNTIL BUF-IX > BUF-SIZE.

    MOVE ZERO TO BUF-SIZE.

FIND-EXC.
        MOVE BUF-RECORD (BUF-IX) TO W-RECORD.

        IF NY-POSITION > NY-LIMIT
        OR LO-POSITION > LO-LIMIT
        OR SI-POSITION > SI-LIMIT
            MOVE 1 TO EXCEPTION-FOUND-SW.

PR-BUF.
        PERFORM PRINT-LINE.
```

Listing 3-2   Coding Loops with Out-of-Line PERFORMs.

program becomes split into small fragments in a manner which no longer reflects the structure chart. Listing 3-2 shows the coding of a paragraph from the outline COBOL program given above which takes this approach.

Another approach is to code all loops using IF, GO TO, and paragraph names. This has the advantage of preserving the PERFORM statement for calling subroutines, and thus preserving the correspondence to the structure chart. On the other hand, the construction of loops in this manner is inelegant, being more reminiscent of assembler than a modern structured programming language. Compared to a PERFORM statement, each loop needs to be read more carefully to ensure that it is a correctly coded standard structure. Listing 3-3 shows the same paragraph as Listing 3-2 from the model program above coded using this approach. Listing 3-4 shows another method of simulating an in-line PERFORM that has sometimes been used. There are other approaches, some of which are variants or hybrids of the two mentioned here, but all are ways of working around a problem in OS COBOL.

```
DO-PARENT SECTION.
* -- ACCUMULATE TO TOTAL LINE
     MOVE 1 TO BUF-IX.

FIND-EXC-LOOP.
     IF BUF-IX > BUF-SIZE
         GO TO FIND-EXC-EXIT.

     MOVE BUF-RECORD (BUF-IX) TO W-RECORD.

     IF NY-POSITION > NY-LIMIT
     OR LO-POSITION > LO-LIMIT
     OR SI-POSITION > SI-LIMIT
         MOVE 1 TO EXCEPTION-FOUND-SW
         GO TO FIND-EXC-EXIT
     ELSE
         ADD 1 TO BUF-IX
         GO TO FIND-EXC-LOOP.

FIND-EXC-EXIT.

     IF NOT EXCEPTION-FOUND
         GO TO PR-BUF-EXIT.

     MOVE 1 TO BUF-IX.

PR-BUF-LOOP.
     IF BUF-IX > BUF-SIZE
         GO TO PR-BUF-EXIT.

     PERFORM PRINT-LINE.
     ADD 1 TO BUF-IX.
     GO TO PR-BUF-LOOP.

PR-BUF-EXIT.
     MOVE ZERO TO BUF-SIZE.
```

Listing 3-3   Coding Loops with GO TO and IF.

3.2   THE IN-LINE PERFORM STATEMENT

3.2.1   Simple In-Line PERFORM

In COBOL II, you can code any PERFORM statement in-line, ended
by an END-PERFORM statement. Listing 3-5 shows some simple examples. Any executable statements can be enclosed between the

```
      PERFORM PR-BUF
      VARYING BUF-IX FROM 1 BY 1
      UNTIL BUF-IX > BUF-SIZE.

      GO TO PR-BUF-EXIT.

   PR-BUF.
      PERFORM PRINT-LINE.

   PR-BUF-EXIT.
```

Listing 3-4   Simulated In-Line PERFORM.

PERFORM and END-PERFORM statements. If these are conditional, their scope terminators must be used.

The simple in-line PERFORM shown in Listing 3-5 appears to have no real value. The examples given execute exactly as if the PERFORM/END-PERFORM statements were not there. Oddly enough, there is a situation where this construction might be of use. Within the scope of an in-line PERFORM, it is necessary to use scope terminators on all conditional statements. This can be used to check that all statements end correctly. Consider the example in Listing 3-6. The first example compiles cleanly. The second does not, highlighting the logic error. You might use this to check code for this type of error.

3.2.2   In-Line PERFORM VARYING

The purpose of the in-line PERFORM is to use it to express loops with PERFORM . . . TIMES and PERFORM . . . VARYING. You can

```
      PERFORM
          MOVE 100 TO W-PERCENT
          MOVE 'A' TO W-GRADE
      END-PERFORM

      PERFORM
          IF W-GRADE = 'A' OR 'B'
              DISPLAY 'WELL DONE!'
          END-IF
      END-PERFORM
```

Listing 3-5   Basic In-Line PERFORM.

```
* THIS COMPILES CLEANLY
* BUT IS IN ERROR
ADD MONTH-TOTAL TO YEAR-TOTAL
ON SIZE ERROR
       ADD MONTH-TOTAL TO OVERFLOW-TOTAL
       DISPLAY 'OVERFLOW OCCURRED'
END-ADD
ADD YEAR-TOTAL TO GRAND-TOTAL

* THIS GENERATES AN ERROR BECAUSE THE FIRST ADD HAS NO
* SCOPE TERMINATOR
PERFORM
ADD MONTH-TOTAL TO YEAR-TOTAL
ON SIZE ERROR
       ADD MONTH-TOTAL TO OVERFLOW-TOTAL
       DISPLAY 'OVERFLOW OCCURRED'
END-ADD
ADD YEAR-TOTAL TO GRAND-TOTAL
END-PERFORM
```

Listing 3-6   Checking Code with PERFORM/END-PERFORM.

now use the in-line PERFORM to express all loops in place. The program is clearer because the body of statements in the loop, which are being performed, are kept together with the conditions leading to their execution. Listing 3-7 shows some in-line PERFORM statements expressing simple loops. In each case, the separate paragraph which would have been necessary in OS COBOL is eliminated, making the program easier to follow. The second example uses the new verb CONTINUE, which is a null statement covered fully in Chapter 5. Listing 3-8 shows the program paragraph from Listings 3-4 and 3-5 written in COBOL II.

3.2.3   Style Issues with PERFORM

In writing new programs, almost all loops should be expressed with in-line PERFORMs. Out-of-line PERFORMs should be reserved for routines that do some discrete thing, often one called from several different places. You will continue to use the PERFORM statement to express subroutine calls in the same manner as before.

In OS COBOL, some programmers "rolled their own" loops. The justification for this was usually a desire to keep the body of the code together with the conditions in one place. Listing 3-9 shows two simple examples of this technique, which is no longer necessary. The

```
COBOL II:
* -- 1. PRINT SEVEN DAYS FROM ARRAY
            PERFORM VARYING DAY FROM 1 BY 1 UNTIL DAY > 7
                  DISPLAY DAY-NAME (DAY)
            END-PERFORM


* -- 2. POSITION INDEX AT FIRST SPACE IN STRING
            PERFORM VARYING CH-IX FROM 1 BY 1
            UNTIL CHAR (CH-IX) = SPACE
                  CONTINUE
            END-PERFORM


* -- 3. REPEAT LINE 500 TIMES
            PERFORM 500 TIMES
                  DISPLAY 'I WILL NOT COME LATE TO SCHOOL'
            END-PERFORM

OS COBOL:
* -- 1. PRINT SEVEN DAYS FROM ARRAY
            PERFORM DISPLAY-DAY
            VARYING DAY FROM 1 BY 1 UNTIL DAY > 7
            GO TO DISPLAY-DAY-EXIT.
      DISPLAY-DAY.
            DISPLAY DAY-NAME (DAY)
      DISPLAY-DAY-EXIT.


* -- 2. POSITION INDEX AT FIRST SPACE IN STRING
            PERFORM DUMMY-PARA VARYING CH-IX FROM 1 BY 1
            UNTIL CHAR (CH-IX) = SPACE

                  ...
      DUMMY-PARA.
* -- THIS PARAGRAPH DOES NOTHING
            EXIT.


* -- 3. REPEAT LINE 500 TIMES
            PERFORM LATE-LINE 499 TIMES
      LATE-LINE.
            DISPLAY 'I WILL NOT COME LATE TO SCHOOL'
```

Listing 3-7   COBOL II In-Line PERFORMs Compared to OS COBOL.

desired effect is now achieved with the in-line PERFORM, as is also shown in Listing 3-9.

Many loops have a beginning, a loop body with conditions, and an end. In OS COBOL, some programmers would repeat the beginning and end in several places to avoid coding an extra PERFORM statement. In other words, the loop would be split up as in Listing 3-10.

```
DO-PARENT SECTION.
*-- ACCUMULATE TO TOTAL LINE
    PERFORM VARYING BUF-IX FROM 1 BY 1
    UNTIL BUF-IX > BUF-SIZE
    OR EXCEPTION-FOUND
        MOVE BUF-RECORD (BUF-IX) TO W-RECORD
        IF NY-POSITION > NY-LIMIT
        OR LO-POSITION > LO-LIMIT
        OR SI-POSITION > SI-LIMIT
            MOVE 1 TO EXCEPTION-FOUND-SW
        END-IF
    END-PERFORM

    IF EXCEPTION-FOUND
        PERFORM VARYING BUF-IX FROM 1 BY 1
        UNTIL BUF-IX > BUF-SIZE
            PERFORM PRINT-LINE
        END-PERFORM
    END-IF

    MOVE ZERO TO BUF-SIZE.
```

Listing 3-8   Coding Loops with COBOL II In-Line PERFORMs.

In COBOL II, you code all the loop codes, initialization, conditions, and body, as in Listing 3-11.

3.3 PERFORM WITH TEST BEFORE

Traditionally in structured programming, there are two types of loops available. The difference is whether the conditional test is performed before or after the body of the loop.

In COBOL II, you can optionally add the clause WITH TEST BEFORE or WITH TEST AFTER to any perform statement which includes an UNTIL test. This states whether to perform the test before or after the body of the loop controlled by the PERFORM statement. This clause affects the starting and ending of the loop.

PERFORM WITH TEST BEFORE is the default; in other words, it is what you get if you code neither BEFORE nor AFTER. This is what you coded with OS COBOL, and it continues to work the same way. Coding this, you will execute the loop zero or more times; if the condition fails on first entry, you will not execute the statements in the body at all. One reason that this is the default case is because it is compatible with OS COBOL; another is because it is what is

```
OS COBOL:
          MOVE 1 TO DAY.
     DAY-LOOP.
          DISPLAY DAY-NAME (DAY)
          ADD 1 TO DAY.
          IF DAY NOT > 7
               GO TO DAY-LOOP.


          SET CH-IX TO 1
     CHAR-LOOP.
          IF CHAR (CH-IX) NOT = SPACE
               SET CH-IX UP BY 1
               GO TO CHAR-LOOP.


COBOL II:

          PERFORM VARYING DAY FROM 1 BY 1 UNTIL DAY > 7
               DISPLAY DAY-NAME (DAY)
          END-PERFORM

          PERFORM VARYING CH-IX FROM 1 BY 1
          UNTIL CHAR (CH-IX) = SPACE
               CONTINUE
          END-PERFORM
```

Listing 3-9   Loops with "GO TO."

desired in most cases. More than 90% of program loops are TEST
BEFORE. As an example of TEST BEFORE, the two perform loops
in Listing 3-12 are identical in their effect.

3.4   PERFORM WITH TEST AFTER

PERFORM WITH TEST AFTER is the new option introduced with
COBOL II. The effect of coding this is to ensure that the code in the
loop body executes at least once, since the UNTIL condition is not
checked until the code in the body is executed. In the example in
Listing 3-13 below, there is no need to set the switch before the loop
on the first time through. The routine RECEIVE-MAP can be left to
do this as necessary, since we know it will be executed at least once.
    In the example in Listing 3-14, there is a personnel file containing
a mixture of applicants, retirees, subcontractors, and employees.
This listing shows the code to read the next employee, skipping the
other types.

```
PART-1.
     .....
     SET IY TO 1
     PERFORM GET-WORD VARYING IX FROM 1 BY 1
     UNTIL IX > 20 OR CH1 (IX) = SPACE
 .....
PART-2.
     .....
     SET IY TO 1
     PERFORM GET-WORD VARYING IX FROM 1 BY 1
     UNTIL IX > 20 OR CH1 (IX) = SPACE
     .....
PART-3.
     .....
     SET IY TO 1
     PERFORM GET-WORD VARYING IX FROM 1 BY 1
     UNTIL IX > 20 OR CH1 (IX) = SPACE
     .....
GET-WORD.
     MOVE CH1 (IX) TO CH2 (IY)
     SET IY UP BY 1.
```

Listing 3-10   Performing a Loop in OS COBOL.

```
PART-1.
     ...
     PERFORM GET-WORD
     ...
PART-2.
     ...
     PERFORM GET-WORD
     ...
PART-3.
     ...
     PERFORM GET-WORD
     ...
GET-WORD.
     SET IY TO 1
     PERFORM VARYING IX FROM 1 BY 1
     UNTIL IX > 20 OR CH1 (IX) = SPACE
         MOVE CH1 (IX) TO CH2 (IY)
         SET IY UP BY 1
     END-PERFORM.
```

Listing 3-11   Performing a Loop in COBOL II.

```
PERFORM UNTIL LOOP-OVER
    PERFORM DISPLAY-SCREEN
    PERFORM ACCEPT-DATA
END-PERFORM

PERFORM WITH TEST BEFORE UNTIL LOOP-OVER
    PERFORM DISPLAY-SCREEN
    PERFORM ACCEPT-DATA
END-PERFORM
```

Listing 3-12   PERFORM WITH TEST BEFORE in COBOL II.

Without the "WITH TEST AFTER" clause, this would find the first employee and then get stuck. You would have to force the RECORD-IS-EMPLOYEE switch off each time to keep going.

Listing 3-15 shows two equivalent PERFORM loops, one with test before and one with test after. Each displays the numbers from 1 to 10. As the example shows, the test condition has to change because the test is now performed at a different place in the loop.

3.4.1   TEST BEFORE/AFTER in Other Languages

Most programming languages support this concept, using different keywords to distinguish whether the test is before or after. Listing 3-16 shows the equivalent code to Listing 3-13 in PL/I (which uses DO . . . WHILE and DO . . . UNTIL) and C (which uses while (. . .) and do . . . while (. . .)).


```
MOVE SPACE TO TIME-TO-QUIT-SW
PERFORM UNTIL TIME-TO-QUIT
    PERFORM SEND-MAP
    PERFORM RECEIVE-MAP
END-PERFORM

PERFORM WITH TEST AFTER
UNTIL TIME-TO-QUIT
    PERFORM SEND-MAP
    PERFORM RECEIVE-MAP
END-PERFORM
```

Listing 3-13   PERFORM WITH TEST AFTER in COBOL II.

```
*** -- GET NEXT EMPLOYEE RECORD
       PERFORM WITH TEST AFTER
          UNTIL RECORD-IS-EMPLOYEE OR EOF-EMP
             READ PERSONNEL-FILE
             AT END
                    SET EOF-EMP TO TRUE
             END-READ
       END-PERFORM
```

Listing 3-14   COBOL II TEST AFTER with READ.

3.5   NESTING PERFORM STATEMENTS

PERFORM statements can be freely nested within IFs, other PERFORMs, and any other conditional statements. For instance, Listing 3-17 sums all elements of a three-dimensional table. In Release 3.0, tables can have as many as seven dimensions, as discussed in Chapter 20.

3.6   A COMPLETE EXAMPLE: AN INTERNAL SORT

At this point, we have looked at a lot of program fragments and covered significant changes in some old familiar verbs (IF, READ, PERFORM). It is time for a complete program that illustrates the style rules we have discussed up to now.

The program in Listing 3-18 shows a small but moderately complex program with examples of IFs and PERFORMs nested inside

```
PROCEDURE DIVISION.

       PERFORM WITH TEST BEFORE
       VARYING A-COUNTER FROM 1 BY 1
       UNTIL A-COUNTER > 10
          DISPLAY A-COUNTER
       END-PERFORM

       PERFORM WITH TEST AFTER
       VARYING A-COUNTER FROM 1 BY 1
       UNTIL A-COUNTER = 10
          DISPLAY A-COUNTER
       END-PERFORM
```

Listing 3-15   COBOL II PERFORM WITH TEST BEFORE and AFTER.

PL/I:

```
            DO WHILE (^TIME_TO_QUIT);
                   CALL SEND_MAP;
                   CALL RECEIVE_MAP;
            END;

            DO UNTIL (TIME_TO_QUIT);
                   CALL SEND_MAP;
                   CALL RECEIVE_MAP;
            END;
```

C:

```
            time_to_quit = 0;
            while (!time_to_quit) {
                   send_map();
                   receive_map();
            }

            do {
                   send_map();
                   receive_map();
            }
            while (!time_to_quit);
```

Listing 3-16   TEST BEFORE/AFTER in Other Languages.

PERFORMs. It is a complete program to sort a table using the Shell sort procedure.

Of course, you usually don't write your own sort program when there is a system sort available that is faster and fully debugged. However, there are situations where you cannot call the system sort, such as CICS programs, and this is a useful and very fast routine for those times.

After the listing, the program is annotated using the line numbers to the left.

Program Name: SHELLSRT
Input: A file of record length 80 containing words in columns 7-72 (such as a COBOL program).
Output: A print file of record length 132 containing all input words in sorted order.
Processing: Reads words from the input file into a table, then calls a sort routine to order them, then prints them.

```
DATA DIVISION.
01  YEAR-PAY.
    02  YEAR-TOTAL                PIC S9(15) COMP-3.
    02  WEEK-PAY                  OCCURS 52 INDEXED BY W-IX.
        03  WEEK-TOTAL            PIC S9(15) COMP-3.
        03  DAY-PAY               OCCURS 7  INDEXED BY D-IX.
            04  DAY-TOTAL         PIC S9(15) COMP-3.
            04  HOUR-PAY          PIC S9(07) COMP-3
                                  OCCURS 24 INDEXED BY H-IX.


PROCEDURE DIVISION.
    PERFORM VARYING W-IX FROM 1 BY 1 UNTIL W-IX > 52
        PERFORM VARYING D-IX FROM 1 BY 1
        UNTIL D-IX > 7
            PERFORM VARYING H-IX FROM 1 BY 1
            UNTIL H-IX > 24
                ADD HOUR-PAY (W-IX, D-IX, H-IX)
                TO DAY-TOTAL (W-IX, D-IX)
            END-PERFORM
            ADD DAY-TOTAL (W-IX, D-IX)
            TO WEEK-TOTAL (W-IX)
        END-PERFORM
        ADD WEEK-TOTAL (W-IX) TO YEAR-TOTAL
    END-PERFORM.
```

Listing 3-17   Three-Dimensional Table.

Comments: This is a very artificial program set up to test
                   the sort routine in SHELL-SORT SECTION.
                   The routine would be more useful in an on-line
                   program (i.e., CICS) where system sort pro-
                   grams are not available.

3.6.1 Notes on Listing 3-18

The Shell sort program in this listing was chosen because it is not a
typical short program. It is an example of many PERFORM loops
and a complex level of nesting in a small space.

The bulk of the program sets up the data to test the sort routine.
GET-TEST-DATA (line 71) reads words from a file into the table for
sorting. The file is 80 characters with data in columns 7–72; in other
words, it could be a COBOL source program.

GET-NEXT-WORD (line 84) breaks out the words in the file by the
simple method of stopping on spaces and periods and keeping only
those which are alphabetic. This finds a lot of words but misses

```
000001 ID DIVISION.
000002 PROGRAM-ID. SHELLSRT.
000003 ENVIRONMENT DIVISION.
000004 INPUT-OUTPUT SECTION.
000005 FILE-CONTROL.
000006     SELECT INPUT-FILE ASSIGN TO INFILE.
000007     SELECT PRINT-FILE ASSIGN TO PRINTER.
000008 DATA DIVISION.
000009 FILE SECTION.
000010 FD  INPUT-FILE
000011     RECORDING MODE F
000012     RECORD CONTAINS 80 CHARACTERS
000013     BLOCK CONTAINS 0 RECORDS
000014     DATA RECORD IS INPUT-RECORD
000015     LABEL RECORDS ARE STANDARD.
000016
000017 01  INPUT-RECORD.
000018* INPUT RECORD IS ASSUMED TO BE COBOL WITH LINE NUMBERS
000019*   IN COLUMNS 1-6
000020     05  FILLER                      PIC X(06).
000021     05  INPUT-REC-DATA.
000022         10  IR-LETTER   PIC X OCCURS 74 INDEXED BY IR-IX.
000023
000024 FD    PRINT-FILE
000025       RECORD CONTAINS 133 CHARACTERS
000026       RECORDING MODE F
000027       LABEL RECORDS ARE STANDARD.
000028
000029 01    PRINT-LINE.
000030       05  SKIP-CHAR                 PIC X(01).
000031       05  PRINT-DATA                PIC X(132).
000032
000033 WORKING-STORAGE SECTION.
000034* THIS TABLE IS THE ITEMS TO SORT. ONE EXTRA ITEM
000035* IS DEFINED FOR SWAPPING. WORDS MUST BE <= 30
000036 01    W-ITEMS.
000037       02  SWAP-ITEM.
000038           03  SWAP-S-KEY            PIC X(30).
000039       02  W-ITEM OCCURS 20001
000040               ASCENDING KEY IS S-KEY
000041               INDEXED BY S1-IX, S2-IX, S3-IX.
000042           03  S-KEY                     PIC X(30).
000043* THE NEXT TWO FIELDS USED BY THE SHELL SORT PROCEDURE
000044 01    GAP               PIC S9(9) COMP.
000045 01    LOOP-OVER-SW      PIC X VALUE ZERO.
000046       88  LOOP-OVER              VALUE '1'.
000047       88  LOOP-NOT-OVER          VALUE ZERO.
000048* ARRAY-SIZE INDICATES THE SIZE OF THE TABLE. SEE CHAPTER
000049* FIVE FOR A METHOD OF CALCULATING THIS FROM THE TABLE
```

Listing 3-18   Shell Sort. (Continued)

```
            DECLARATION
000050 01     ARRAY-SIZE            PIC S9(9) COMP VALUE 20000.
000051* THE NEXT THREE FIELDS ARE USED IN THE ROUTINES TO GET
000052* WORDS FROM A FILE AND BUILD THE TABLE
000053 01     NEXT-WORD.
000054        02  NEXT-LETTER   PIC X OCCURS 70 INDEXED BY NL-IX.
000055 01  END-OF-FILE-SW            PIC X VALUE ZERO.
000056        88  END-OF-FILE        VALUE '1'.
000057        88  NOT-END-OF-FILE    VALUE ZERO.
000058 01     NUMBER-WORDS           PIC S9(9) COMP.
000059
000060 PROCEDURE DIVISION.
000061 0000-MAIN SECTION.
000062* GET TEST DATA, THEN PERFORM SORT
000063     OPEN OUTPUT PRINT-FILE
000064
000065     PERFORM GET-TEST-DATA
000066     PERFORM SHELL-SORT
000067
000068     CLOSE PRINT-FILE
000069     GOBACK.
000070
000071 GET-TEST-DATA SECTION.
000072* READ WORDS FROM A FILE INTO THE TABLE FOR SORTING
000073     OPEN INPUT INPUT-FILE
000074     MOVE HIGH-VALUES TO W-ITEMS
000075     SET S1-IX TO 1
000076     SET IR-IX TO 70
000077     PERFORM GET-NEXT-LETTER
000078
000079     PERFORM GET-NEXT-WORD UNTIL END-OF-FILE
000080     SET S1-IX DOWN BY 1
000081     SET NUMBER-WORDS TO S1-IX
000082     CLOSE INPUT-FILE.
000083
000084 GET-NEXT-WORD SECTION.
000085* READ ONE WORD FROM FILE
000086     PERFORM UNTIL IR-LETTER (IR-IX) NOT = SPACE
000087     OR END-OF-FILE
000088         PERFORM GET-NEXT-LETTER
000089     END-PERFORM
000090
000091     MOVE SPACES TO NEXT-WORD
000092     SET NL-IX TO 1
000093
000094     PERFORM WITH TEST AFTER UNTIL END-OF-FILE
000095     OR IR-LETTER (IR-IX) = SPACE OR '.'
000096         MOVE IR-LETTER (IR-IX) TO NEXT-LETTER (NL-IX)
000097         SET NL-IX UP BY 1
```

Listing 3-18   Shell Sort. (Continued)

```
000098           PERFORM GET-NEXT-LETTER
000099     END-PERFORM
000100
000101     IF NEXT-WORD ALPHABETIC
000102         MOVE NEXT-WORD TO S-KEY (S1-IX)
000103         SET S1-IX UP BY 1
000104         IF S1-IX > ARRAY-SIZE
000105             SET END-OF-FILE TO TRUE
000106         END-IF
000107     END-IF.
000108
000109 GET-NEXT-LETTER SECTION.
000110* GET ONE LETTER FROM FILE
000111     SET IR-IX UP BY 1
000112
000113     IF IR-IX > 65
000114         READ INPUT-FILE
000115         AT END
000116             SET END-OF-FILE TO TRUE
000117         END-READ
000118         SET IR-IX TO 1
000119     END-IF.
000120
000121 SHELL-SORT SECTION.
000122* SORT TABLE
000123*1. SET GAP TO SUITABLE NUMBER
000124     MOVE 1 TO GAP
000125     PERFORM UNTIL GAP > ARRAY-SIZE
000126         COMPUTE GAP = (3 * GAP) + 1
000127     END-PERFORM
000128
000129*2. SORT
000130     PERFORM WITH TEST AFTER UNTIL GAP = 1
000131         COMPUTE GAP = GAP / 3
000132         SET S1-IX TO GAP
000133         SET S1-IX UP BY 1
000134         PERFORM UNTIL S1-IX > ARRAY-SIZE
000135             MOVE S-KEY (S1-IX) TO SWAP-ITEM
000136             SET S2-IX TO S1-IX
000137             MOVE ZERO TO LOOP-OVER-SW
000138             PERFORM UNTIL LOOP-OVER
000139                 IF S2-IX > GAP
000140                     SET S3-IX TO S2-IX
000141                     SET S2-IX DOWN BY GAP
000142                     IF S-KEY (S2-IX) > SWAP-ITEM
000143                         MOVE S-KEY (S2-IX) TO S-KEY (S3-IX)
```

Listing 3-18   Shell Sort. (Continued)

```
000144                         ELSE
000145                             SET S2-IX TO S3-IX
000146                             SET LOOP-OVER TO TRUE
000147                         END-IF
000148                     ELSE
000149                         SET LOOP-OVER TO TRUE
000150                     END-IF
000151                 END-PERFORM
000152                 MOVE SWAP-ITEM TO S-KEY (S2-IX)
000153                 SET S1-IX UP BY 1
000154             END-PERFORM
000155     END-PERFORM.
```

Listing 3-18   Shell Sort.

some, which is good enough for test data but wouldn't do for a word count program, for instance.

GET-NEXT-LETTER (line 109) reads one character, getting a new record when necessary.

SHELL-SORT (line 121) is the routine which sorts the table. This can be taken out of the program and used elsewhere. This is a variation on the insertion sort. An insertion sort works the way people sort cards: It looks at each element in turn and places it in sequence with the already sorted ones. This variant starts with comparisons over a large gap, resulting in a set of interleaved sorted files. It reduces the gap in steps, eventually to one, when the file will be completely sorted. The first loop finds a starting gap number for the exchanges, using the fact that a declining sequence like 124,40,13,4,1 has been found by experiment to work well. The main loop then performs the insertion sorts using these declining gaps. This method makes some very big exchanges quickly, and finishes up with a gap of one doing a standard insertion sort.

Periods are avoided except where necessary. Lines 69, 82, 107, 119, and 155 are the only ones terminated by periods, because they are required at the end of a paragraph.

Lines 65, 66, 77, and 79 feature PERFORM statements calling clearly defined subroutines. The PERFORM in line 79 is also a loop.

Lines 86, 94, 125, 134, and 138 feature PERFORM statements expressing loops.

In line 94, use of PERFORM WITH TEST AFTER ensures that at least one letter is read.

In general, notice the use of END-IF and END-READ consistently in the program. Terminators on other statements, such as END-COMPUTE, are not used unless needed. The program is broken into logical units with out-of-line PERFORMs, and all loops in the program are coded as in-line PERFORMs except the one beginning on line 79, which is a natural break as well as a loop.

4

The EVALUATE Statement

In this chapter, we will briefly review the generally understood principles of structured programming. We will consider how OS COBOL and COBOL II support them. We will then examine the EVALUATE statement which has been introduced to implement one of the structures.

4.1 STRUCTURED PROGRAMMING CONSTRUCTS

There is general agreement on the set of control structures which are the basic building blocks of structured programming. There are three basic types of control statements for the expression of sequence, iteration, and selection. It is necessary to be able to combine these structures freely.

Sequence simply refers to the fact that the default flow of control in a program is from one statement to the next until the bottom of the code is reached. This is actually not as obvious as it seems. In languages such as PROLOG, for instance, statements are not executed in sequence, but in an order determined by a problem-resolution mechanism. Even in COBOL, declaratives (the USE statement) are not executed in sequence. And most languages other than COBOL do not allow control to fall through performed paragraphs. Figure 4-1 illustrates the sequence structure.

Sequence

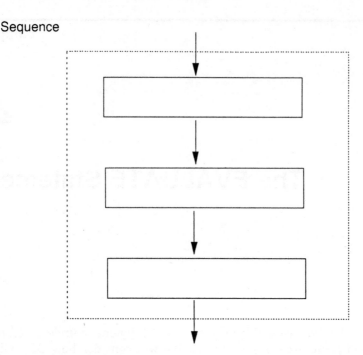

Figure 4-1   The Sequence Structure.

Iteration is the controlled repetition of a body of code while some set of conditions applies. The test for the conditions can occur before (DO . . . WHILE) or after (DO . . . UNTIL) the body of code. Figures 4-2 and 4-3 illustrate these two iteration structures.

Selection refers to the choice of different paths of execution based on a set of conditions. The choice could be of one path or not (IF), between two paths (IF . . . ELSE), or between many paths (CASE). Figures 4-4 and 4-5 illustrate these two selection structures.

An essential point of structured programming is that you should be able to combine these structures in any manner you choose. You can combine them as building blocks into arbitrarily complex programs. It has been proved that if you can do this in a computer language, you can code anything that can be programmed. Figure 4-6 illustrates an example of this combination of structures.

Selection

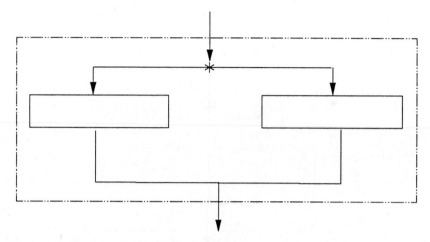

Figure 4-2   The IF/ELSE Selection Structure.

Selection

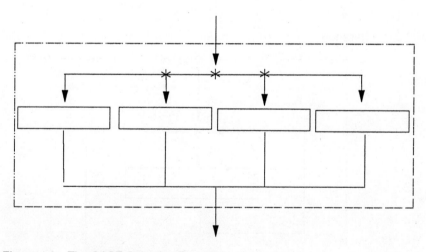

Figure 4-3   The CASE Selection Structure.

Iteration

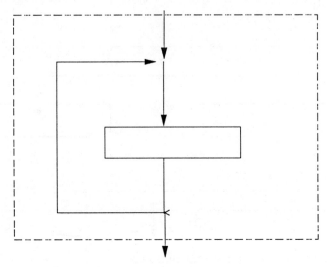

Figure 4-4   The DO . . . UNTIL Iteration Structure.

Iteration

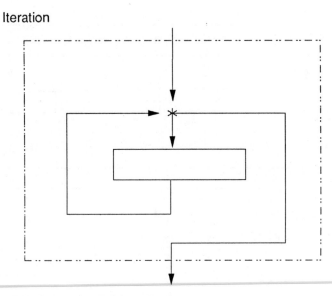

Figure 4-5   The DO . . . WHILE Iteration Structure.

Unlimited
Combination

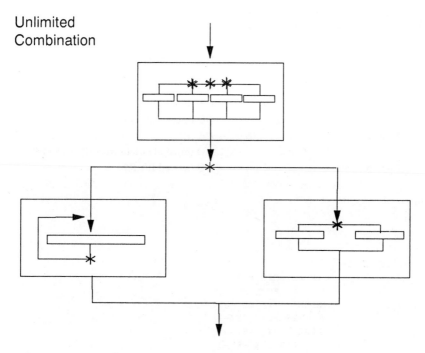

Figure 4-6   Unlimited Combination of Simple Structure.

4.1.1   Structured Programming in OS COBOL

OS COBOL (like any COBOL compiler conforming to the ANSI 1974 standard) was not a very good vehicle for coding using these structured programming principles. The PERFORM statement had iteration with test before, but not with test after. There is no implementation of the CASE construct. It is not possible to combine blocks of code, because of the problems with nested conditional statements and the period. Table 4-1 summarizes these areas of weakness.

4.2   THE CASE STRUCTURE IN OS COBOL AND COBOL II

Listing 4-1 shows possible OS COBOL case structures. The example nests the IF . . . ELSE structure in two different ways because there are different schools of thought on the right way to do it. The first

Table 4-1   OS COBOL and Structured Concepts.

Principle	Detail	COBOL Compliance
Sequence		OK
Iteration	test before	OK (Perform)
	test after	NO (must simulate)
Selection	IF . . . ELSE	OK (If)
	CASE	NO (must simulate with IF . . . ELSE)
Combination		NO (nested IFs fail)

```
1. IF/ELSE:
                IF KEY-HIT = 1
                    PERFORM KEY-1
                ELSE    IF KEY-HIT = 2
                    PERFORM KEY-2
                ELSE    IF KEY-HIT = 3
                    PERFORM KEY-3
                ELSE
                    PERFORM OTHER-KEY.

2. IF/ELSE:
                IF KEY-HIT = 1
                    PERFORM KEY-1
                ELSE
                    IF KEY-HIT = 2
                        PERFORM KEY-2
                    ELSE
                        IF KEY-HIT = 3
                            PERFORM KEY-3
                        ELSE
                            PERFORM OTHER-KEY.

3. GO TO DEPENDING:
            CASE-STRUCTURE.
                GO TO KEY-1
                    KEY-2
                    KEY-3
                DEPENDING ON KEY-HIT.
                GO TO OTHER-KEY.
        * -- KEY FUNCTIONS MUST END BY GOING TO HERE
            END-CASE.
```

Listing 4-1   Possible OS COBOL Case Structures.

```
1. IF ... ELSE IF ... ELSE IF:

        IF KEY-HIT = 1
                PERFORM KEY-1
        ELSE
                IF KEY-HIT = 2
                        PERFORM KEY-2
                ELSE
                        IF KEY-HIT = 3
                                PERFORM KEY-3
                        ELSE
                                PERFORM OTHER-KEY
                        END-IF
                END-IF
        END-IF

2. EVALUATE:

        EVALUATE TRUE
        WHEN KEY-HIT = 1
                PERFORM KEY-1
        WHEN KEY-HIT = 2
                PERFORM KEY-2
        WHEN KEY-HIT = 3
                PERFORM KEY-3
        WHEN OTHER
                PERFORM OTHER-KEY
        END-EVALUATE
```

Listing 4-2   Possible COBOL II Case Structures.

way seems to express the situation more clearly, since all the statements are at the same level of nesting, logically. After all, they could
be in any order. Furthermore, the second method will fall off the
right-hand side of the page when there are many cases to consider.
The third method would be rejected by most people but is recommended by some writers as the way to code a case structure in
COBOL.

Listing 4-2 shows additional possible COBOL II case structures.
The series of IF statements has to be nested now for consistency
with the string of END-IFs at the end, but this makes it even more
untidy than the previous example. One solution would be to drop the
rule that every IF has an END-IF for this case, and use Example 1
from Listing 4-1 which still works.

A better answer is to use the EVALUATE statement instead of a
string of nested IFs. The second example in Listing 4-2 shows an

```
IF KEY-HIT = 1
    PERFORM KEY-1
ELSE
    IF KEY-HIT = 2
        PERFORM KEY-2
    ELSE
        IF KEY-HIT = 3
            IF SHIFT-KEY-HELD
                PERFORM SPECIAL-CASE
            ELSE
                PERFORM KEY-3
        ELSE
            PERFORM OTHER-KEY
        END-IF
    END-IF
END-IF
```

Listing 4-3   Not Equivalent to EVALUATE.

equivalent EVALUATE statement. Using this will remove us from the disputes on how to indent nested IFs.

4.3 THE EVALUATE STATEMENT

The example in Listing 4-2 shows a typical simple EVALUATE statement, starting with EVALUATE TRUE, containing several WHEN clauses, and ending with a WHEN OTHER clause and END-EVALUATE. The scope terminator END-EVALUATE is required, since this is always a conditional statement.

This form of EVALUATE is easier to read than the IF . . . ELSE structure because it is more regular. It is immediately apparent what is going on, even if the statement spans several pages. The IF . . . ELSE IF . . . ELSE IF structure is logically equivalent, but it is not easy to see this. For instance, compare Listing 4-3. This is not the same multi-way branch structure—there is a different special case coded in the middle. This has to be discovered by inspecting each line of code.

```
EVALUATE TRUE
WHEN LOCATION = 'NY'
        PERFORM NEW-YORK-ROUTINE
WHEN LOCATION = 'LO'
        PERFORM LONDON-ROUTINE
WHEN LOCATION = 'PA'
        PERFORM PARIS-ROUTINE
WHEN OTHER
        PERFORM DEFAULT-ROUTINE
END-EVALUATE

EVALUATE TRUE
WHEN LOCATION = 'NY'
        PERFORM NEW-YORK-ROUTINE
WHEN LOCATION = 'LO'
        PERFORM LONDON-ROUTINE
WHEN LOCATION = 'PA'
        PERFORM PARIS-ROUTINE
END-EVALUATE
```

Listing 4-4   WHEN OTHER Clauses.

4.4   THE WHEN OTHER CLAUSE

The WHEN OTHER clause is optional. If present, this clause is executed if no other condition is matched. This guarantees that exactly one clause of the statement will be executed. If the WHEN OTHER clause is missing, it is possible for no clause to be matched and executed. Listing 4-4 has examples of these cases. If location is 'HK', for instance, in the first case DEFAULT-ROUTINE will be executed, and in the second nothing. In either case, control will then pass to the following statement.

4.5   THE TRUE AND FALSE RESERVED WORDS

The reserved words TRUE and FALSE are introduced in COBOL II. (A list of the reserved words in COBOL II, with the new ones highlighted, is included in Appendix C.) When used with an EVALUATE clause, they indicate whether a condition on a following WHEN clause must be true or false to cause execution of the statements following it.

```
EVALUATE TRUE
WHEN RET-CODE = '10'
        PERFORM END-OF-FILE
WHEN RET-CODE = '21'
        PERFORM NOT-FOUND
WHEN OTHER
        PERFORM FILE-ERROR
END-EVALUATE
```

Listing 4-5   EVALUATE TRUE.

4.5.1   EVALUATE TRUE

In Listing 4-5, if RET-CODE is '10', END-OF-FILE will be performed. If RET-CODE is '21', NOT-FOUND will be performed. In any other case, for instance if RET-CODE is '30', FILE-ERROR will be performed.

4.5.2   EVALUATE FALSE

In Listing 4-6, the reserved word FALSE is used instead of TRUE. In this case, a condition must be untrue for its following statements to be executed. If RET-CODE is any value other than '00', for instance '10', FILE-ERROR will be performed. If RET-CODE is '00', then FILE-OK will be performed. You might want to restrict your use of this form of EVALUATE, as it is not easy to read and comprehend. This example would be better as an IF statement, for instance.

4.6   EVALUATE EXPRESSION

Besides the reserved words TRUE and FALSE, the EVALUATE clause can contain an expression. If a single expression is being

```
EVALUATE FALSE
WHEN RET-CODE = '00'
        PERFORM FILE-ERROR
WHEN OTHER
        PERFORM FILE-OK
END-EVALUATE
```

Listing 4-6   EVALUATE FALSE.

```
EVALUATE TRUE
WHEN RET-CODE = '10'
          PERFORM END-OF-FILE
WHEN RET-CODE = '21'
          PERFORM NOT-FOUND
WHEN OTHER
          PERFORM FILE-ERROR
END-EVALUATE


EVALUATE RET-CODE
WHEN '10'
          PERFORM END-OF-FILE
WHEN '21'
          PERFORM NOT-FOUND
WHEN OTHER
          PERFORM FILE-ERROR
END-EVALUATE
```

Listing 4-7   EVALUATE Expression.

evaluated, as in all the preceding examples, it is possible to code this expression once in the EVALUATE clause, rather than repeat it in each WHEN clause. The two fragments in Listing 4-7 are equivalent.

This technique has the advantage of constraining the code even further, making it easier to read. If you see the statement "EVALU-ATE KEY-HIT" followed by five pages of code and ended with "END-EVALUATE," you know immediately that every WHEN clause on those pages refers to a value of KEY-HIT.

4.6.1   EVALUATE and Condition Names

Condition names (88 levels) can be freely used in the EVALUATE statement. For example, if you have a variable that can take different values that control execution flow, you can set up 88 levels and test for them as in the example in Listing 4-8. The advantage of this approach, as compared to Listing 4-7, is that the "magic" values (10, 21, etc.) of RET-CODE have disappeared from the procedure code. A disadvantage is that it is no longer clear that all branches of the EVALUATE statement are based on the value of the same variable. The best way to do this will be a question of judgment or style in many cases.

```
DATA DIVISION.
01  RET-CODE                      PIC XX.
        88 RC-ENDFILE             VALUE '10'.
        88 RC-NOTFND              VALUE '21'.
PROCEDURE DIVISION.
        EVALUATE TRUE
        WHEN RC-ENDFILE
                PERFORM END-OF-FILE
        WHEN RC-NOTFND
                PERFORM NOT-FOUND
        WHEN OTHER
                PERFORM FILE-ERROR
        END-EVALUATE
```

Listing 4-8   Using Condition Names.

4.7   EVALUATE WITH COMPOUND CONDITIONS

The preceding examples have used simple conditions on the EVALU-
ATE and WHEN clauses. Compound conditions can also be easily
handled by the EVALUATE statement in several ways. One possibility is use of the ALSO clause, which is mentioned in the next two
sections.

Conditions in the WHEN clauses of an EVALUATE statement can
be simple or compound. In the example in Listing 4-9, assume the
user of the program pressed the page-forward key. If he is already at
end-of-file, the compound condition is true and INVALID-KEY will
be performed. Otherwise, PAGE-FORWARD will be performed.

4.7.1   Using EVALUATE with Several Conditions

If a WHEN clause evaluates to TRUE, the next imperative
statement following the WHEN will be executed. There can be

```
EVALUATE TRUE
WHEN PAGING-FORWARD AND END-OF-FILE-REACHED
        PERFORM INVALID-KEY
WHEN PAGING-FORWARD
        PERFORM PAGE-FORWARD
    ...
    END-EVALUATE
```

Listing 4-9   Compound Condition.

```
DATA DIVISION.
01  YEAR-CODE        PIC XX.

PROCEDURE DIVISION.
    EVALUATE YEAR-CODE
    WHEN '17'
    WHEN '18'
        PERFORM FIRST-WORLD-WAR
    WHEN '41'
    WHEN '42'
    WHEN '43'
    WHEN '44'
    WHEN '45'
        PERFORM SECOND-WORLD-WAR
    WHEN OTHER
        PERFORM AT-PEACE
    END-EVALUATE
```

Listing 4-10   WHEN Clause Fall-Through.

intervening conditions. It follows that when one WHEN clause immediately follows another without any executable statement between, the two conditions are effectively "OR"ed. In Listing 4-10, if the year-code is 17 or 18, the procedure FIRST-WORLD-WAR will execute. If the year is from 41 to 45 inclusive, SECOND-WORLD-WAR will be performed.

4.7.2   The Order of WHEN Clauses Is Significant

The "fall-through" effect discussed above is a useful feature which can save a lot of redundant typing in certain cases. But you should bear in mind that the correct execution of this code is totally dependent on the order in which the WHEN clauses were coded. If you want to make 1943 a (nonhistorical) year of peace, you must do more than add the phrase "PERFORM AT-PEACE" under "WHEN '43'." You must either reorder the WHEN clauses or add PERFORM SECOND-WORLD-WAR under "WHEN '42'."

In many forms of the EVALUATE clause, the order of the WHEN clauses is not significant to the results. However, this is certainly not guaranteed. Evaluation of WHEN clauses proceeds sequentially from top to bottom. You can take advantage of this, as in the code in Listing 4-11.

```
EVALUATE TRUE
WHEN PAGING-FORWARD AND END-OF-FILE-REACHED
    PERFORM INVALID-KEY
WHEN PAGING-FORWARD
    PERFORM PAGE-FORWARD
...
END-EVALUATE
```

Listing 4-11   Order of Evaluation.

4.8 THE ALSO CLAUSE

Using ALSO, you can extend the EVALUATE expression form to
handle several expressions in one statement. This enables the or-
derly coding of sets of alternatives that would otherwise require a
series of nested IF statements. Listing 4-12 shows two examples of
the use of this statement.

```
PROCEDURE DIVISION.

    EVALUATE TRUE ALSO TRUE
    WHEN PAGING-FORWARD ALSO END-OF-FILE-REACHED
            PERFORM INVALID-KEY
    WHEN PAGING-FORWARD
            PERFORM PAGE-FORWARD
    ...
    END-EVALUATE

    EVALUATE VSAM-STATUS-1 ALSO VSAM-STATUS-2
    WHEN '0' ALSO '0'
    WHEN '0' ALSO '2'
            PERFORM SUCCESSFUL-PROCESS
    WHEN '1' ALSO '0'
            PERFORM END-OF-FILE-PROCESS
    WHEN '2' ALSO '1'
            PERFORM NOTFND-PROCESS
    WHEN '2' ALSO '2'
            PERFORM DUPREC-PROCESS
    ...
    END-EVALUATE
```

Listing 4-12   ALSO Clause.

```
EVALUATE VSAM-STATUS-1 ALSO VSAM-STATUS-2
WHEN '0' ALSO ANY
          PERFORM SUCCESSFUL-PROCESS
   WHEN '1' ALSO '0'
             PERFORM END-OF-FILE-PROCESS
   WHEN '2' ALSO '1'
             PERFORM NOTFND-PROCESS
   WHEN '2' ALSO '2'
             PERFORM DUPREC-PROCESS
   WHEN '2' ALSO ANY
             PERFORM INVALID-KEY-PROCESS
END-EVALUATE
```

Listing 4-13   ALSO with ANY.

4.8.1   The ANY Reserved Word

In addition to TRUE and FALSE, there is a reserved word ANY for use in the EVALUATE statement. This will match any value in the evaluate clause. Listing 4-13 shows Listing 4-12 recoded and simplified by use of the ANY clause.

4.8.2   Early Compiler Versions

Release 1.0 of the VS COBOL II compiler did not include the ALSO statement at all or mention it in the documentation. You may need to review EVALUATE statements in COBOL II programs written for this compiler.

4.8.3   EVALUATE as a Decision Table Processor

Decision tables are a method of representing a series of conditions. In the past, they have been used as a step in analysis of systems. There have been languages based on decision tables, and many people have regarded the method as one of the most understandable ways of laying out a process design for review by users. There are

Table 4-2   Customer Discount Table.

Ann Purch > $10M	Categ A/B	Order in $K	# O/S Inv > 3	Disc %
Y	Y	<50	Y	10
Y	Y	50-500	Y	12
Y	Y	>500	Y	15
Y	Y	<50	N	9
Y	Y	50-500	N	11
Y	Y	>500	N	13
Y	N	<50	Y	9
Y	N	50-500	Y	11
Y	N	>500	Y	13
Y	N	<50	N	8
Y	N	50-500	N	10
Y	N	>500	N	7
N	Y	<50	Y	8
N	Y	50-500	Y	11
N	Y	>500	Y	11
N	Y	<50	N	8
N	Y	50-500	N	9
N	Y	>500	N	7
N	N	<50	Y	4
N	N	50-500	Y	6
N	N	>500	Y	8
N	N	<50	N	0
N	N	50-500	N	3
N	N	>500	N	6

simple methods for determining completeness and consistency of such tables.

It is possible to use EVALUATE to encode a decision table directly into COBOL. The following is a typical medium-sized decision table from a purchase order system. The customer discount percentage depends on the customer category, his annual purchases, the size of the order, and the number of outstanding invoices in a somewhat arbitrary manner, as described in Table 4-2. The program of Listing 4-14 carries out this decision table using the EVALUATE statement.

```
000001 ID DIVISION.
000002 PROGRAM-ID. DECTABLE.
000003 ENVIRONMENT DIVISION.
000004 INPUT-OUTPUT SECTION.
000005 FILE-CONTROL.
000006     SELECT CUST-FILE  ASSIGN TO INFILE.
000007     SELECT PRINT-FILE ASSIGN TO PRINTER.
000008 DATA DIVISION.
000009 FILE SECTION.
000010 FD CUST-FILE
000011    RECORDING MODE F
000012    RECORD CONTAINS 80 CHARACTERS
000013    BLOCK CONTAINS 0 RECORDS
000014    DATA RECORD IS INPUT-RECORD
000015    LABEL RECORDS ARE STANDARD.
000016
000017 01 INPUT-RECORD.
000018    02  CUST-ID                PIC 9(10).
000019    02  CUST-ANNUAL-PURCHASE   PIC 9(12).
000020        88  CUST-ANNUAL-SMALL     VALUES 0 THRU 9999999.
000021    02  CUST-CATEGORY          PIC X.
000022    02  CUST-INV-OS            PIC 999.
000023    02  CUST-ORDER             PIC 9(08).
000024        88  CUST-ORDER-SMALL  VALUES 0 THRU 49999.
000025        88  CUST-ORDER-MEDIUM VALUES 50000 THRU 500000.
000026        88  CUST-ORDER-BIG    VALUES 500000 THRU 99999999.
000027    02  CUST-DISCOUNT          PIC 9(04).
000028    02  FILLER                 PIC X(42).
000029
000030 FD     PRINT-FILE
000031        RECORD CONTAINS 133 CHARACTERS
000032        RECORDING MODE F
000033        LABEL RECORDS ARE STANDARD.
000034
000035 01     PRINT-LINE.
000036        02  PR-SKIP-CHAR        PIC X(01).
000037        02  FILLER              PIC X(02).
000038        02  PR-CUST-ID          PIC 9(10).
000039        02  FILLER              PIC X(02).
000040        02  PR-CUST-ANNUAL-PURCHASE PIC $$$,$$$,$$$,$$9.99.
000041        02  FILLER              PIC X(02).
000042        02  PR-CUST-CATEGORY    PIC X.
000043        02  FILLER              PIC X(02).
000044        02  PR-CUST-INV-OS      PIC 999.
000045        02  FILLER              PIC X(02).
```

Listing 4-14 Decision Table. (Continued)

```
000046           02  PR-CUST-ORDER        PIC $$,$$$,$$9.99.
000047           02  FILLER               PIC X(02).
000048           02  PR-CUST-DISCOUNT     PIC 9(04).
000049           02  FILLER               PIC X(70).
000050
000051 WORKING-STORAGE SECTION.
000052 01  END-OF-FILE-SW         PIC X VALUE ZERO.
000053     88  END-OF-FILE                VALUE '1'.
000054
000055 PROCEDURE DIVISION.
000056 0000-MAIN SECTION.
000057* GET TEST DATA, THEN PERFORM SORT
000058     OPEN INPUT CUST-FILE
000059     OPEN OUTPUT PRINT-FILE
000060
000061     READ CUST-FILE
000062     AT END
000063         SET END-OF-FILE TO TRUE
000064     END-READ
000065
000066     PERFORM UNTIL END-OF-FILE
000067         PERFORM FIGURE-DISCOUNT
000068         PERFORM DISPLAY-OUTPUT
000069         READ CUST-FILE
000070         AT END
000071             SET END-OF-FILE TO TRUE
000072         END-READ
000073     END-PERFORM
000074
000075     CLOSE CUST-FILE
000076     CLOSE PRINT-FILE
000077     GOBACK.
000078
000079 FIGURE-DISCOUNT SECTION.
000080     EVALUATE NOT CUST-ANNUAL-SMALL
000081         ALSO CUST-CATEGORY = "A" OR "B"
000082         ALSO TRUE
000083         ALSO CUST-INV-OS > 3
000084     WHEN TRUE  ALSO TRUE ALSO CUST-ORDER-SMALL   ALSO TRUE
000085         MOVE 10 TO CUST-DISCOUNT
000086     WHEN TRUE  ALSO TRUE  ALSO CUST-ORDER-MEDIUM ALSO TRUE
000087         MOVE 12 TO CUST-DISCOUNT
000088     WHEN TRUE  ALSO TRUE  ALSO CUST-ORDER-BIG    ALSO TRUE
000089         MOVE 15 TO CUST-DISCOUNT
000090     WHEN TRUE  ALSO TRUE  ALSO CUST-ORDER-SMALL  ALSO FALSE
000091         MOVE  9 TO CUST-DISCOUNT
```

Listing 4-14   Decision Table. (Continued)

```
000092      WHEN TRUE  ALSO TRUE  ALSO CUST-ORDER-MEDIUM ALSO FALSE
000093          MOVE 11 TO CUST-DISCOUNT
000094      WHEN TRUE  ALSO TRUE  ALSO CUST-ORDER-BIG    ALSO FALSE
000095          MOVE 13 TO CUST-DISCOUNT
000096      WHEN TRUE  ALSO FALSE ALSO CUST-ORDER-SMALL  ALSO TRUE
000097          MOVE  9 TO CUST-DISCOUNT
000098      WHEN TRUE  ALSO FALSE ALSO CUST-ORDER-MEDIUM ALSO TRUE
000099          MOVE 11 TO CUST-DISCOUNT
000100      WHEN TRUE  ALSO FALSE ALSO CUST-ORDER-BIG    ALSO TRUE
000101          MOVE 13 TO CUST-DISCOUNT
000102      WHEN TRUE  ALSO FALSE ALSO CUST-ORDER-SMALL  ALSO FALSE
000103          MOVE  8 TO CUST-DISCOUNT
000104      WHEN TRUE  ALSO FALSE ALSO CUST-ORDER-MEDIUM ALSO FALSE
000105          MOVE 10 TO CUST-DISCOUNT
000106      WHEN TRUE  ALSO FALSE ALSO CUST-ORDER-BIG    ALSO FALSE
000107          MOVE  7 TO CUST-DISCOUNT
000108      WHEN FALSE ALSO TRUE ALSO CUST-ORDER-SMALL   ALSO TRUE
000109          MOVE  8 TO CUST-DISCOUNT
000110      WHEN FALSE ALSO TRUE  ALSO CUST-ORDER-MEDIUM ALSO TRUE
000111          MOVE 11 TO CUST-DISCOUNT
000112      WHEN FALSE ALSO TRUE  ALSO CUST-ORDER-BIG    ALSO TRUE
000113          MOVE 11 TO CUST-DISCOUNT
000114      WHEN FALSE ALSO TRUE  ALSO CUST-ORDER-SMALL  ALSO FALSE
000115          MOVE  8 TO CUST-DISCOUNT
000116      WHEN FALSE ALSO TRUE  ALSO CUST-ORDER-MEDIUM ALSO FALSE
000117          MOVE  9 TO CUST-DISCOUNT
000118      WHEN FALSE ALSO TRUE  ALSO CUST-ORDER-BIG    ALSO FALSE
000119          MOVE  7 TO CUST-DISCOUNT
000120      WHEN FALSE ALSO FALSE ALSO CUST-ORDER-SMALL  ALSO TRUE
000121          MOVE  4 TO CUST-DISCOUNT
000122      WHEN FALSE ALSO FALSE ALSO CUST-ORDER-MEDIUM ALSO TRUE
000123          MOVE  6 TO CUST-DISCOUNT
000124      WHEN FALSE ALSO FALSE ALSO CUST-ORDER-BIG    ALSO TRUE
000125          MOVE  8 TO CUST-DISCOUNT
000126      WHEN FALSE ALSO FALSE ALSO CUST-ORDER-SMALL  ALSO FALSE
000127          MOVE  0 TO CUST-DISCOUNT
000128      WHEN FALSE ALSO FALSE ALSO CUST-ORDER-MEDIUM ALSO FALSE
000129          MOVE  3 TO CUST-DISCOUNT
000130      WHEN FALSE ALSO FALSE ALSO CUST-ORDER-BIG    ALSO FALSE
000131          MOVE  6 TO CUST-DISCOUNT
000132      END-EVALUATE.
000133
000134 DISPLAY-OUTPUT SECTION.
000135      MOVE SPACES                TO   PRINT-LINE
000136
000137      MOVE CUST-ID               TO   PR-CUST-ID
```

Listing 4-14   Decision Table. (Continued)

```
000138        MOVE  CUST-ANNUAL-PURCHASE  TO   PR-CUST-ANNUAL-PURCHASE
000139        MOVE  CUST-CATEGORY         TO   PR-CUST-CATEGORY
000140        MOVE  CUST-INV-OS           TO   PR-CUST-INV-OS
000141        MOVE  CUST-ORDER            TO   PR-CUST-ORDER
000142        MOVE  CUST-DISCOUNT         TO   PR-CUST-DISCOUNT
000143
000144        WRITE PRINT-LINE.
```

Listing 4-14   Decision Table.

4.9   SUMMARY OF EVALUATE STATEMENT

4.9.1   EVALUATE in Other Languages

The EVALUATE statement brings to COBOL the case structure of traditional structured programming. There are similar statements in most programming languages. The PL/I SELECT statement is similar to EVALUATE TRUE and EVALUATE expression, with the difference that if you leave off the OTHERWISE clause (like COBOL WHEN OTHER) and there is no match, a run-time error (abend) will occur. The C language SWITCH statement is similar to EVALUATE expression, with the difference that control will fall through from one case to another unless you explicitly force it out of the statement. Listing 4-15 shows the COBOL example of Listing 4-9 expressed in PL/I and C.

4.9.2   Summary of EVALUATE Statement

The EVALUATE statement varies from the simple to the very complex. The simplest case, EVALUATE . . . TRUE, is a good replacement for the nested IF structure. EVALUATE with a variable is a tidy way of coding a test for many values of a switch variable. By using ALSO, or coding complex conditions, or multiple WHEN clauses, some very complicated choices can be expressed in a single EVALUATE statement. A single EVALUATE statement can contain up to 64 subjects and up to 256 WHEN clauses.

PL/I:

```
SELECT YEAR_CODE;
WHEN ('17' '18')
        CALL FIRST_WORLD_WAR;
WHEN ('41' '42' '43' '44' '45')
        CALL SECOND_WORLD_WAR;
OTHERWISE
        CALL AT_PEACE
END;
```

C:

```
switch (year_code) {
case 17:
case 18:
        first_world_war();
case 41:
case 42:
case 43:
case 44:
case 45:
        second_world_war();
default:
        at_peace();
}
```

Listing 4-15   EVALUATE in Other Languages.

The simplest forms of the EVALUATE statement are the best ones to use regularly. Use of the more exotic flavors may not be advisable, as they can be difficult to understand.

4.9.3   COBOL II and Structured Programming

In Chapter 2, we saw that the introduction of scope terminators solved the combination problem. In Chapter 3, we saw that WITH TEST AFTER solves the iteration problem. In this chapter, we covered the EVALUATE statement, which introduces to COBOL the structured programming construct CASE. Table 4-3 summarizes the manner in which COBOL II complies with structured programming principles.

Table 4-3   COBOL II and Structured Concepts.

Principle	Detail	COBOL Compliance
Sequence		OK
Iteration	test before	OK (Perform with test before)
	test after	OF (Perform with test after)
Selection	IF . . . ELSE	OK (If)
	CASE	OK (Evaluate)
Combination		OK

5

Further Features Added in COBOL II

This chapter introduces several new language features which have been added in COBOL II but which do not fall into a convenient category. These are:

• the INITIALIZE statement and its option REPLACING
• explicit setting of 88-levels to TRUE
• the LENGTH special register
• the CONTINUE statement

5.1 THE INITIALIZE STATEMENT

The INITIALIZE verb is used to assign values to a group or elementary item. It is equivalent to a series of MOVE statements. In the simplest form, numeric fields have zero moved to them and alphanumeric fields are filled with spaces. Other fields are unchanged, as is FILLER.

A simple example of INITIALIZE is illustrated in Listing 5-1. After the INITIALIZE statement executes, the five numeric fields (S-PACKED, S-NUMERIC, S-BINARY, S-FLOAT, S-FLOAT2) are initialized to zero. S-CHARS is initialized to all spaces. FILLER, S-INDEX, and S-POINTER are untouched.

```
DATA DIVISION.
01  BIG-STRUCTURE
    02  S-PACKED    PIC S9(07)       COMP-3.
    02  S-NUMERIC   PIC 9(08).
    02  S-BINARY    PIC S9(08)       COMP.
    02  S-FLOAT                      COMP-1.
    02  S-FLOAT2                     COMP-2.
    02  S-CHARS     PIC X(40).
    02  FILLER      PIC X(100).
    02  S-INDEX                      INDEX.
    02  S-POINTER                    POINTER.

PROCEDURE DIVISION.
    INITIALIZE BIG-STRUCTURE.
```

Listing 5-1   Example of INITIALIZE.

5.1.1   Elementary Items and INITIALIZE

INITIALIZE can be used on elementary items, when it will just be equivalent to one MOVE statement. In the example in Listing 5-1, five separate INITIALIZE statements could have been used to initialize the five fields.

When INITIALIZE is used on group items, it initializes the elementary fields contained in them, in other words, the fields at the lowest level. Table 5-1 lists the effects of INITIALIZE on each elementary field.

5.1.2   Uninitialized Fields

Since the INITIALIZE statement doesn't act on some data types, the contents of variables of those types will depend on the prior operation of the program. Possibly the program has assigned values to them previously. If they have not been assigned values and they are in working storage, they will contain binary zeroes (low values). If they have not been assigned values and they are in the linkage or file sections, their contents will be unpredictable.

One way to assign a value prior to the INITIALIZE statement is with the VALUE clause.

Table 5-1   Default Operation of Initialize.

Data Type	Value Moved In
PIC 9	ZERO
PIC 9 COMP	ZERO
COMP-1	ZERO
COMP-2	ZERO
PIC 9 COMP-3	ZERO
PIC X	SPACES
INDEX	not affected
POINTER	not affected
named FILLER	not affected

5.1.3   INITIALIZE with FILLER

INITIALIZE doesn't do anything with fields named FILLER. As discussed above, this means they could contain various kinds of garbage. Although you are not going to reference filler fields in the program, you will not want to write fields like this to shared common areas and external files.

One approach you can take is to name all filler fields something other than FILLER (e.g., Filler-1, Filler-2, etc.). You could even name them all F, for instance, since you won't be referring to them. The first example in Listing 5-2 shows this.

A second approach is to move spaces to the area first. Now any area not touched by INITIALIZE, including FILLER, will contain spaces. This also puts spaces in indexes and pointers (see below). The second example in Listing 5-2 shows this.

A third approach is to use VALUE statements on all the FILLER items. These will be unaffected by INITIALIZE. Of course, this only works if the area in question is in working storage (not file or linkage section) and the filler areas are not subscripted. This approach can be used in conjunction with the REPLACING option (discussed in Section 5.2). The first example in Listing 5-2 also shows this technique.

```
DATA DIVISION.
01  BIG-RECORD.
    02  BR-ITEM-1       PIC X(80).
    02  FILLER-1        PIC X(40).
    02  FILLER          PIC X(11) VALUE 'Section One'.
    .....
    02  BR-ITEM-2       PIC X(50).
    02  F               PIC X(05).
    02  FILLER          PIC X(11) VALUE 'Section Two'
    .....
    02  F               PIC X(35).


PROCEDURE DIVISION.
    INITIALIZE BIG-RECORD.
*  -- NOW ALL FIELDS CONTAIN SPACES
*  -- EXCEPT THE FILLER FIELDS
```

Example of MOVE SPACES with INITIALIZE:

```
DATA DIVISION.
01  BIG-STRUCTURE
02  S-PACKED    PIC S9(07)      COMP-3  OCCURS 100.
02  S-NUMERIC   PIC 9(08)               OCCURS 100.
02  S-CHARS     PIC X(40)               OCCURS 50.
02  FILLER      PIC X(100).
02  S-INDEX                             INDEX.
02  S-POINTER                           POINTER.


PROCEDURE DIVISION.
    MOVE SPACES TO BIG-STRUCTURE
    INITIALIZE BIG-STRUCTURE
*  -- NOW FILLER, INDEX AND POINTER CONTAIN SPACES
        SET S-INDEX TO 1
        SET S-POINTER TO NULL.
*  -- NOW INDEX AND POINTER CONTAIN REASONABLE VALUES
```

Listing 5-2   Example of Named FILLER Fields and VALUE clauses.

5.1.4   INITIALIZE with POINTER and INDEX

The INITIALIZE statement doesn't do anything to fields with usage POINTER or INDEX. As discussed in 5.1.2, this means they could contain garbage, in particular leftover pointers to areas that have been freed. While default values are not very useful for these data types, the most reasonable values are zero or 1 for the INDEX and

NULL for the POINTER data type. These could be assigned with VALUE clauses or SET statements.

5.1.5 INITIALIZE with Numeric Fields

The main use of INITIALIZE is to put zeroes into arrays or records containing many numeric fields. In OS COBOL, initialization of numeric fields was irritating because you had to code it differently for each data type. Packed decimal and floating-point fields could not be initialized at the group level. The examples in Listing 5-3 show the code to initialize a group of numeric fields, first in OS COBOL then in COBOL II.

COBOL II has an option PFDSGN, which instructs the compiler that all numeric data has the IBM-preferred signs. Fields with IBM-preferred signs contain hexadecimal 'F0', 'F1', etc., in character (PIC X) fields, and hexadecimal 'C0', 'C1', 'D0', 'D1', etc., in numeric (PIC 9) fields. This instruction allows a performance enhancement by letting the compiler avoid redundant sign-checking code. To use this option, you should ensure that numeric fields are initialized either with the INITIALIZE statement or with individual MOVE statements. Numeric fields should not be initialized with group move statements. For example, a group move of zeroes will put the value X'F0' in fields which should contain 'C0'. Since the PFDSGN option might be used on a program without your knowledge, or even in another program on data generated by your program, you should always initialize numeric fields in this manner.

Rather than the loop coded in Listing 5-3, you will sometimes meet an old trick for packed decimals shown in the example in Listing 5-4. The second move statement initializes the last 99 occurrences in a single statement, relying on the way the System/370 performs a character move. This dubious practice still works, generating a compile-time warning, but is no longer necessary; one INITIALIZE statement will do the job.

5.1.6 Initializing Elementary and Subscripted Items

While you can initialize an elementary item, there is no point to it; a single MOVE statement is as good.

If an item is defined as subscripted, you must use a subscript with INITIALIZE. This will only affect the single item referred to.

```
OS COBOL:

    DATA DIVISION.
    01  DATA-RECORD.
        02  DISPLAY-NUMERICS.
            03  DN-NUMERIC      PIC 9(09)           OCCURS 100.
        02  BINARY-NUMERICS.
            03  BN-NUMERIC      PIC S9(09) COMP     OCCURS 100.
        02  PACKED-NUMERICS.
            03  PN-NUMERIC      PIC S9(09) COMP-3 OCCURS 100.


    PROCEDURE DIVISION.
        MOVE ZEROES TO DISPLAY-NUMERICS.

        MOVE LOW-VALUES TO BINARY-NUMERICS.

        PERFORM  0000-ZERO-PACKED-FIELD
        VARYING PN-IX FROM 1 BY 1
        UNTIL PN-IX > 100.

    0000-ZERO-PACKED-FIELD.
        MOVE ZERO TO PN-NUMERIC (PN-IX).

COBOL II:

    DATA DIVISION.
    01  DATA-RECORD.
        02  DISPLAY-NUMERICS.
            03  DN-NUMERIC      PIC 9(09)           OCCURS 100.
        02  BINARY-NUMERICS.
            03  BN-NUMERIC      PIC S9(09) COMP     OCCURS 100.
        02  PACKED-NUMERICS.
            03  PN-NUMERIC      PIC S9(09) COMP-3 OCCURS 100.

    PROCEDURE DIVISION.
        INITIALIZE DATA-RECORD
```

Listing 5-3   Numeric Field Initialization.

To initialize a whole array, you must identify a group item which contains it. Listing 5-5 contains examples which illustrate this.

5.1.7   INITIALIZE with Redefine and 88-Levels

INITIALIZE will act on the first definition of an area, not on any redefinition. In the example in Listing 5-6, REDEF-NUM will

```
OS COBOL:

    DATA DIVISION.
    01  PACKED-NUMERICS.
        02  PN-NUMERIC        PIC S9(08) COMP-3 OCCURS 100.

    01  FILLER REDEFINES PACKED-NUMERICS.
        02  FILLER                 PIC X(05).
        02  REST-OF-IT             PIC X(495).

    PROCEDURE DIVISION.
        MOVE ZERO TO PN-NUMERIC (1).
        MOVE PACKED-NUMERICS TO REST-OF-IT.

COBOL II:

    DATA DIVISION.
    01 PACKED-NUMERICS.
        02  PN-NUMERIC          PIC S9(08) COMP-3 OCCURS 100.

    PROCEDURE DIVISION.
        INITIALIZE PACKED-NUMERICS.
```

Listing 5-4   Initializing a Packed Decimal Array.

```
    DATA DIVISION.
    01  SINGLE-ITEM      PIC S9(07) COMP.
    01  GROUP-ITEM.
    02  SUBSCRIPTED-ITEM      OCCURS 50 INDEXED BY BB-IX.
            03 SI-1      PIC S9(07) COMP-3.
            03 SI-2      PIC S9(07) COMP-3.

    PROCEDURE DIVISION.
    * -- SET SINGLE-ITEM TO ZERO
        INITIALIZE SINGLE-ITEM

    * -- THIS STATEMENT SETS ALL OCCURRENCES TO ZEROES
        INITIALIZE GROUP-ITEM

        SET BB-IX TO 1
    * -- THESE STATEMENTS EACH SET ONE OCCURRENCE TO ZEROES
        INITIALIZE SUBSCRIPTED-ITEM (20)
        INITIALIZE SUBSCRIPTED-ITEM (BB-IX)

    * -- THIS IS INVALID (NEEDS A SUBSCRIPT)
        INITIALIZE SUBSCRIPTED-ITEM
```

Listing 5-5   Initializing Items in Arrays.

```
DATA DIVISION.
01  GROUP-ITEM.
    02  REDEF-ALPHA                 PIC X(05).
    02  REDEF-NUM
            REDEFINES REDEF-ALPHA   PIC 9(05).
    02  AA-CODE             PIC X.
        88  VALID-CODES             VALUE '1', '2', '3'.


PROCEDURE DIVISION.
    INITIALIZE GROUP-ITEM.
```

Listing 5-6   Redefinition with INITIALIZE.

contain five spaces, not five zeroes, because the area was first defined as alphanumeric.

Condition names (88-level items) have no effect on the operation of the INITIALIZE verb, and of course it has no effect on them. In the previous example, AA-CODE is simply set to space because it is an alphanumeric item.

5.1.8 INITIALIZE REPLACING

The simple INITIALIZE statement defined above moves zero to all numeric fields and spaces to all alphabetic and alphanumeric fields. This suffices in the majority of cases. If something other than this is needed, you use the REPLACING option.

With REPLACING you can initialize categories of data to the values you specify. These categories are:

```
ALPHABETIC
ALPHANUMERIC
NUMERIC
ALPHANUMERIC-EDITED
NUMERIC-EDITED
EGCS
```

In Listing 5-7, we first set all the subscripts to 1. Then the alphanumeric and numeric fields in LAST-RECORD are set to their highest possible values. Then some literals are moved into SCREEN-RECORD that might be useful for a program that prompts for a screen of text from a user.

```
DATA DIVISION.
01  SUBSCRIPTS.
        02  S1-SUB              PIC S9(9) COMP.
        .....
        02  S9-SUB              PIC S9(9) COMP.

01  LAST-RECORD.
        02  SR-ITEM-1           PIC X(80).
        .....
        02  SR-ITEM-10          PIC 9(12).
        .....
        02  SR-ITEM-20          PIC 9(08).
        .....
01  SCREEN-RECORD.
        02  SC-LINE             OCCURS 20.
            03  SC-PROMPT       PIC X(5)B.
            03  SC-ENTRY        PIC X(60).

PROCEDURE DIVISION.
        INITIALIZE SUBSCRIPTS REPLACING NUMERIC BY 1

        INITIALIZE LAST-RECORD
        REPLACING ALPHANUMERIC DATA BY HIGH-VALUES

        INITIALIZE LAST-RECORD
        REPLACING NUMERIC DATA BY 99999999999999

        INITIALIZE SCREEN-RECORD
        REPLACING ALPHANUMERIC-EDITED BY 'Text: '

        INITIALIZE SCREEN-RECORD
        REPLACING ALPHANUMERIC BY ALL '_'.
```

Listing 5-7   INITIALIZE ... REPLACING.

5.1.9   INITIALIZE REPLACING with FILLER

You can exploit the fact that INITIALIZE doesn't touch fields defined as FILLER. You can define a data entry form or print layout, for instance, with all the constant values named FILLER. You then use INITIALIZE to set all the variable values when you want to, as in Listing 5-8.

The moves implied by the INITIALIZE verb follow the normal rules for a MOVE statement. For instance, alphanumeric literals will be truncated if too long and space-padded if too short. Numeric fields should receive numeric values. The statement in Listing 5-9 is illegal

```
DATA DIVISION.
01  PRINT-RECORD.
    02  FILLER          PIC X(06) VALUE 'Name: '.
    02  PR-NAME         PIC X(30).
    02  FILLER          PIC X(07) VALUE 'Street: '.
    02  PR-NAME         PIC X(30).
        . . . . .
    02  FILLER          PIC X(13) VALUE 'Income Code: '.
    02  PR-NAME         PIC X(02).
    02  FILLER          PIC X(05) VALUE 'Age: '.
    02  PR-NAME         PIC X(03).

PROCEDURE DIVISION.
    INITIALIZE PRINT-RECORD
    REPLACING ALPHANUMERIC BY ALL '_'.
*   -- THE FILLER FIELDS STILL CONTAIN LITERAL VALUES
```

Listing 5-8   INITIALIZE REPLACING with FILLER.

because it generates illegal moves of the alphanumeric value '_' to numeric fields.

A limitation of REPLACING is that you must put the same value into every field of the same data type. The example above worked around this by defining some fields as EDITED and giving them a separate value. But in most cases where the default values of INITIALIZE are not adequate, this extension is not enough either. As a result the REPLACING option is not often used.

5.1.10   Summary: Why Use INITIALIZE?

The INITIALIZE verb is not a solution to all problems of field initialization, particularly considering POINTER, INDEX, and FILLER. It does provide a better default than leaving LOW-VALUES or SPACES everywhere. It is particularly useful with numeric fields. The advantages of the INITIALIZE verb are:

```
INITIALIZE LAST-RECORD
REPLACING NUMERIC DATA BY ALL '_'
```

Listing 5-9   Illegal INITIALIZE Statement.

```
OS COBOL:

        DATA DIVISION.
        01  ITEM-NAME       PIC X VALUE ZERO.
        88  ITEM-88         VALUE '1'.


        PROCEDURE DIVISION.
            MOVE '1' TO ITEM-NAME.


            IF ITEM-88
            ...
COBOL II:

        DATA DIVISION.
        01  ITEM-NAME       PIC X value zero.
        88  ITEM-88         VALUE '1'.


        PROCEDURE DIVISION.
            SET ITEM-88 TO TRUE


            IF ITEM-88
            ...
```

Listing 5-10   Condition Names.

- It is economical to code (it can replace hundreds of MOVE statements).
- It is easy to maintain, because the purpose is more explicit than the equivalent string of moves and the program is smaller.
- It is more likely to be complete; the compiler is not going to forget a field. For instance, if numeric fields are added during maintenance, zeroes will be moved into them without coding changes as soon as the program is recompiled.

The INITIALIZE statement sets the signs correctly on all fields, whereas a group move does not.

5.2 SET TO TRUE

In OS COBOL, you could only refer to a condition-name (an 88-level item) to find its value, not to set it. When you updated it, it was by another name, the data name (the 01-level). In COBOL II, you can set the value with SET . . . TO TRUE. Listing 5-10 shows a simple example of this statement.

```
DATA DIVISION.
01  MASTER-RECORD.
    .....
    02  SUB-SECTION
        .....
        03  MR-SEX-CODE          PIC X.
            88  SEX-IS-MALE           VALUE 'M'.
            88  SEX-IS-FEMALE         VALUE 'F'.
            88  SEX-IS-UNKNOWN        VALUE 'X'.


PROCEDURE DIVISION.
    MOVE SPACES TO MASTER-RECORD
    ...
    INITIALIZE MASTER-RECORD
    ...
    MOVE SPACES TO SUB-SECTION
    ...
    MOVE 'M' TO MR-SEX-CODE
    ...
    SET SEX-IS-FEMALE TO TRUE
```

Listing 5-11   Updating a Condition Name.

5.2.1   Conditions Can Be Set Indirectly

Using SET . . . TO TRUE consistently in a program makes it easier
to follow the logic during maintenance. For instance, you can search
the program text with an editor looking for the condition-name, or
look it up in the cross-reference listing. However, you cannot really
know that the condition-name wasn't set indirectly. For example, in
the program in Listing 5-11, all the statements update the condition-
name.

5.2.2   Setting Conditions FALSE

There is no SET . . . TO FALSE, although FALSE is a reserved word
used with EVALUATE. This is because in VS COBOL II any value
other than the TRUE one would be false. The compiler has no way to
pick which one you want. For example, consider the first invalid code
in Listing 5-12. If you want to achieve the effect of setting an 88-
level item to false, you can define a condition-name that is the

```
Invalid (SET TO FALSE):

    DATA DIVISION.
    01  HAIR-COLOR.
        88  BLONDE       VALUE '1'.
        88  BRUNETTE     VALUE '2'.
        88  RED          VALUE '3'.

    PROCEDURE DIVISION.
        SET BLONDE TO TRUE

  * -- BUT THIS IS INVALID -- IS IT BRUNETTE OR RED?
        SET BLONDE TO FALSE

Correct:

    DATA DIVISION.
    01  TIME-TO-QUIT-SW      PIC X VALUE SPACE.
        88  NOT-TIME-TO-QUIT  VALUE SPACE.
        88  TIME-TO-QUIT      VALUE 'Q'.

    PROCEDURE DIVISION.
        SET NOT-TIME-TO-QUIT TO TRUE
```

Listing 5-12   Setting a Condition Not True.

negation of this one and set that to true, as in the second part of Listing 5-12.

5.2.3   Conditions with Indexing

You can use indexes or subscripts freely with condition-names, when referring to them and when setting them, as in the example in Listing 5-13.

5.2.4   SET with Multiple 88 Values

If an 88-level item has multiple values and you set it TRUE, the first value will be used. In the following example (Listing 5-14), DAY-OF-WEEK is set to 'MON'. However, this is not very good style; it is rather unnatural to think of the order of the 88-values as having an

```
DATA DIVISION.
01  NUMBER-ARRAY.
    02  NA-NUMBER    PIC X OCCURS 500 INDEXED BY NA-IX.
        88  IS-EVEN    VALUE '1'.

PROCEDURE DIVISION.
    PERFORM VARYING NA-X1 FROM 2 BY 2
    UNTIL NA-X1 > 500
        SET IS-EVEN (NA-X1) TO TRUE
    END-PERFORM.
```

Listing 5-13   Indexed Condition Names.

effect on execution. It would be better to set the day explicitly to Monday.

5.2.5   Setting Several Conditions at Once

You can set several conditions in one statement. This has the same effect as coding each one in a separate statement. The two IF statements in the program in Listing 5-15 do the same thing.

5.2.6   Why Use SET . . . TO TRUE?

The old method of setting a condition name, using the MOVE statement, still works but is not recommended. The SET . . . TO TRUE method has several advantages:

• It treats the condition name consistently. You set and read the value in the same manner.

```
DATA DIVISION.
01  DAY-OF-WEEK VALUE X(03).
    88  WEEK-DAY VALUE 'MON', 'TUE',
                       'WED', 'THU', 'FRI'.

PROCEDURE DIVISION.
    SET WEEK-DAY TO TRUE
```

Listing 5-14   Multiple 88 Values.

```
DATA DIVISION.
01  HAIR-TYPE    PIC X.
    88  LONG-HAIR VALUE 'L'.
    88  SHORT-HAIR VALUE 'S'.
01  HAIR-COLOR  PIC X.
    88  BLOND-HAIR VALUE 'B'.
    88  DARK-HAIR   VALUE 'D'.
01  CLOTHING-TYPE PIC X.
    88  LIGHT-CLOTHING VALUE 'L'.
    88  HEAVY-CLOTHING VALUE 'H'.

PROCEDURE DIVISION.
    IF LADY-GODIVA
        SET LONG-HAIR TO TRUE
        SET BLOND-HAIR TO TRUE
        SET LIGHT-CLOTHING TO TRUE
    END-IF

    IF LADY-GODIVA
        SET LONG-HAIR, BLOND-HAIR, LIGHT-CLOTHING TO TRUE
    END-IF.
```

Listing 5-15   Setting Several Conditions in One Statement.

- Within the procedure division, you can refer to a condition name without considering its representation as a PICTURE.
- If you find a reference to a condition name in a program and want to search for where it was set, you can find it without looking up aliases.
- When you set the condition this way, it must be one of the defined values; it cannot be invalid.

5.3 THE LENGTH SPECIAL REGISTER

LENGTH acts like a special register which tells you the length of a group or elementary item. Prior to COBOL II, you would simply calculate this yourself, either by adding up all the PICTURE fields or by consulting the data division map. You would then be responsible for ensuring the value was correct after any maintenance operations, although there was no way to search for the reference (which was a hard-coded integer somewhere). Now you use the LENGTH register and let the compiler do the work for you.

```
Valid Uses:

                MOVE LENGTH OF PRODUCT-AREA TO PA-LENGTH
                COMPUTE TOTAL-AREA = LENGTH OF PRODUCT-AREA
                                   + LENGTH OF CUSTOMER-AREA
                CALL 'PR0140' USING PRODUCT-AREA,
                                 BY CONTENT LENGTH OF PRODUCT-AREA
Invalid Uses:

    ***   THESE ARE INVALID REFERENCES TO LENGTH   ***
          MOVE PA-LENGTH TO LENGTH OF PRODUCT-AREA
          ADD 50 TO LENGTH OF PRODUCT-AREA
          CALL 'PR0140' USING PRODUCT_AREA,
                          LENGTH OF PRODUCT-AREA
          ADD 1 TO PRODUCT-COUNT (LENGTH OF PRODUCT-AREA)
```

Listing 5-16   Using LENGTH.

5.3.1   Using LENGTH

LENGTH acts essentially like a predefined PIC 9(9) COMP variable, but with restrictions because it makes no sense to alter it.
  You can use length:

• as a source value in a MOVE statement
• as a source value in an arithmetic statement
• in a call BY CONTENT

  You cannot use length:

• as a target value in a MOVE statement
• as a target value in an arithmetic statement
• in a call BY REFERENCE
• as a subscript

  Listing 5-16 contains examples of all these.

5.3.2   LENGTH and Addressability

It is not necessary to have addressability to an item to use LENGTH. You can find the length of any item in the DATA DIVISION of the program, working-storage, or linkage, at any time. This is because unlike the ADDRESS register it is calculated at compile-

```
DATA DIVISION.
WORKING-STORAGE SECTION.
01  WORK-LENGTH        PIC S9(08) COMP.
LINKAGE SECTION.
01  WORK-AREA.
    .....
    02  WORK-SECTION.
PROCEDURE DIVISION.
    MOVE LENGTH OF WORK-SECTION TO WORK-LENGTH
*   - NOW GET ADDRESSABILITY TO WORK-AREA
    EXEC CICS
            GETMAIN
                SET (ADDRESS OF WORK-AREA)
                LENGTH (LENGTH OF WORK-AREA)
    END-EXEC
```

Listing 5-17   Addressability.

time. An item does not have to be a 01-level, either. The example in Listing 5-17 illustrates both of these points.

5.3.3   LENGTH and OCCURS

The LENGTH of a table element is the length of one item. It does not need to be subscripted. To get the length of a whole table, you must give a group name that contains it.

Because the value in the LENGTH register is a constant determined at compile-time, it is not useful with OCCURS DEPENDING ON items, simply giving the largest possible value. The program in Listing 5-18 will display the value 500 each time, because that is the maximum value.

5.3.4   When Wouldn't You Use LENGTH?

Sometimes the LENGTH of an item is externally determined, rather than being the sum of its elements. For instance, a file might be 200 bytes long whatever the record type. It may be more appropriate to hard-code the LENGTH. In the example in Listing 5-19, suppose that during maintenance you add a field after LAST-REAL-FIELD in MISC-FILE. If you forget to recalculate the FILLER field length, you will be O.K.—your filler will be truncated. If you had coded LENGTH OF (or left the translator to default it for you), you would

```
DATA DIVISION.
01  FIXED-RECORD.
    02  FIXED-ITEM  PIC X OCCURS 500 INDEXED BY FI-IX.
01  VARIABLE-RECORD.
    02  ODO-FIELD.
    02  ODO-ARRAY.
        03  ODO-ITEM    PIC X OCCURS 1 TO 500
                            DEPENDING ON ODO-FIELD.
01  F-LENGTH            PIC S9(09) COMP.


PROCEDURE DIVISION.
    COMPUTE F-LENGTH = 500 * (LENGTH OF FIXED-ITEM)
    DISPLAY F-LENGTH
    DISPLAY LENGTH OF FIXED-RECORD
    MOVE 1 TO ODO-FIELD
    DISPLAY LENGTH OF ODO-ARRAY
    MOVE 300 TO ODO-FIELD
    DISPLAY LENGTH OF ODO-ARRAY
```

Listing 5-18   LENGTH with OCCURS DEPENDING.

probably be in for a run-time error (CICS will give a LENGERR if the file is fixed-length or if your length is too long).

5.3.5   Using LENGTH to Avoid Hard-Coding

You can use LENGTH when you anticipate changes in a specification—to avoid hard-coding the length of arrays, for instance. The

```
DATA DIVISION.
01  MISCFILE-LENGTH         PIC S9(08) COMP VALUE 200.

01  MISC-FILE.
02  ......
02  LAST-REAL-FIELD     PIC X.
02  FILLER              PIC X(75).


PROCEDURE DIVISION.
    EXEC CICS
        WRITE DATASET ('MISCFILE')
        FROM (MISC-FILE)
        LENGTH(200)
    END-EXEC
```

Listing 5-19   Example of Hard-Coded LENGTH.

```
DATA DIVISION.
01  NUMBER-ARRAY.
02  NA-LINE   OCCURS 1000.
    03  NA-NUMBER     PIC X.
        88  IS-PRIME       VALUE '1'.
        88  IS-NOT-PRIME VALUE ZERO.
    03  NA-PROOF      PIC S9(08) COMP.
01  CANDIDATE     PIC S9(08) COMP.
01  CPRIME        PIC S9(08) COMP.
01  ARRAY-SIZE    PIC S9(08) COMP.


PROCEDURE DIVISION.
    INITIALIZE NUMBER-ARRAY REPLACING ALPHANUMERIC BY '1'
    INITIALIZE NUMBER-ARRAY REPLACING NUMERIC BY ZERO
    COMPUTE ARRAY-SIZE = LENGTH OF NUMBER-ARRAY / 5

    PERFORM VARYING CPRIME FROM 2 BY 1
    UNTIL CPRIME > ARRAY-SIZE
        IF IS-PRIME (CPRIME)
            COMPUTE CANDIDATE = CPRIME + CPRIME
            PERFORM UNTIL CANDIDATE > ARRAY-SIZE
                SET IS-NOT-PRIME (CANDIDATE) TO TRUE
                MOVE CPRIME TO NA-PROOF (CANDIDATE)
                ADD CPRIME TO CANDIDATE
            END-PERFORM
        END-IF
    END-PERFORM

    PERFORM VARYING CANDIDATE FROM 1 BY 1
    UNTIL CANDIDATE > ARRAY-SIZE
        IF IS-PRIME (CANDIDATE)
            DISPLAY CANDIDATE ' IS PRIME'
        ELSE
            DISPLAY CANDIDATE ' DIVISIBLE BY '
                NA-PROOF (CANDIDATE)
        END-IF
    END-PERFORM.
```

Listing 5-20   Calculate Prime Numbers by Eratosthenes' Sieve.

program in Listing 5-20 uses LENGTH to localize the size of the table to one place so that it can be easily changed from run to run. This type of coding can minimize maintenance problems.

Listing 5-20 also illustrates the use of INITIALIZE . . . REPLACING and SET . . . TO TRUE with indexed variables in a (somewhat) practical context. The sieve program has been made famous from computer magazine performance tests. It generates a list of prime numbers, also printing for each nonprime its largest divisor. The

```
DATA DIVISION.
01   ITEM-TABLE.
     02   S-LINE            OCCURS 100 INDEXED BY S-IX.
          03   S-ITEM            PIC X(08).
          .....
          03   S-PRICE          PIC 9(7)V99.
01   TARGET-ITEM             PIC X(08).
01   TARGET-PRICE            PIC Z,ZZZ,ZZ9.99.

PROCEDURE DIVISION.
     PERFORM VARYING S-IX FROM 1 BY 1
     UNTIL S-ITEM (S-IX) = TARGET-ITEM
        CONTINUE
     END-PERFORM
* -- NOW S-IX POINTS TO OUR ITEM
     MOVE S-PRICE (S-IX) TO TARGET-PRICE.
```

Listing 5-21   Example of NULL Statement.

process begins by assuming every number is prime, then taking each
prime in turn, starting with 2, marks off all its multiples. What is
left at the end really are prime numbers; these are printed.

5.4   THE CONTINUE STATEMENT

The CONTINUE statement is new in COBOL II. It has no effect on
the operation of the program, but can be placed where an executable
statement is needed. In other words, CONTINUE is a null statement.

The code in Listing 5-21 looks up the price of an item in a list. We
don't want to do any processing in the loop.

In Listing 5-22, we insert an item in a table if it's not a duplicate.
The CONTINUE statement is necessary because if we find the item
already, we don't want to do anything.

5.4.1   CONTINUE and NEXT SENTENCE

NEXT SENTENCE is still legal in COBOL II. Whereas CONTINUE
is legal wherever a COBOL statement can be placed, NEXT SEN-
TENCE is only valid in IF and SEARCH statements. You can use
CONTINUE and NEXT SENTENCE in the same program, and may

```
DATA DIVISION.
01  ITEM-LIST-ARRAY.
    02  ITEM-LIST    PIC X(30) OCCURS 200
                               INDEXED BY IL-IX.
01  NEW-ITEM         PIC X(30.

PROCEDURE DIVISION.
    MOVE HIGH-VALUES TO ITEM-LIST-ARRAY
    ....
    SET IL-IX TO 1
    SEARCH ITEM-LIST
    WHEN ITEM-LIST (IL-IX) = HIGH-VALUES
        MOVE NEW-ITEM TO ITEM-LIST (IL-IX)
    WHEN ITEM-LIST (IL-IX) = NEW-ITEM
        CONTINUE
    END-SEARCH.
```

Listing 5-22 CONTINUE.

well do so when adding new code to a program in maintenance. However, you will do best to avoid NEXT SENTENCE entirely in new code because it is more restricted in its use and dependent on the period, which is now obsolete. NEXT SENTENCE is known to be bug-prone. Using NEXT SENTENCE, you lose the ability to freely move code around between blocks because it is affected by nesting. Also, the two constructs are very similar and using both can confuse people.

Sometimes within a simple IF statement or at the end of a nested IF, the two constructs would be equivalent; but in general they operate quite differently. Whereas CONTINUE is a null statement, NEXT SENTENCE is a branch to the statement after the next period. If the program is currently within a nested IF, NEXT SENTENCE will jump around code. Notice how in Listing 5-23 the addition of another IF statement changes the effect of NEXT SENTENCE in the block. This implies a maintenance headache.

5.4.2 CONTINUE and Program Stubs

Continue is useful in top-down program development. Undeveloped paragraphs can be left as stubs, perhaps with comments explaining their eventual role.

```
DATA DIVISION.
.....
PROCEDURE DIVISION.
* -- CONTINUE can be replaced by NEXT SENTENCE here
    IF EXEMPT-STATUS
        CONTINUE
    ELSE
        PERFORM TAX-ROUTINE
    END-IF
    PERFORM GENERAL-ROUTINE

* -- CONTINUE can not be replaced by NEXT SENTENCE here
* -- because GENERAL-ROUTINE will not be performed
    IF MAJOR-ACCOUNT
        IF EXEMPT-STATUS
            CONTINUE
        ELSE
            PERFORM TAX-ROUTINE
        END-IF
        PERFORM GENERAL-ROUTINE
    END-IF.
```

Listing 5-23   Examples of CONTINUE and NEXT SENTENCE.

5.5 SUMMARY: MISCELLANEOUS ADDITIONAL FEATURES

All of the new features presented in this chapter have their uses in many, perhaps most, new programs. INITIALIZE simplifies the use of large groups of numeric variables. SET . . . TO TRUE improves the consistency of condition names. The LENGTH register helps in the maintainability of programs, but is most useful with CICS. CONTINUE has a small role in improving program readability. The features we will look at in the next chapter, by contrast, are mostly fairly obscure.

6

Changed Features in COBOL II

This chapter contains many detailed changes in the new compiler. Many of these will only cause changes to programs which are very old or which exploit unusual features of OS COBOL. They include changes to:

• Identification and Environment Division entries
• Sequential file processing
• COPY statement
• Declaratives
• Occurs Depending On
• SEARCH statement
• IF statement

6.1 IDENTIFICATION AND ENVIRONMENT DIVISION CHANGES

6.1.1 SPECIAL-NAMES

There are new function names supported in the "function-name IS mnemonic-name" clause of the SPECIAL-NAMES paragraph. Table 6-1 lists the function names supported in OS COBOL and COBOL II. Asterisked function-names (*) are new with COBOL II.

Table 6-1   Allowable Function Names for SPECIAL-NAMES.

Function Name	Statement Using	Used For
CONSOLE	ACCEPT	
	DISPLAY	operator console
CSP	WRITE ADVANCING	suppress spacing
C01-12	WRITE ADVANCING	skip to printer channel 1-12
SYSIN	ACCEPT	standard input
* SYSIPT	ACCEPT	standard input
* SYSLST	DISPLAY	standard output
SYSOUT	DISPLAY	standard output
* SYSPCH	DISPLAY	punch device
SYSPUNCH	DISPLAY	punch device
S01-S02	WRITE ADVANCING	pocket select on punch
* S03-S05	WRITE ADVANCING	pocket select on punch
* UPSI0-UPSI7	any condition	test user-set switch

The UPSI switches are User Programmable Status Indicator switches. These switches are contained in a 1-byte area set prior to execution of the program. Historically, these were once hardware switches which were used to set conditions for the program. It would be more common nowadays to use parameters to control processing, but COBOL II allows you to declare condition names for the eight UPSI switches in the SPECIAL-NAMES paragraph and then test them in the Procedure Division. This feature is compatible with the DOS/VS COBOL compiler.

COBOL II does not support the Report Writer, so support in the SPECIAL-NAMES paragraph for literals used by report writer code has been dropped.

Listing 6-1 gives an example of a SPECIAL-NAMES paragraph containing some of the new features.

6.1.2   Select Statement Clauses

Several clauses of the select statement have been deleted or changed in COBOL II.

The reserve clause specifies the number of buffers and is coded as:

RESERVE n AREAS

```
ENVIRONMENT DIVISION.
CONFIGURATION SECTION.
SPECIAL-NAMES.
    C01 IS TOP-OF-PAGE
    SYSIPT IS STANDARD-INPUT
    UPSI-0 ON  STATUS IS FIRST-SWITCH-SET-ON
    UPSI-0 OFF STATUS IS FIRST-SET-SWITCH-OFF

...


PROCEDURE DIVISION.

    WRITE PRINT-FILE AFTER ADVANCING TOP-OF-PAGE

    IF FIRST-SWITCH-SET-ON
        ACCEPT SYS-DATE FROM STANDARD-INPUT
    END-IF
```

Listing 6-1   SPECIAL-NAMES.

The formats RESERVE NO ALTERNATE AREAS and RESERVE n ALTERNATE AREAS are no longer accepted. If replacing this phrase, one should be added to the integer. For example, RESERVE 2 ALTERNATE AREAS should be replaced by RESERVE 3 AREAS to have the same effect.

The FILE-LIMITS and PROCESSING MODE clauses, previously accepted by OS COBOL as documentation, are no longer accepted in COBOL II and should be deleted.

Since COBOL II no longer supports ISAM files, the NOMINAL KEY and TRACK-AREA clauses which were for ISAM use only are no longer supported.

The TOTALED AREA and TOTALING AREA options of the LABEL RECORDS clause are no longer supported. These options automatically placed record counts into multivolume user tape labels. This feature is no longer available.

6.2   SEQUENTIAL FILE PROCESSING

6.2.1   Deleted OPEN Options

The options LEAVE, REREAD, and DISP on the OPEN statement, which referred to the disposition of multireel tape files, have been removed. In addition, the REVERSED option is no longer allowed for multivolume files.

6.2.2   Changes to START, SEEK, and WRITE

The USING option of the START statement has been dropped in COBOL II. The SEEK statement is no longer accepted in COBOL II. This statement has been obsolete for a long time; the previous OS COBOL compiler treated it as comments.

On sequential files opened for I/O processing, it is no longer possible to use the WRITE statement. The REWRITE statement should be used instead. This is clearer, as a rewrite is what actually occurs, since it is not possible to insert new records into a sequential file.

6.2.3   Deleted CLOSE Options

The options FOR REMOVAL, POSITIONAL, and DISP on the CLOSE statement, which referred to the disposition of tape files, have been removed. These options are now ignored (treated as comments).

6.3   THE COPY STATEMENT

COPY statements can now be nested; that is, you can now put COPY statements in files that are copied themselves. Listing 6-2 shows an example of this.

6.3.1   Portability and Nested Copies

OS/VS COBOL doesn't support nested COPY statements. Since copy members are generally of most value when they describe shared code, you will not want to use this feature unless you can guarantee that no old programs will share the code. In practice, use of this feature should be reserved for systems which are all VS COBOL II. Also, the ANSI 1985 standard does not define nested COPY statements, so you will not want to use this feature in programs which will be ported to non-IBM environments.

```
-- File EXNEST1 in copy library --
    01  MASTER-REC.
    02  MR-TYPE          PIC X.
  COPY EXNEST2
            COPY EXNEST3

-- File EXNEST2 in copy library --
    02  R2-NAME          PIC X(20).
    02  R2-FILE          PIC X(10).

-- File EXNEST3 in copy library --
    02  R3-NAME

-- Code Sample with Nested Copies --
    DATA DIVISION.
    COPY EXNEST1

-- Result after Compilation --
    DATA DIVISION.
    COPY EXNEST1
01  MASTER-REC.
C           02  MR-TYPE          PIC X.
C           COPY EXNEST2
C           02  R2-NAME          PIC X(20).
C           02  R2-FILE          PIC X(10).
C           COPY EXNEST3
C           02  R3-NAME
```

Listing 6-2   Example of the COPY Statement Using Nesting.

6.3.2   The REPLACING Option and Nesting

If you want to use the REPLACING option of the copy statement (which is the same as in OS/VS COBOL), you cannot nest. That is, neither the top-level COPY nor those included in the copybooks can have the replacing option. In the example given in Listing 6-2, none of the three COPY statements could have the REPLACING option.

6.3.3   No Self-Reference

You must avoid recursive references, that is, copy members calling themselves either directly or indirectly. The compiler will not act on these because if such a process were tried, it would have no way to

```
Files:

        -- File FILE1 --
           COPY FILE1

        -- File FILE2 --
           COPY FILE3

        -- File FILE3 --
           COPY FILE2

Program:

           DATA DIVISION.
    *   -- DIRECT RECURSIVE REFERENCE
           COPY FILE1.

    *   -- INDIRECT RECURSIVE REFERENCE
           COPY FILE2.
```

Listing 6-3   Recursive COPY Statements.

terminate. For example, in Listing 6-3, given the three files in the copy library, the statements in the following program are illegal.

6.3.4   Why Use Nested Copies?

You use nested copies for the same reasons that you segment a program using CALLS. They enable you to keep each unit of code small and easy to understand. A master file can be several thousand lines long, which is too much code for one person to develop or maintain. Using nested copies, you can have different people working concurrently on the same object, since it is split into conveniently sized pieces. The different pieces can reflect natural boundaries in the object, such as large related groups of data in a file or alternate record layouts.

You can also reuse the same code from more than one place. If FILE A and FILE B both contain an area C, you can COPY C in the layouts of A and B. You don't have to put the definition in two places.

In the past, many people used an independent library product such as Panvalet or Librarian to provide this feature. Otherwise in OS COBOL you had no alternative but to use very large copy members and repeated code in different files. With VS COBOL II, you can use

```
Copy file (PRODCOPY):

    01  PROD-CD.
        02  PRODUCT-NUMBER    PIC 9(8).
        02  PRODUCT-NAME      PIC X(20).

Source file:
    01  PRODUCT-CODE COPY "PRODCOPY".

Result under OS COBOL:

    01  PRODUCT-CODE.
        02  PRODUCT-NUMBER    PIC 9(8).
        02  PRODUCT-NAME      PIC X(20).
```

Listing 6-4   Old (ANSI 1968) COPY Statement in OS COBOL.

nested copies to split large code objects into pieces of a convenient size. However, because of the REPLACING and portability issues discussed earlier, you will have to consider whether to adopt this feature.

6.3.5   Missing Features in COPY

The COPY statement in COBOL II fully supports the ANSI 1974 standard. It no longer supports the ANSI 1968 standard, although this was supported in OS COBOL. This means that one format of the COPY statement is no longer valid. You cannot use text on the line containing the COPY statement to override the first line of the included file. See the example in Listing 6-4. Alternatively, you may choose to begin copy members at the 02 or 05 level, so that the 01-level name is always defined in the calling program.

6.3.6   Partial Replacement of Data Names

One undocumented feature of OS COBOL is missing in COBOL II in Release 2.0 or prior. This is a technique which allows you to replace part of the name of data items. This is very useful when you want to change all the prefixes of a record layout to something else. This feature is part of the ANSI definition, so it is supported in Release 3.0, which complies with ANSI-85. A patch is available to allow use of this in Release 2.0.

```
          DATA DIVISION.
      01  (PFX)-REC.
          02  (PFX)-X1      PIC X(10).
          02  (PFX)-X2      PIC X(10).

          COPY REPLACING == (PFX) == BY == MYPREFIX ==
```

Listing 6-5   Text Substitution (OS COBOL and COBOL II Release 3).

To use this trick, you must code the prefix you may want to re-place in parentheses. Then any program copying this layout must use the REPLACING option to convert the prefix to what is needed. It works because any item enclosed in parentheses is defined as being a COBOL word. Listing 6-5 gives an example of the technique.

6.4   CHANGES TO DECLARATIVES

There are several changes to the declarative statements introduced with COBOL II.

USE BEFORE STANDARD, which caused the writing of user la-bels before the standard tape labels, is dropped. USE AFTER STAN-DARD is still available. Application programs which used this fea-ture will need review to determine their requirements for nonstan-dard tape labeling.

The GIVING clause of USE AFTER EXCEPTION/ERROR is no longer available. This option made available a data area which con-tained error information regarding a failed I/O operation. This should be replaced by FILE STATUS. Some of the information which this option made available (for instance, unit address and device type) will not be easily available to a COBOL program. Applications which use this will have to be reviewed to see if they actually require the information. If so, a call to an Assembly language routine might be needed.

6.5   CHANGES TO OCCURS DEPENDING ON

6.5.1   ODO Length Calculation

The manner in which the compiler computes the length of an Occurs-Depending-On (ODO) object has changed. COBOL II now calculates

```
DATA DIVISION.
01  SERVICE-RECORD.
    02  CURRENT-SERVICE.
    ...
    02  HISTORY-COUNT                PIC S9(04) COMP.
    02  SERVICE-HISTORY OCCURS 0 TO 30 TIMES
                        DEPENDING ON HISTORY-COUNT.
...
PROCEDURE DIVISION.
    EXEC CICS
        READ ... UPDATE
    END-EXEC

    MOVE HISTORY-COUNT TO HISTORY-COUNT

    EXEC CICS
        REWRITE ...
    END-EXEC
```

Listing 6-6   Occurs-Depending-On Length.

the length of ODOs at the time of reference. OS COBOL would do the calculation when the value of the ODO object changed. Unfortunately, it was possible to fool the old COBOL compiler, because it did not know all the ways in which the length of an object could change. Listing 6-6 shows an example of a program which reads a record using CICS. It was necessary with OS COBOL to include the odd statement MOVE HISTORY-COUNT TO HISTORY-COUNT to set the ODO up properly. This statement is no longer required.

6.5.2   ODO and Early COBOL II

Early versions of COBOL II (prior to Release 2.0) provide minimal support for Occurs Depending On. They are restricted to data records with a single ODO as the last component in the structure. If you work with programs written for these compiler versions, you may find cumbersome code written to get around this limitation.

6.6   CHANGES TO THE SEARCH STATEMENT

In COBOL II, there are new limitations on use of the SEARCH ALL statement (but not on the SEARCH statement) that were not present in OS COBOL.

In COBOL II, the WHEN phrase condition on a SEARCH ALL statement must be one of:

- a single-valued condition name associated with a dataname in the KEY phrase of the table
- a relational condition of the form A = B, where A is a dataname in the KEY phrase of the table being searched and B is not

In OS COBOL, the WHEN condition could be any valid condition. Because of the way in which the binary search works, only conditions that contain an equality test with reference to a key item of the table could give useful results, but the order of coding was less restrictive. The examples in Listing 6-7 will compile under OS COBOL but must all be recoded in COBOL II to conform to the more restrictive rules above.

6.7 OTHERWISE NOT SUPPORTED

There is one small change to the IF statement other than the structured programming changes discussed in Chapter 2. The reserved word OTHERWISE is no longer supported and must be replaced by ELSE wherever it occurs.

6.8 MISCELLANEOUS CHANGES

6.8.1 UNSTRING with Numeric Edited Fields

It is no longer possible to use UNSTRING with numeric edited fields. They must be redefined as elementary alphanumeric items.

6.8.2 RERUN

With RERUN under COBOL II, a checkpoint is not taken on the first record. It is advisable not to use RERUN, which is obsolete, but to achieve the same effect with external facilities.

```
DATA DIVISION.
01 CURRENCY-TABLE.
   02   CURRENCY-ENTRY          OCCURS 50
                                INDEXED BY CE-IX
                                ASCENDING KEY IS CURRENCY-CODE.
        03   CURRENCY-CODE             PIC X(03).
        88   CURRENCY-IS-DEUTSCHMARK   VALUES 'DEM', 'DMK'.
        03   CURRENCY-NAME             PIC X(30).


PROCEDURE DIVISION.

*** -- SUBJECT AND OBJECT OF WHEN CLAUSE INVERTED
SEARCH ALL CURRENCY-ENTRY
AT END
    PERFORM ERROR-ROUTINE
WHEN 'DEM' = CURRENCY-CODE (CE-IX)
    CONTINUE.


*** -- NOT A SINGLE-VALUED CONDITION NAME
SEARCH ALL CURRENCY-ENTRY
AT END
    PERFORM ERROR-ROUTINE
HEN CURRENCY-IS-DEUTSCHMARK
    CONTINUE.


*** -- CONDITION TEST IN WHEN CLAUSES NOT EQUAL (=)
SEARCH ALL CURRENCY-ENTRY
AT END
    PERFORM ERROR-ROUTINE
WHEN CURRENCY-CODE (CE-IX) > 'DE'
AND  CURRENCY-CODE (CE-IX) < 'DN'
    CONTINUE.
```

Listing 6-7   Invalid Binary Searches in COBOL II.

6.8.3   Change in the WHEN-COMPILED Format

The WHEN-COMPILED special register format has been changed
from OS COBOL for compatibility with other IBM compilers. The
two new formats are given below.
    WHEN-COMPILED OS COBOL Format:

```
hh.mm.ssMMM DD,YYYY
```

WHEN-COMPILED COBOL II Format:

```
MM/DD/YYhh.mm.ss
```

where hh = hours (24-hour clock), mm = minutes, ss = seconds, DD = days in month, MM = month in year, YY = year in century, MMM = first three chars of month, YYYY = year.

In each format case, WHEN-COMPILED is an alphanumeric item which can only be used as the source field of a MOVE statement.

6.9   THE USAGE CLAUSE

While changes in the USAGE clause are discussed elsewhere in this book, they are assembled here so they can be reviewed in one place.

The precise usage options available have changed a little between releases. Table 6-2 is a list of all the valid usage options under IBM VS COBOL II Release 2 with an explanation of their meaning.

6.10   OBSOLETE LANGUAGE ELEMENTS

Many COBOL language elements were regarded as obsolete by the ANSI 1985 standards committee, but retained in order to minimize the changes to existing programs. The ANSI 1985 standard declares all of the following to be obsolete. They are expected to be deleted at the next revision. It would, therefore, be good practice to avoid these elements. The obsolete elements are listed below by division.

6.10.1   Obsolete ID DIVISION Elements

All the following documentation paragraphs should be replaced by comments (asterisk in column 7).

```
AUTHOR
INSTALLATION
DATE-WRITTEN
DATE-COMPILED
SECURITY
OBJECT-COMPUTER. MEMORY SIZE IS.
```

Table 6-2   Usage in COBOL II.

Usage	*Meaning*
BINARY	Binary
COMP*	Binary
COMP-1	4-byte floating-point
COMP-2	8-byte floating-point
COMP-3	Packed decimal
COMP-4	Binary
DISPLAY	EBCDIC (default)
DISPLAY-1	DBCS
INDEX	Index
PACKED-DECIMAL	Packed Decimal
POINTER	Pointer

*COMP, COMP-1, etc. can also be written in full as COMPUTATIONAL, COMPUTATIONAL-1, etc..

Notes:

COMP-4 is equivalent to COMP with this compiler.
If USAGE is omitted, DISPLAY is implicit.
POINTER and DISPLAY-1 are new with COBOL II.
COMP-1 and COMP-2 were unavailable with early versions (1.0 and 1.1) of COBOL II.
BINARY and PACKED-DECIMAL available in Release 3.0 only.

6.10.2   Obsolete DATA DIVISION Elements

All of the following are obsolete:

I/O-CONTROL.

RERUN clause.

MULTIPLE FILE TAPE. Job Control Language is the place to determine tape handling, rather than COBOL.

In FD entries, the following documentation items are obsolete:

LABEL RECORDS

VALUE OF

DATA RECORDS

ALL literal where literal is longer than one character numeric. For example, ALL '25' is obsolete.

6.10.3 Obsolete PROCEDURE DIVISION Elements

ALTER (this has been regarded as bad programming practice for years).

GO TO without procedure-name (this exists only to support the ALTER statement).

DISABLE—KEY phrase

ENABLE—KEY phrase

ENTER (This was never used. Inter-language communication is done with the CALL statement.)

OPEN REVERSED

STOP literal (this displays a message on the operator console, which is an inappropriate practice for modern operating systems). Segmentation module. This has been made obsolete by virtual storage. Numbers on sections, for instance, are part of the segmentation feature.

WITH DEBUGGING MODE/USE FOR DEBUGGING. These options should be avoided because their use disables the interactive debugger COBTEST (see Chapter 14). Since COBTEST is more flexible and more powerful, it should be used instead.

Chapter

7

Using Pointers and Addresses

In this chapter we look at the language elements added to COBOL II to support the explicit manipulation of machine addresses. These are the new data type POINTER, the ADDRESS special register, and the associated reserved word NULL. We then see some examples of the use of pointers to construct advanced data types, which can be more efficient or flexible in their use of storage.

All the discussion in this chapter can apply to COBOL programs running in any environment (that is, batch, CICS, IMS/DC, TSO, and CMS). However, as a practical matter such pointer manipulation is rarely encountered except under CICS. The reasons for this include:

- In CICS, many programs are sharing the same address space and may wish to share data.
- Storage can be acquired dynamically (by the CICS GETMAIN statement). This allows and sometimes requires address manipulation.
- CICS often has performance constraints requiring efficient techniques. Passing pointers to data areas between programs is more efficient than passing copies of the data around, particularly when the data areas are large.
- In order to use pointers in batch programs, you will normally need some assembler support for access to dynamic memory allocation (GETMAIN).

117

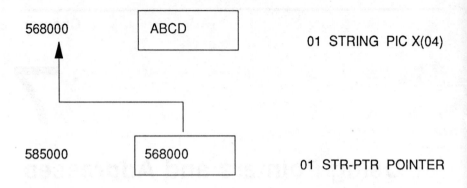

Figure 7-1   Pointer.

7.1   THE POINTER DATA TYPE

The POINTER data type is new in COBOL II. It is an IBM extension for the MVS and VM environments. It is not in the ANSI 1974 or 1985 standards, nor in SAA, and should be regarded as not portable to any other environment.

The POINTER data type refers to an area in which an address can be stored. Figure 7-1 shows the way a pointer refers to a variable. An alphanumeric variable STRING which is at storage location 568000 contains the value "ABCD." A pointer variable STR-PTR which is at storage location 585000 contains the value 568000. Since it contains the address of STRING, it is said to point to STRING.

A pointer variable is defined in the data division as in Listing 7-1. Pointers have no associated PICTURE clause; all pointers are the same size, 4 bytes long.

7.1.1   The Purpose of Pointers

Often, it is necessary in a program to refer to the address of a variable (its physical location in the computer) rather than its contents. This chapter gives examples which use pointers for reasons of flexibility and efficiency. A pointer is a field which contains an address.

```
DATA DIVISION.
01  POINTER-INSTANCE                USAGE IS POINTER.
01  POINTER-INSTANCE-2              POINTER.
```

Listing 7-1   Pointer Definition.

7.1.2   The Dangers of Pointers

Pointers are very dangerous things. It is very easy to make mistakes using them. There is no concept of the type of a pointer. A pointer simply contains a number which represents an address in storage. There is no check that this address is of a variable or record of the desired type. In fact, there is no check that the address is valid at all. Incorrect pointers can lead to corruption of data, to corruption of areas of system storage leading to inefficiencies or system crashes, or to protection exceptions (CICS 0C4) leading to task abends. When you combine these dangers with the lack of storage protection in CICS, you are headed for trouble. Because of this, it is wise to review the use of pointer-based designs and measure the difficulties introduced against the efficiencies in storage use and speed that can be offered.

This said, however, it is true that use of pointers offers great performance advantages. CICS itself uses them extensively. One compromise is to use the techniques, but ensure that access to data areas using pointers is confined to a group of service modules rather than allowed to proliferate through the system.

7.2   INITIALIZING POINTERS

You store an address in a POINTER in one of four ways:

• initialization in the Data Division
• the COBOL SET statement
• subroutine call
• CICS SET statement

7.2.1   Initialization in the Data Division

Any value can be assigned to a pointer with a VALUE clause. Normally, only NULL will be a useful value for initializing a pointer. In large IBM computers, one does not normally code machine addresses directly.

7.2.2   Using the SET Statement

The SET statement can be used to assign a value to a pointer. This could be a constant such as NULL, the value in another pointer variable, or the contents of an ADDRESS register.

7.2.3   Subroutine Call

A pointer can be set by calling a subroutine using the address of a pointer variable as an argument and having the subroutine obtain it. This is the only practical way for a batch COBOL program to obtain addresses.

7.2.4   CICS Set Clause

CICS programs have options to allow the setting of pointer variables in many EXEC CICS statements. To the COBOL compiler, this is a form of subroutine call (see Section 7.2.3 above), since the translator generates CALL statements.

Listing 7-2 shows examples of all these ways of assigning values to a pointer.

7.2.5   Pointers in Groups

The POINTER data type can only refer to an elementary field. If a group is given the usage POINTER, this will be taken as applying to each elementary item in the group in the same manner as other attributes, like COMP. Listing 7-3 illustrates this.

```
DATA DIVISION.

01  DATA-POINTER           POINTER VALUE NULL.
01  DATA-POINTER-2         POINTER VALUE NULL.


PROCEDURE DIVISION.

    SET DATA-POINTER    TO 40000
    SET DATA-POINTER    TO NULL
    SET DATA-POINTER    TO ADDRESS OF DATA-AREA
    SET DATA-POINTER-2 TO DATA-POINTER

    CALL "SUBPGM" USING DATA-POINTER

    EXEC CICS
        GETMAIN
            SET (DATA-POINTER)
            LENGTH (500)
    END-EXEC
```

Listing 7-2   Assigning Values to a Pointer.

7.3   USING POINTERS

A POINTER item can only be used:

• in a SET statement
• in a relation condition
• in a CALL statement, under USING . . . BY REFERENCE

7.3.1   Use of Pointers in Relation Conditions

Pointers can always be usefully compared to the reserved word
NULL. Most other comparisons are of no value. It is occasionally, in


```
DATA DIVISION.

*** -- ALL THESE ARE POINTERS
01  SET-OF-POINTERS        POINTER.
    02  PTR-1.
    02  PTR-2.
    02  PTR-3.
```

Listing 7-3   Pointer on Group-Level Item.

```
Calling Program:

    PROCEDURE DIVISION.
        CALL 'COPYTREE' USING AREA-1 AREA-2

Called Program:

    DATA DIVISION.
    LINKAGE SECTION.
    01  AREA-1.
    ...
    01  AREA-2.
    ...
    PROCEDURE DIVISION USING AREA-1 AREA-2.
        IF ADDRESS OF AREA-1 = ADDRESS OF AREA-2
            GOBACK
        END-IF
 *** -- SO AREAS ARE DIFFERENT. CODE TO COPY AREAS FOLLOWS
    ...
        GOBACK.
```

Listing 7-4   Comparing Two ADDRESSES.

some special circumstances, useful to compare two pointers to see if they are equal. An example is given in Listing 7-4. This is a subroutine which copies a data area and checks to see if the two areas to copy are actually the same.

There are also special circumstances where you might test to see if one pointer is greater than another, but these are very unusual and will not be covered here.

7.3.2   Redefining a Pointer

The pointer is equivalent in size to a full-word binary field, and can be redefined as such, as in Listing 7-5. There are two reasons for doing this. First, it is sometimes necessary in order to communicate with OS COBOL programs. If a file or data area is to be read by OS COBOL programs, pointers must be defined in this way or as PIC X(4), since OS COBOL programs will not compile if they contain POINTER declarations.

Second, it is forbidden to perform arithmetic on pointer items, but you may sometimes want to do this. You could acquire a large pool of storage, then calculate addresses for separate blocks.

```
DATA DIVISION.
01  POINTER-EXAMPLE                    POINTER.
01  COMP-POINTER REDEFINES POINTER-EXAMPLE
                                       PIC S9(09) COMP.

PROCEDURE DIVISION.
    ADD 100 TO COMP-POINTER.
```

Listing 7-5   Redefining a Pointer.

7.4   THE ADDRESS SPECIAL REGISTER

The ADDRESS register is introduced with COBOL II. One AD-
DRESS register is reserved for each 01-level and 77-level item in the
Linkage Section. Using this register, a program can obtain the ad-
dress of every variable in the Linkage Section.

7.4.1   ADDRESS and Working Storage

The ADDRESS is not available for items in the Working Storage
Section.

7.4.2   Accessing the ADDRESS Register

The contents of this register can be accessed using the SET statement, or with a CALL USING . . . BY REFERENCE. Listing 7-6 is
an example of saving the address of a Linkage Section item in a
pointer, then restoring it.

```
DATA DIVISION.
WORKING-STORAGE SECTION.
01  WORK-PTR                     POINTER.
LINKAGE SECTION.
01  WORK-AREA                    PIC X(1000).

PROCEDURE DIVISION.
    SET WORK-PTR TO ADDRESS OF WORK-AREA
    ...
    SET ADDRESS OF WORK-AREA TO WORK-PTR.
```

Listing 7-6   ADDRESS Register.

```
DATA DIVISION.
01  DATA-POINTER-1          POINTER VALUE IS NULL.
01  DATA-POINTER-2          POINTER.

PROCEDURE DIVISION.
    SET DATA-POINTER-2 TO NULL.
```

Listing 7-7   The NULL Reserved Word.

7.5   THE NULL RESERVED WORD

The reserved word NULL is introduced in COBOL II. This value can be assigned only to POINTER items. It is a value which is guaranteed not to equal any valid address, so that it can be used to represent pointers that do not contain an address.

The NULL value can be assigned either with a VALUE IS NULL clause in the Data Division or with a SET . . . TO NULL statement in the Procedure Division. Listing 7-7 shows both methods of assigning a value.

7.6   USING POINTERS TO PASS ADDRESSES

The examples of pointer use given here are all for CICS systems, because that is where they are generally used. Pointers are used to pass between programs the addresses of:

• system areas, such as the CWA, TCTUA
• areas obtained by user GETMAINs

Listing 7-8 illustrates the manner in which this is done. The two CICS programs communicate by using pointers in a shared Commarea. The first program, CICSMAIN, does a CICS ASSIGN to get the addresses of the two system areas TCTUA and CWA. It also allocates storage with a GETMAIN. These three addresses are all passed in the Commarea to the second program, CICSTWO. Figure 7-2 illustrates this.

```
ID DIVISION.
PROGRAM-ID. CICSMAIN.
ENVIRONMENT DIVISION.
DATA DIVISION.
WORKING-STORAGE SECTION.
01  M-COMMAREA.
    02  CWA-PTR POINTER.
    02  TCTUA-PTR       POINTER.
    02  USER-PTR        POINTER.

LINKAGE SECTION.
01  USER-AREA           PIC X(10000).

PROCEDURE DIVISION.
    EXEC CICS
        ADDRESS
            CWA (CWA-PTR)
            TCTUA (TCTUA-PTR)
    END-EXEC
    EXEC CICS
        GETMAIN
                                    SET (USER-PTR)
            LENGTH (10000)
    END-EXEC

    SET ADDRESS OF USER-AREA TO USER-PTR

    EXEC CICS
        LINK
            PROGRAM ('CICSSUB')
            COMMAREA(M-COMMAREA)
    END-EXEC.


ID DIVISION.
PROGRAM-ID. CICSTWO.
ENVIRONMENT DIVISION.
DATA DIVISION.
LINKAGE SECTION.
01  M-COMMAREA.
    02  CWA-PTR POINTER.
    02  TCTUA-PTR       POINTER.
    02  USER-PTR        POINTER.
01  CWA-AREA            COPY CWACPY.
```

Listing 7-8   Passing Pointers in CICS. (Continued)

```
02  TCTUA-AREA           COPY TCTCPY.
01  USER-AREA            PIC X(10000).

PROCEDURE DIVISION.
    SET ADDRESS OF CWA-AREA   TO CWA-PTR
    SET ADDRESS OF TCTUA-AREA TO TCTUA-PTR
    SET ADDRESS OF USER-AREA  TO USER-PTR.
*** -- NOW THIS PROGRAM CAN FREELY ACCESS
*** -- THESE THREE AREAS.
```

Listing 7-8   Passing Pointers in CICS.

7.7   USING POINTERS TO ADDRESS VARIABLE AREAS

Pointers can be used to allow a program to reference data areas with unusual structures. Data created by other languages, or textual data, often does not have the clearly defined record structure which COBOL handles most conveniently. If the data has a "floating" record structure, where records definable in COBOL occur at unpredictable places, there may be a case for using pointers to address the record. Listing 7-9 is an example of this. It is a program which is

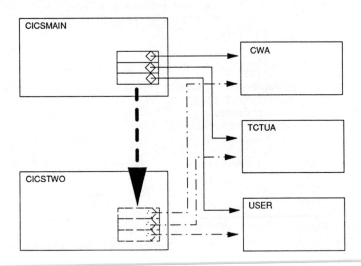

Figure 7-2   Pointers to CICS Work Areas.

```
DATA DIVISION.
WORKING-STORAGE SECTION.
01  SEARCH-HEADER          PIC X(05) VALUE '!KEY!'.
LINKAGE SECTION.
01  RETURN-CODE            PIC X(02).
01  USER-AREA              PIC X(50000).
01  FILLER REDEFINES USER-AREA.
02  USER-CHAR              PIC X(01)
                           OCCURS 10000 INDEXED BY UC-IX.
01  SEARCH-PATTERN-1       PIC X(25).
01  SEARCH-PATTERN-2       PIC X(25).
01  RESULT-TEXT            PIC X(400).
01  TEXT-STRUCTURE.
    02 KEY-LITERAL         PIC X(05).
    02 KEY-VALUE           PIC X(25).
    02 TOPIC                   OCCURS 1 TO 500
                               INDEXED BY T-IX.
        03 TOPIC-KEY       PIC X(20).
        03 TOPIC-TEXT      PIC X(400).

PROCEDURE DIVISION USING RETURN-CODE,
                        USER-AREA,
                        SEARCH-PATTERN-1,
                        SEARCH-PATTERN-2,
                        RESULT-TEXT.

*** -- SEARCH THE WHOLE AREA
    PERFORM VARYING UC-IX FROM 1 BY 1
    UNTIL UC-IX > 10000
*** -- POSITION TO AN ENTRY
        SET ADDRESS OF TEXT-STRUCTURE TO USER-CHAR (UC-IX)
        IF  KEY-LITERAL = SEARCH-HEADER
        AND KEY-VALUE = SEARCH-PATTERN-1
            SEARCH TOPIC
            AT END
                MOVE '10' TO RETURN-CODE
            WHEN TOPIC-KEY = SEARCH-PATTERN-2
*** -- ENTRY MATCHED: RETURN IT
                MOVE TOPIC-TEXT (T-IX) TO RESULT-TEXT
                MOVE '00' TO RETURN-CODE
                GOBACK
            END-SEARCH
        END-IF
    END-PERFORM

    MOVE '20' TO RETURN-CODE
    GOBACK.
```

Listing 7-9   Using Pointers to Access Floating Areas.

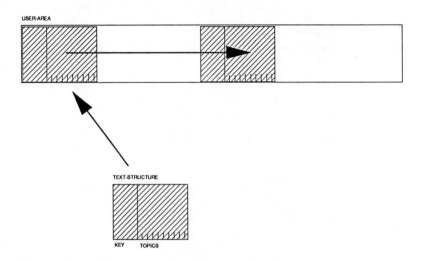

Figure 7-3   Using Pointers to Address Variable Areas.

passed a large text area and a pair of keys with which to search, and returns a piece of text. The program uses SET ADDRESS to position the structure which it uses in the text area. Figure 7-3 diagrams the process used here.

7.8 LINKED LISTS

Pointers can be used to implement sophisticated data addressing schemes such as the linked list. This is a structure where various records are chained together with pointers. This type of code allows a program to process an arbitrary number of items, each of an arbitrary size. This is efficient in many circumstances compared to the array (or table), because it is more flexible. A conventional table stores a fixed number of fixed length items.

The linked list achieves its efficiency at the expense of not allowing direct access to an item. To find a single item, it is necessary to follow the chain of pointers from the beginning until the item is reached.

Figure 7-4 shows a linked list structure. Figures 7-5 and 7-6 show the operations of storage and retrieval on this structure.

The example in Listing 7-10 assumes that a linked list has already been created, and that the start address can be obtained by calling the program GETFIRST. GETFIRST either gets the linked list start

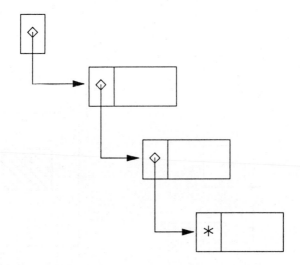

Figure 7-4   Pointers in a Linked List.

address or returns NULL. In batch systems, this would probably be an assembler program. In a CICS system, such an address would usually be stored in a CICS common area such as the CWA.

The two programs in Listings 7-11 and 7-12 show how a linked list can be built and manipulated using CICS GETMAINs. The first

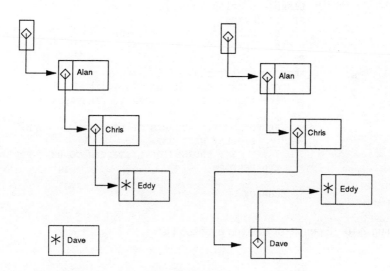

Figure 7-5   Adding an Item to a Linked List.

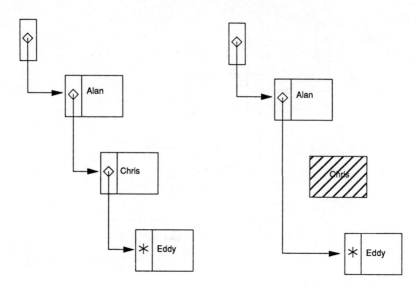

Figure 7-6   Deleting an Item from a Linked List.

```
ID DIVISION.
PROGRAM-ID.  READLIST.
ENVIRONMENT DIVISION.
DATA DIVISION.
WORKING-STORAGE SECTION.
01  FIRST-PTR           POINTER VALUE IS NULL.
LINKAGE SECTION.
01  LIST-ITEM.
    02  NEXT-PTR        POINTER.
    02  NEXT-DATA   PIC X(75).

PROCEDURE DIVISION.
    CALL 'GETFIRST' USING FIRST-PTR
    SET ADDRESS OF LIST-ITEM TO FIRST-PTR

    PERFORM UNTIL ADDRESS OF LIST-ITEM = NULL
        DISPLAY NEXT-DATA
            SET ADDRESS OF LIST-ITEM TO NEXT-PTR
    END-PERFORM

    GOBACK.
```

Listing 7-10   Example of Reading a Linked List.

```
ID DIVISION.
PROGRAM-ID.  MAKELIST.
ENVIRONMENT DIVISION.
DATA DIVISION.
FILE SECTION.
FD LOAD-FILE.
01  LOAD-RECORD PIC X(75).
WORKING-STORAGE SECTION.
01  FIRST-PTR          POINTER VALUE IS NULL.
LINKAGE SECTION.
01  LIST-ITEM.
    02  NEXT-PTR       POINTER.
    02  NEXT-DATA   PIC X(75).
01  EOF-LOAD-SW        PIC X VALUE ZERO.
        88  EOF-LOAD            VALUE '1'.


PROCEDURE DIVISION.
    OPEN LOAD-FILE
    READ LOAD-FILE
    AT END
        SET EOF-LOAD TO TRUE
    END-READ

    SET FIRST-PTR TO NULL
    PERFORM UNTIL EOF-LOAD
        PERFORM GET-NEW-ITEM
        SET NEXT-PTR TO FIRST-PTR
        MOVE LOAD-DATA TO NEXT-DATA
        SET FIRST-PTR TO ADDRESS OF LIST-ITEM
        READ LOAD-FILE
        AT END
            SET EOF-LOAD TO TRUE
        END-READ
    END-PERFORM

    CLOSE LOAD-FILE
    GOBACK.

GET-NEW-ITEM.
    EXEC CICS GETMAIN
        SET    (ADDRESS OF LIST-ITEM)
        LENGTH(LENGTH  OF LIST-ITEM)
    END-EXEC.
```

Listing 7-11   Generating a Linked List.

program (MAKELIST) loads the list from a file. Each entry is pointed to by the one before it. Figure 7-4 shows the addition of one item. The second program (SRCHLIST) performs maintenance on a linked list. It is passed a single record for insertion or deletion. It searches the list for the given key value. If it is found, it updates or deletes it depending on the action requested. If it is not found, it inserts it or does nothing depending on the action requested. Figure 7-5 shows the deletion of an item.

```
ID DIVISION.
PROGRAM-ID.  SRCHLIST.
ENVIRONMENT DIVISION.
DATA DIVISION.
FILE SECTION.
FD SEARCH-FILE.
01  SEARCH-RECORD.
        02 SEARCH-ACTION        PIC X.
            88 INSERT-DATA       VALUE 'I'.
            88 DELETE-DATA       VALUE 'D'.
        02 SEARCH-KEY           PIC X(5).
        02 SEARCH-DATA          PIC X(70).
WORKING-STORAGE SECTION.
01  FIRST-PTR            POINTER VALUE IS NULL.
LINKAGE SECTION.
01  LIST-ITEM.
        02  NEXT-PTR        POINTER.
        02  NEXT-KEY        PIC X(05).
        02  NEXT-DATA   PIC X(70).
01  LIST-ITEM-2.
        02  NEXT-PTR2       POINTER.
        02  NEXT-KEY2       PIC X(05).
        02  NEXT-DATA2  PIC X(70).
01  EOF-SEARCH-SW       PIC X VALUE ZERO.
        88  EOF-SEARCH          VALUE '1'.

PROCEDURE DIVISION.
    OPEN SEARCH-FILE
    READ SEARCH-FILE
    AT END
        SET EOF-SEARCH TO TRUE
    END-READ

    PERFORM UNTIL EOF-SEARCH
```

Listing 7-12   Searching a Linked List, Inserting, and Deleting. (Continued)

```
      EVALUATE SEARCH-ACTION
      WHEN 'I' PERFORM INSERT-DATA-PROCESS
      WHEN 'D' PERFORM DELETE-DATA-PROCESS
      END-EVALUATE
      READ SEARCH-FILE
      AT END
              SET EOF-SEARCH TO TRUE
      END-READ
   END-PERFORM

   CLOSE SEARCH-FILE
   GOBACK.

INSERT-DATA-PROCESS.
   PERFORM FIND-KEY
   IF NEXT-KEY = SEARCH-KEY
      EXEC CICS GETMAIN
          SET    (ADDRESS OF LIST-ITEM-2)
          LENGTH(LENGTH  OF LIST-ITEM-2)
      END-EXEC
      MOVE NEXT-ITEM TO NEXT-ITEM-2
      SET NEXT-KEY   TO SEARCH-KEY
      SET NEXT-DATA TO SEARCH-DATA
      SET NEXT-PTR  TO ADDRESS OF NEXT-ITEM-2
   ELSE
      MOVE SEARCH-DATA TO NEXT-DATA
   END-IF


DELETE-DATA-PROCESS.
   PERFORM FIND-KEY
   IF NEXT-KEY = SEARCH-KEY
      SET NEXT-PTR TO NEXT-PTR2
      EXEC CICS FREEMAIN
              DATA (NEXT-ITEM-2)
      END-EXEC
   END-IF.

FIND-KEY.
   SET NEXT-PTR TO FIRST-PTR
   PERFORM UNTIL NEXT-PTR = NULL
   OR NEXT-KEY NOT < SEARCH-KEY
      SET ADDRESS OF LIST-ITEM TO NEXT-PTR
   END-PERFORM.
```

Listing 7-12   Searching a Linked List, Inserting, and Deleting.

8

Calling Sub-Programs

In COBOL II, a new option has been introduced on the CALL statement. Parameters can now be passed either BY CONTENT or BY REFERENCE. The presence of the new option BY CONTENT has allowed some other improvements: the ability to pass a literal and to pass the contents of special registers such as LENGTH and AD-DRESS.

The new MVS/XA environment has introduced some complications in the matter of sub-program linkage, so in this chapter we also review some terminology for discussing calls and linkage, and then look at the concept of the CALL in its different forms.

8.1 CALL BY REFERENCE OR CONTENT

With COBOL II, parameters are passed either BY REFERENCE or BY CONTENT.

8.1.1 CALL BY REFERENCE

When parameters are passed to a called program in OS COBOL, the program receives the address of the parameter. Any changes made to the parameter are made immediately in the calling program. This is illustrated on the left side of Figure 8-1. This method of passing

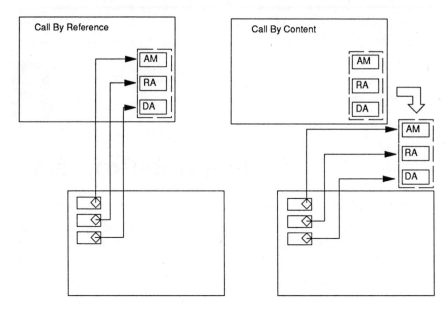

Figure 8-1   CALL BY REFERENCE and CALL BY CONTENT.

parameters is termed "call by reference," because the called program gets a reference to, or address of, each parameter. In COBOL II, you can code BY REFERENCE explicitly on any parameter you previously passed with OS COBOL. Call by Reference is the explicit name of the default call mechanism. All CALL statements which compiled under OS COBOL are automatically call by reference.

8.1.2   CALL BY CONTENT

CALL BY CONTENT is a new feature on the call statement introduced in COBOL II. Certain parameters can be passed BY CONTENT. Parameters which are passed BY CONTENT are protected from alteration by the called program. This is done by passing a copy down to the called program which is not copied back, as illustrated on the right side of Figure 8-1.

```
CALL 'PROGRAM' USING PARAMETER-1
            BY CONTENT    PARAMETER-2
                          PARAMETER-3
            BY REFERENCE  PARAMETER-4
                          PARAMETER-5
            BY CONTENT    PARAMETER-6
```

Listing 8-1   Transitive Call Type.

8.1.3   Call Type Is Transitive

BY CONTENT and BY REFERENCE are transitive. This means that once one is coded, all following parameters are of that type until another one is coded. In the example in Listing 8-1 (which is not correct COBOL, but illustrates this point), Parameter-1 is BY REFERENCE because that is the default. Parameter-3 is BY CONTENT because it follows Parameter-2, and Parameter-5 is BY REFERENCE because it follows Parameter-4.

It is probably clearer, as a matter of style, to explicitly code the call type on each parameter if the types are mixed.

8.1.4   BY CONTENT Parameters Must Match Exactly

The data description must be the same on the BY CONTENT parameters in the called and calling programs. No conversion, extension, or truncation will take place. In particular, when coding literals, their length should be coded correctly, with any necessary spaces inserted.

8.1.5   Passing Literals BY CONTENT

CALL BY CONTENT also allows the passing of constants because these are defended against any alteration. Listing 8-2 gives examples of the use of BY CONTENT to pass literals to a subprogram. In the second case, the subprogram is IMS and the literals are used to specify the DL/I call. Notice that I-O-AREA is called BY REFERENCE because the prior parameter was.

```
DATA DIVISION.
01  REC-AREA              PIC X(128).
01  DB-PCB                PIC X(128).
01  I-O-AREA              PIC X(400).


PROCEDURE DIVISION.
*  -- PASSING A LITERAL
            CALL 'FMAINT' USING BY CONTENT 'DELETE',
                                  BY REFERENCE REC-AREA


*  -- IMS CALL
            CALL 'CBLTDLI' USING
                 BY CONTENT     'GU',
                 BY REFERENCE DB-PCB,
                                  I-O-AREA,
                 BY CONTENT     'LIMITS(LOCATION = NY)'
```

Listing 8-2   CALL BY CONTENT Using Literals.

8.1.6   CALL BY CONTENT and LENGTH

In a CALL statement the LENGTH special register must always be
passed BY CONTENT because it must be protected against update
by the called program. Listing 8-3 gives examples of incorrect and
correct usage of the LENGTH register being used in a CALL statement.

8.1.7   Review and Comparison to Other Languages

It is important to remember that in VS COBOL II Release 2, CALL
BY CONTENT only applies to literals and the special register
LENGTH. In Release 3, it can be applied to any parameter.

The distinction between these two types of CALL statements is
recognized in many other languages. Listing 8-4 shows examples in
PL/I, which defaults to reference like COBOL, and C, which defaults
to content.

✓ CALL BY CONTENT can be simulated in general by copying the
parameters to a separate area and calling using this area. However,
this method does not allow literals to be passed in OS COBOL.

```
      DATA DIVISION.
      01   CALL-PARM        PIC X(200).
      01   STR-1                       PIC X(40).
      01   STR-2                       PIC X(40).

      PROCEDURE DIVISION.
*     -- INVALID CALL (BY REFERENCE)
            CALL 'SUBPGM' USING CALL-PARM,
                                      LENGTH OF CALL-PARM
*     -- VALID CALL   (BY CONTENT)
            CALL 'SUBPGM' USING CALL-PARM,
                      BY CONTENT LENGTH OF CALL-PARM

*     -- PASSING THE LENGTH OF AN ITEM
            CALL 'STRCPY' USING STR-1, STR-2,
                      BY CONTENT LENGTH OF STR-1
```

Listing 8-3   CALL BY CONTENT with LENGTH.

8.2   TERMINOLOGY OF CALLS AND LINKAGE

Before talking about changes introduced with MVS/XA, let's briefly review the terminology used in program preparation. When you start to create a program, you make SOURCE FILES using an editor. When you compile these, the compiler produces OBJECT FILES, one for each source file. These will generally have the same name but a different type or extension (OBJ or TEXT).

Object files are not executable; they must be passed through a linkage editor (or linker, sometimes called a loader) to produce an EXECUTABLE FILE, which can be run. An executable file may be created from one source file, but this is not necessary. The linker can take one or many object files as input; it combines these with code

```
  PL/I:
            /* by Content   */    CALL MODULE( (A), (B) );
            /* by Reference */    CALL MODULE( A, B );

  C:
            /* by Content   */    module(a, b);
            /* by Reference */    module(&a, &b);
```

Listing 8-4   CALL BY CONTENT/REFERENCE in Other Languages.

from the COBOL LIBRARY into a single executable file. One of these object files must be the MAIN PROGRAM, which receives control first. The linker assumes that this is the first one unless told otherwise.

In order to combine programs, the linker resolves EXTERNAL REFERENCES. An external reference is a reference within a program to a procedure or variable not contained within it. In a COBOL program, such a reference can be created by a CALL statement, and will refer to another COBOL program or to an ENTRY statement within another program. In addition, external references to routines in the COBOL library are generated by the compiler.

8.2.1 Dynamic and Static Linking

You can instruct the linker either to resolve external references or to leave them. In either case, the result of a successful use of the linkage editor is the creation of an executable file or RUN UNIT. If the linker resolved all external references, the run unit is a single, statically bound object which needs no external support to run. This is STATIC LINKING. Alternatively, the linker may have left references unresolved, relying on their resolution at run-time. In this case, the program will need to resolve these references when run, by searching the run-time libraries provided. This is DYNAMIC LINKING.

Compared to static linking, dynamic linking has some disadvantages. First, a program created in this manner needs the external support of a run-time library. It will fail if this is missing, which could be caused by a JCL error, or more seriously because the program is distributed to a site which has not licensed the library. Second, there can be a time penalty in loading copies of subroutines from libraries. Third, an unchanged tested program can fail because a subroutine it calls dynamically was changed.

The advantages of dynamic linking, on the other hand, are considerable. In program maintenance, if dynamically called subroutines are changed, it is not necessary to relink all programs which call them. Considerable memory savings can be realized if the dynamically called programs are large and not always used, or if they are reusable so that they can be shared between different programs. You can ensure that dynamically called programs are in an initialized state by using CANCEL appropriately. CANCEL is not available for static calls. All of the disadvantages mentioned above can be controlled with appropriate documentation and management.

In an MVS/XA environment, an additional advantage is that by using dynamic calls you can mix 24-bit and 31-bit programs.

Instructions to the COBOL compiler and linker control whether external references are resolved at compile-time or run-time. (A full reference of options to the compiler is in Chapter 16.) If they are to be resolved at run-time, the linkage editor "LET" option is required. This allows unresolved references; otherwise the program will be marked as nonexecutable. CICS programs always have an unresolved reference to the CICS interface program, so they are always marked "LET."

8.3 COMPILER AND LINKER OPTIONS

The COBOL compiler options RESIDENT and DYNAM are the options which control resolution of references, as follows:

NORESIDENT, NODYNAM: Library subroutines and called programs are linked into the run unit. No dynamic calls are possible.

RESIDENT, NODYNAM: Called programs are linked into the run unit where possible, but library subroutines are not.

NORESIDENT, DYNAM: not possible, will be treated as NODYNAM.

RESIDENT, DYNAM: neither library subroutines nor programs are included in the run unit.

The ability to dynamically link routines from the COBOL subroutine library is termed the COBOL Library Management Feature. Figure 8-2 illustrates the operation of the compiler, linker, and run-time loader on programs. Figure 8-3 illustrates the sharing of code in library routines and COBOL modules.

8.4 STATIC CALLS

A static call is a call to another program module in the same run unit. Static calls will be made if the NODYNAM compiler option is in effect, and the program to be called is coded in the statement as a literal rather than an identifier. All static CALL statements will be resolved by the linker. If the modules are not found, linkage editor

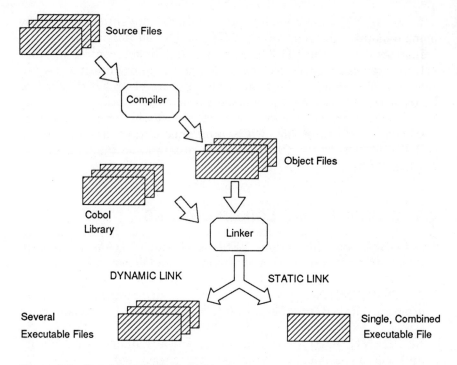

Figure 8-2   Dynamic and Static Linking.

errors will occur. The module will then be marked nonexecutable unless the "LET" linkage option was coded. If there are no errors, a single load module will be generated, containing the called and calling programs.

8.4.1 Mixing Static and Dynamic Calls

If the NODYNAM and RESIDENT options were coded, it is still possible to force a dynamic call by placing a variable in the CALL statement. Listing 8-5 illustrates the use of both types of call in a single program. In order to do this, the program must be compiled NODYNAM.

No Shared Code

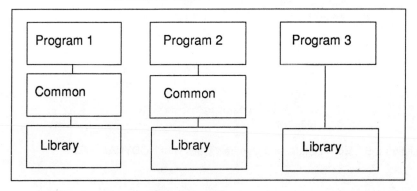

Shared Library Routines

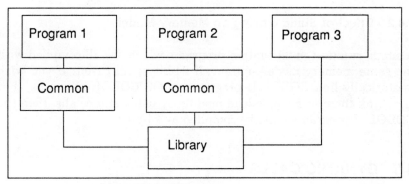

Shared Cobol Modules

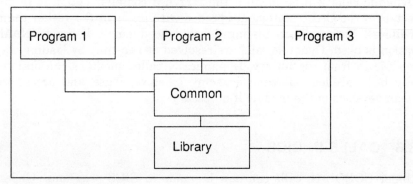

Figure 8-3   Shared Code.

```
DATA DIVISION.
01  XXX-PROGRAM PIC X(08) VALUE 'XXX1000'.
01  XXX-PARMS          PIC X(100).

PROCEDURE DIVISION.
* -- STATIC CALL
            CALL 'XXX1000'    USING XXX-PARMS

* -- DYNAMIC CALL
            CALL XXX-PROGRAM USING XXX-PARMS
            GOBACK.
```

Listing 8-5   Mixing Static and Dynamic Calls with NODYNAM,RES.

8.4.2   Effect of Static Linking on Memory Model

A single run unit must contain programs which are all compiled with the same memory model—either all 24-bit or all 31-bit. If you wish to statically link COBOL II programs to OS COBOL programs, that is, to link them in a single load module by using static calls, then the COBOL II programs must be compiled as 24-bit.

8.5   DYNAMIC CALLS

Dynamic calls will be made if the DYNAM compiler option is in effect, or if the CALL statement is coded with an identifier rather than a literal. Both calls in Listing 8-5 will be dynamic if the DYNAM option is used. Dynamic calls are resolved at run-time by loading the module in from the library. Dynamically called modules can optionally be cancelled, allowing economy of storage use and access to clean versions of the module if necessary.

8.6   CALLS IN CICS

Under COBOL II, calls can now be made in CICS programs. Under CICS 1.6.1 or above, one COBOL II program can issue static calls to another COBOL II program. Both programs can go through the CICS translator, and both programs can reference CICS data areas and issue EXEC CICS requests. They will appear as a single run unit to CICS, and have one entry in the CICS PPT.

Under CICS 1.7 with MVS/XA, COBOL II programs can issue dynamic calls to programs. These called programs may not contain references to CICS data areas or issue EXEC CICS requests. They will not be known to CICS, and will not appear in the PPT.

Coding changes for CICS programs, including calls, are fully covered in Chapter 10.

8.7 CALLS WITH MIXED ADDRESSING MODES

Dynamic calls can connect modules with different addressing modes. It is necessary to be careful, because you cannot pass above-the-line data to programs running below the line. One way to do this is to compile the program with the DATA(24) option, which ensures that all Working Storage is below the line. If you do not want to do this, remember that a program which is running above the line cannot reliably determine whether data items in its working storage are above or below. If you wish to pass data from a program running above the line to one running below, you must use a data area in the Linkage Section which is known to be below the line. One method in CICS is to allocate an area of less than 4K, because all areas less than 4096 bytes are allocated below the line in CICS. In other words, define an area of less than 4096 characters in the Linkage Section and perform a CICS GETMAIN to obtain addressability to it. This area can then be used to communicate with the below-the-line program. Listing 8-6 contains an example of this.

8.8 CALL USING PROCEDURE-NAME

The CALL statement using a procedure-name (a paragraph or section name) has been deleted from COBOL II. This feature was frowned upon and very rarely used in OS COBOL. An example of its use might be a program which called a jump table written in Assembly language. It is certainly the case that any program which relied on this feature will need to be completely rewritten for COBOL II, since there is no analogue to it available.

8.9 SUMMARY: CALLS AND LINKING

CALL statements in OS COBOL programs will compile unchanged using COBOL II unless they refer to procedure-names. OS COBOL

```
31-bit Program:

    DATA DIVISION.
    WORKING-STORAGE SECTION.

    LINKAGE SECTION.
    01  DATA-AREA              PIC X(2000).

    PROCEDURE DIVISION.
    EXEC CICS
            GETMAIN
                    SET (ADDRESS OF DATA-AREA)
                    LENGTH (LENGTH OF DATA-AREA)
    END-EXEC

    CALL 'BELOWPGM' USING DATA-AREA
    GOBACK.

24-bit Program:
    ID DIVISION.
    PROGRAM-ID. BELOWPGM.
    DATA DIVISION.
    WORKING-STORAGE SECTION.

    LINKAGE SECTION.
    01  DATA-AREA              PIC X(2000).

    PROCEDURE DIVISION USING DATA-AREA.

*  -- USES DATA-AREA
    GOBACK.
```

Listing 8-6   Passing Data from Above to Below the Line.

and COBOL II programs cannot be statically linked together, but using the dynamic linkage options discussed in this chapter, you can mix OS COBOL and COBOL II programs and pass data between them. The BY CONTENT option simplifies the coding of CALL statements using literals and the LENGTH register. Call statements are now available in CICS programs. Further changes in interprogram communication and the CALL statement are introduced with the full support of the ANSI 1985 standard contained in Release 3. A review of nested programs in Release 3 is contained in Chapter 20.

9

Double-Byte Character
Set Support

This chapter covers the new double-byte character set (DBCS) introduced with COBOL II. Programmers who are not planning to use this feature can skip this chapter without loss.

9.1   WHAT ARE ALTERNATE CHARACTER SETS?

The normal character set for the System/370 environment in which the VS COBOL II compiler runs is EBCDIC. The other common character set for modern computers (including the IBM PS/2 and IBM AS/400) is, of course, ASCII. Whereas EBCDIC is an 8-bit code defining 256 different characters, ASCII is a 7-bit code defining 128 characters.

English and other European languages have approximately 50–70 alphabetic characters, including upper and lower case, plus 10 numeric digits and a small number of special characters. They fit well into the character sets that use 7 or 8 bits; which is why these character sets were chosen.

There are languages with a much wider choice of characters, which cannot be expressed with a single-byte character set. One prominent example is Japanese (Kanji). It is also convenient to express computer graphic languages and scientific information in larger character sets.

A double-byte character set can contain any of 32,767 characters. COBOL II supports this DBCS in a number of ways.

9.2   SHIFT-OUT AND SHIFT-IN

Character strings can be created using the double-byte character set and two control characters called SHIFT-IN and SHIFT-OUT.

In a COBOL II program, SHIFT-OUT and SHIFT-IN are two special registers available to specify these control characters. SHIFT-OUT represents the single character X'0E' and SHIFT-IN represents X'0F'. They can be used wherever a data-item defined as PIC X can be used.

The presence of a SHIFT-OUT character means that the following characters until the next SHIFT-IN character are to be interpreted as being from the double-byte character set. The SHIFT-IN character indicates the return to single-byte characters. At present, a string cannot contain an arbitrary mixture of character types. It must begin with a single SHIFT-OUT and end with a single SHIFT-IN. In early releases of VS COBOL II, a compiler option GRAPHIC enabled the SHIFT-OUT and SHIFT-IN character values to be changed. This option is not available with Release 2. The values are fixed as described above.

9.3   THE DISPLAY-1 DATA TYPE

The DISPLAY-1 usage option defines a DBCS item.
Example of DBCS definition:

```
01  JAPANESE-NAME       PIC G(20) DISPLAY-1.
```

The new picture G is introduced for display-1 items and cannot be used for items which are not declared as display-1. The only other picture allowed for DBCS is B, which represents spaces. If B is used, the item is referred to as DBCS-edited.

9.4   DBCS USER-DEFINED WORDS

Any word in a COBOL II program can be constructed using DBCS characters, except one which refers to an external entity and has to conform to the external rules. Library, program, or text names cannot be DBCS, but all of the following can:

```
Alphabet-name
Condition-name
Data-name
Record-name
File-name
Index-name
Mnemonic-name
Paragraph-name
Section-name
```

These words do have to follow a more restricted set of rules than DBCS literals. They must be no longer than 30 characters, like their EBCDIC equivalents. The first and last characters must be SHIFT-OUT and SHIFT-IN, respectively. The 2 bytes of the DBCS characters may only contain values between X'41' and X'FE'. Double-byte EBCDIC characters are allowed; these have the first character X'42' and the second character one of A–Z, 0–9, and "-" (the same rule as for EBCDIC names). At least one non-EBCDIC double-byte character must be included. DBCS words cannot be extended over more than one line.

Using these rules, a program can be constructed where only level numbers, reserved words, operators, and external names are not from the double-byte character set.

9.5   SPECIFYING DBCS LITERALS

DBCS literals are specified as follows:

```
G'SO .............. SI'
```

where G followed by a quote (or apostrophe if that compiler option has been chosen) is the opening delimiter, and quote (or apostrophe) is the closing delimiter. The SHIFT-OUT and SHIFT-IN control char-acters must be the first and last characters, respectively, in the string. The SHIFT-OUT and SHIFT-IN characters are X'0E' and X'0F', respectively.

The maximum length of a DBCS literal is 56 bytes (28 characters). The literal cannot be extended over more than one line. There are no restrictions on the characters which can be used within a literal; they can range from X'00' to X'FF' for both bytes.

In the Data Division, DBCS literals can only be specified in the VALUE clause of DBCS (DISPLAY-1) data items. In the Procedure Division, DBCS literals can only be used as the sending field when the target is a DBCS or group item, or in a relation condition with a DBCS or group item. SPACE or SPACES can be DBCS literals, when they represent the value X'4040'. No other figurative constant is allowed.

Only EQUAL and NOT EQUAL comparisons can be made on DBCS fields. In other words, there is no ordering defined for them. When DBCS fields are used in MOVE statements, they are padded with the extended space characters X'4040' when too short and truncated as necessary when too long, but no other conversions will occur.

9.5.1 DBCS Literals and CICS

DBCS literals must not be included in CICS statements, or on the same line as CICS statements. The CICS preprocessor does not recognize them.

9.6 THE KANJI CLASS CONDITION

The Kanji class condition determines whether a data item contains any KANJI (Japanese) characters. The data item being tested must be a DBCS (DISPLAY-1) item. A data item qualifies as Kanji if all characters in the data portion meet these conditions:

both bytes equal to X'40' (SPACES)

or

first byte between X'41' and X'7F' inclusive and
second byte between X'41' and X'FE' inclusive

9.7 COMMENTS AND DBCS CHARACTERS

Comments may contain DBCS character strings, which cannot be continued across lines. The following optional paragraphs in the Identification Division may contain DBCS character strings:

```
Author
Date-Written
Date-Compiled
Installation
Security
```

9.8 CONCLUSION

This facility is of great value to native speakers of Japanese and other foreign languages, when combined with other software such as an editor which supports the character set. It also has some other specialist applications enabling COBOL to manipulate nontextual data.

10

CICS Considerations

This chapter covers the changes in the design and coding of CICS programs introduced as a result of COBOL II. Remember that COBOL II can be used with CICS versions 1.6, 1.6.1, 1.7, or 2.1. There are some relevant differences in programming introduced with CICS 1.7.

Of course, the changes discussed in other parts of the book apply to CICS programs also. All the structured programming changes can be used. Programs can take advantage of access to above-the-line storage. The ADDRESS and LENGTH registers are available, making the coding of many EXEC CICS statements simpler.

Perhaps surprisingly, the changes in the debugging facilities discussed elsewhere in the book also apply to CICS programs. Formatted dumps requested with the FDUMP compile option will be produced on a Temporary Storage Queue, and the interactive debugger can be used on CICS programs in its batch mode. However, most programmers will prefer to use debuggers written specifically for CICS, such as CEDF and Intertest, when they are available.

10.1 PROGRAM REENTRANCE

A program is serially reusable if several different tasks can execute one copy of the code one after the other without interfering with each other. A program is reentrant if several different tasks can execute one copy of the code simultaneously without interfering with each other. Under CICS, it is normal for many tasks to run at the same time. It is a goal of CICS to allow them to share the same code.

✓ OS COBOL programs were not reentrant because all tasks shared the same working storage areas. CICS achieved a simulation of reentrancy by loading a separate copy of Working Storage for each program and sharing the Procedure Division code. ⋀

Under COBOL II, programs can be compiled as truly reentrant, whether they are to run in the CICS or batch environment. The COBOL compiler manages the storage to ensure that different tasks do not alter each other's storage. One advantage of this is that VS COBOL II programs can be placed in an area of MVS called the Link Pack Area (LPA). In this area, they can be shared by several CICS systems and are immune from corruption because this area cannot be overwritten.

Under COBOL II, many COBOL library routines are loaded at system initialization and located dynamically. These also can be placed in the MVS LPA and shared between regions. Some of the library routines have been written specifically for CICS, using CICS rather than MVS GETMAINs, for instance. These routines are termed ESMs (environment-specific modules). ESMs are the reason that with COBOL II, CICS programs can include statements like INSPECT and STRING statements that were previously not allowed. By the way, these ESMs use the ordinary CICS Command-level interface. Because of these changes in library and program management, all CICS programs must be compiled as RES (resident) and RENT (reentrant).

10.2 USING CALLS INSTEAD OF LINKS

Until now, you could not use CALL statements in CICS COBOL programs unless they were calls to assembler modules which did not use CICS services. With COBOL II, you can now code calls to other COBOL programs in CICS. These called programs have full access to CICS areas, such as the Exec Interface Block and Commarea, and can make any CICS calls they wish. This means that you can freely segment large programs using CALL statements.

One restriction is that CALL statements in CICS must in general be static calls—see Chapter 8 for a full discussion of static calls. (We discuss the limited dynamic call option in CICS 1.7 [see 10.2.6].)

10.2.1   Efficiency of CALL Statements

Using the CALL statement to segment programs makes possible an improvement in efficiency over the CICS LINK. The EXEC CICS LINK instruction has to establish a new run-unit, including setting up the environment and doing CICS table-searches. This executes about 1400 machine-code instructions. This compares with a dozen or so for a CALL, which is simply a branch to a piece of code linked in the same module. A set of COBOL II programs can provide improved performance over an identical set of OS COBOL programs in two ways: because they run above the line and because they can be easily rewritten to use calls rather than links. Table 10-1 shows some tested efficiency improvements published by IBM. These improvements were gained solely by compiling the programs with COBOL II rather than OS COBOL, running the COBOL II programs above the line, and changing all LINK statements to CALLs. No other changes were made to the programs.

10.2.2   CALL Statements and Modular Code

The LINK instruction is very inefficient. Many shops solved this problem by simply not using it. Then they could segment programs with CICS XCTL statements, which leads to an unstructured "spaghetti"-like system. Alternatively, they could choose not to segment programs at all, leading to large monolithic programs which were daunting to maintain. Because the CALL statement is as efficient as a simple PERFORM, it is now possible to build CICS systems efficiently from small modules.

If you switch from the use of EXEC CICS LINK statements to CALL statements, you will have some decisions to make about the management of software. In CICS programs, it is common for control to pass between many programs and to go several levels deep. It is advisable to carefully manage the source and object code configurations to avoid problems. There are many products sold for library management and source code control.

10.2.3   GOBACK, STOP RUN, and EXIT PROGRAM
✓

With COBOL II, it is now possible to code and execute GOBACK or STOP RUN statements in CICS programs. Remember that previously, execution of such a statement would bring down the CICS

Table 10-1   Improvements Using COBOL II Above the Line with Calls.

Internal Transaction Response Time	23–78 %
Total CPU Time	15–23 %
Dynamic Storage Use	11–30 %

region. Most programmers coded a GOBACK or STOP RUN somewhere in their OS COBOL programs (the compiler inserts one anyway if you don't), but made sure it didn't execute, for instance, by putting an EXEC CICS RETURN immediately before it. While it is not necessary to change this practice, there are several advantages to the GOBACK statement.

GOBACK ends a program in the same way, whether it was invoked with a CALL or an EXEC CICS LINK.

GOBACK ends a program in the same way in both CICS and batch environments.

GOBACK is more efficient than EXEC CICS RETURN because it doesn't go through the CICS Execute Interface Program.

There is one problem with the use of the GOBACK statement at present. If you use the CEDF debugger with subprograms which return using GOBACK rather than EXEC CICS RETURN, you may experience storage violations which can cause random problems in the CICS region, even as serious as bringing it down. Apparently the CEDF product is not able to tell that the called program has ended. If you plan to use run units composed of several modules statically linked together, it is important to be aware of the differences between the EXIT PROGRAM, GOBACK, and STOP RUN statements. EXIT PROGRAM returns to the calling program if invoked by a CALL statement, and will be ignored if there was no CALL. STOP RUN has the same effect as EXEC CICS RETURN, returning to the last invoking run unit, which is a program that used a CICS LINK, or CICS itself. GOBACK returns to the calling program, whether invoked by a CALL or a CICS LINK.

10.2.4   Coding Programs for Batch or CICS

Using CALL and GOBACK statements to communicate, it is possible to write modules which have no difference in source code and run in both batch and CICS environments. Of course, such programs must avoid sequential, VSAM, and terminal I/O statements, but substantial subroutines can be written in this way.

10.2.5   Coding for CALL or LINK

A problem arises using CALL statements with the symbolic debugger Intertest. This product, at the time of writing, does not support the CALL statement. It is not able to track called programs and will at times fail on the call instruction, reporting that it is an invalid instruction. This problem may occur with other debuggers also, since until the advent of COBOL II the CALL statement was not available in CICS COBOL programs. Since it can be a real inconvenience to lose the power of such a debugger, this book suggests a technique for working around the problem.

It is possible to write programs so that they can be switched without recompilation to use either CALL or link statements for communication. This has several advantages. The CALL statement is more efficient than the link; but systems built around static calls can be difficult to administer, particularly in the development phase, because a change in any program requires the relinking of any programs which reference it. Also, as mentioned above, there can be problems debugging programs with CALL statements. With COBOL II support for the CALL and the GOBACK statements in CICS, a program can be written to switch between the two methods. All that is necessary to allow this switching is a careful ordering of the parameters to the called program. Listing 10-1 gives an example of this. After running through the CICS preprocessor, both programs will have the Exec Interface Block inserted in the Linkage Section.

10.2.6   Dynamic Calls in CICS 1.7

In Release 1.7 of CICS using COBOL II, it is possible to code dynamic calls. The advantages of dynamic calls are that a single load

```
Invoking Program:

    DATA DIVISION.
    01  PARAMETERS                     PIC X(100).
    LINKAGE SECTION.
    01  MAP-LAYOUT.
    01  RECORD-LAYOUT.
    01  CWA-AREA.
        ...
        02  CWA-CALL-LINK-SW   PIC X.
            88  USE-CALL                VALUE 'C'.
            88  USE-LINK                VALUE 'L'.

    PROCEDURE DIVISION.
        EXEC CICS
            ASSIGN CWA
                SET (ADDRESS OF CWA-AREA)
        END-EXEC

        IF USE-CALL
            CALL 'SUBPGM'
            USING DFHEIBLK, PARAMETERS
        ELSE
            EXEC CICS
                LINK
                    PROGRAM ('SUBPGM')
                    COMMAREA (PARAMETERS)
            END-EXEC
        END-IF.

Invoked Program:

    DATA DIVISION.
    LINKAGE SECTION.
    01  DFHCOMMAREA.

    PROCEDURE DIVISION.
    * -- USE DFHCOMMAREA, WHICH IS THE SAME AS
    * -- PARAMETERS IN  THE CALLING PROGRAM
        ...
        GOBACK.
```

Listing 10-1   Switching from CALL to LINK.

module can be shared with batch programs, and that they remove
the maintenance issues discussed above. There is a severe limitation
on this option, however; only programs with no CICS dependencies
can be called in this manner. This might include timing routines,

data validation routines such as part numbers, and other simple procedures, particularly if shared with batch programs.

10.3 MOVING ABOVE THE LINE

Chapter 13 includes an explanation of the 16-megabyte line and 31-bit addressing in MVS/XA. Storage above the 16-megabyte line is available to COBOL II programs running under MVS/XA. Of course, COBOL II programs running under MVS/370 gain no advantage in this area. All the following can now be loaded above the line:

- COBOL procedure code
- COBOL working storage
- user storage (greater than 4096 bytes) obtained with GETMAINs
- COBOL II library functions

10.3.1 Taking Advantage of Above-the-Line Storage

With MVS/XA and COBOL II, the effective memory available to CICS programmers changes from an architectural limit of 5–6 megabytes to a great deal more, depending on your attitude towards the cost of memory. It is now an option to redesign your applications to be much freer in their use of system memory. Disk files, at least those which are reference (read-only), can be replaced by in-core areas. The simplest way to do this is by reviewing and being more generous with database and VSAM buffer allocations. Other options to consider are the use of in-core tables, using the EXEC CICS LOAD statement or GETMAIN with the SHARED option to allocate the table and load the data with a program. All programs should be resident, unless it is known they are rarely used. In general, any design trade-off where memory is a factor should be reconsidered when migrating to COBOL II and MVS/XA.

10.4 RELAXED LANGUAGE RESTRICTIONS

Certain statements which were not allowed under CICS with OS COBOL are now allowed. The CALL statement has already been discussed in Chapter 8. The others are the USE FOR DEBUGGING statement and these string-handling statements:

```
INSPECT
STRING
UNSTRING
```

These statements were disallowed in OS COBOL because they issued OS GETMAINs. This is no longer a problem. In COBOL II,
under CICS, they use the new environment-specific CICS library
routines, which issue CICS commands such as GETMAINs where
appropriate. Under COBOL II, the only COBOL language statements
which are restricted are file I-O statements, file related entries in
the Environment and Data Divisions, and the dynamic CALL (but
see the discussion of CALLS in Section 10.2.6).

Listing 10-2 gives examples of the use of the UNSTRING,
INSPECT, and STRING verbs, since some CICS programmers may
never have used them. In COBOL II, you will find that there is no
choice but to use these verbs, because TRANSFORM and EXAMINE,
the staples of COBOL/CICS string-handling in the past, have both
been removed from the language. Chapter 18 covers missing features, and ways to replace them, in more detail. This example program reads a user input line which contains an action, a document
name, and some one-character arguments. It might look like:

```
SAVE MY-FILE -A-F
```

The program parses it using UNSTRING into data areas, and
edits them, using a second UNSTRING to strip out the arguments
and count them. It uses STRING to concatenate any error messages
into a single area. A final INSPECT statement converts the remain-
ing $ signs in the error message to spaces.

10.5   DEBUGGING FEATURES AVAILABLE

A formatted dump is now available for CICS programs. To obtain
one, the program should be compiled with the FDUMP option. If an
abnormal termination occurs, the dump will be produced on the temporary storage queue CEBRterm, where term is the terminal ID of
the abending task. Use of HANDLE ABEND will bypass the dump.

CICS programmers can now use the symbolic debugger COBTEST,
in its batch mode. To use it, you place input commands to the tool on
the temporary storage queue CSCOterm, where term is the terminal
ID where the test is to be performed. You then start the task from
the terminal in the usual way. COBTEST will direct output from the

```
DATA DIVISION.
01  ACTION               PIC X(08).
        88  VALID-ACTION         'SAVE', 'DELETE', 'CHANGE',
                                 'COPY', 'ARCHIVE', 'INDEX'
01  DOCUMENT             PIC X(24).
01  ARGUMENTS            PIC X(12).
01  ARG-TABLE.
        02  ARG              PIC X OCCURS 6 INDEXED BY ARG-IX.
01  ARG-COUNT            PIC S9(09) COMP.
01  ERROR-MESSAGE        PIC X(132).


PROCEDURE DIVISION.

UNSTRING USER-INPUT DELIMITED BY SPACE OR ','
INTO ACTION DOCUMENT ARGUMENTS

MOVE ALL '$' TO ERROR-MESSAGE

IF NOT VALID-ACTION
        STRING ERROR-MESSAGE          DELIMITED BY '$'
              'ACTION ('                    DELIMITED BY SPACES
              ACTION                        DELIMITED BY SIZE
              ') IS NOT RECOGNIZED. ' DELIMITED BY SIZE
        INTO ERROR-MESSAGE
END-IF


PERFORM FIND-DOCUMENT

IF NOT DOCUMENT-FOUND
        STRING ERROR-MESSAGE          DELIMITED BY '$'
              'DOCUMENT ('             DELIMITED BY SPACES
              DOCUMENT                      DELIMITED BY SIZE
              ') DOES NOT EXIST. ' DELIMITED BY SIZE
        INTO ERROR-MESSAGE
END-IF

UNSTRING ARGUMENTS DELIMITED BY '-'
INTO ARG(1) ARG(2) ARG(3) ARG(4) ARG(5) ARG(6)
TALLYING IN ARG-COUNT
ON OVERFLOW
        STRING ERROR-MESSAGE          DELIMITED BY '$'
              'TOO MANY ARGS. '              DELIMITED BY SPACES
        INTO ERROR-MESSAGE
END-UNSTRING

PERFORM ARGUMENT-PROCESS
VARYING ARG-IX FROM 1 BY 1 UNTIL ARG-IX > ARG-COUNT

INSPECT ERROR-MESSAGE REPLACING ALL '$' BY SPACES
```

Listing 10-2   CICS/COBOL II String Handling.

tool to the temporary storage queue CEBRterm, where it can be examined after the task is completed.

The output from the dump or the debugger can be browsed using the CICS transaction CEBR, which defaults to the same queue (CEBRterm) that they both use.

The SSRANGE option, which enables run-time index and subscript boundary checking, is available under CICS.

All the debugging options of COBOL II are covered in Appendix C of this book. One point to remember is that you should generally turn these options off when moving a program over for production. The TEST option is not needed in production. FDUMP facility makes the programs much larger and produces very big dumps. It should only be used with programs running above the line in systems without virtual storage constraints. The SSRANGE incurs a considerable performance overhead, and can increase run-time by 50%.

10.6   ADDRESSABILITY ISSUES

10.6.1   Service Reload

SERVICE RELOAD statements are used by COBOL to keep the correct values in registers after the execution of CICS statements. The COBOL II compiler still supports the SERVICE RELOAD statement, because the CICS preprocessor generates these statements. However, using COBOL II, it is no longer necessary for a programmer to code SERVICE RELOAD statements.

10.6.2   BLL Cells

In OS/VS COBOL, you use the Base Locator for Linkage (BLL) Cells to access any items which were outside the program. Such items include GETMAINed storage, CICS system areas, and files accessed with SET. This mechanism was an extension of the OS PARM facility which is somewhat unnatural to the COBOL programmer. In VS COBOL II there is no longer any reference to BLL cells. The compiler establishes addressability using the ADDRESS special register. (For a full discussion of the ADDRESS special register and pointers, see Chapter 7.)

OS COBOL:

```
            DATA DIVISION.
            LINKAGE SECTION.
            01  BLL-CELLS.
                    02  FILLER       PIC 9(9) COMP.
                    02  REC-PTR      PIC 9(9) COMP.
                    02  REC-PTR2     PIC 9(9) COMP.
                    02  REC-PTR3     PIC 9(9) COMP.
            01  RECORD-LAYOUT  PIC X(12000).


            PROCEDURE DIVISION.
                EXEC CICS
                        READ
                                DATASET ('THE-FILE')
                                RIDFLD (THE-KEY)
                                SET (REC-PTR)
                    END-EXEC
                    SERVICE RELOAD RECORD-LAYOUT
                    COMPUTE REC-PTR2 = REC-PTR + 4096
                    COMPUTE REC-PTR3 = REC-PTR + 8192

                EXEC CICS
                        RETURN
                    END-EXEC

                    GOBACK.
```

COBOL II:

```
            DATA DIVISION.
            LINKAGE SECTION.
            01  RECORD-LAYOUT.

            PROCEDURE DIVISION.
                EXEC CICS
                        READ
                                DATASET ('THE-FILE')
                                RIDFLD (THE-KEY)
                    END-EXEC

                    GOBACK.
```

Listing 10-3 Changes from OS COBOL.

In OS COBOL, a special technique was required when using BLL cells for addressing an area greater than 4096 bytes. It was necessary to assign an additional BLL cell and code in the Procedure Division to keep the second one equal to the first + 4096. An additional

BLL cell was needed for each 4K being addressed. In COBOL II, this is not necessary. The examples in Listing 10-3 show the code to read a 12K record in OS COBOL and in COBOL II.

10.6.3   The ADDRESS Special Register

The two new special registers, LENGTH and ADDRESS, are particularly useful in CICS programs. The ADDRESS register can be used in the SET option of the following CICS commands:

```
ADDRESS
GETMAIN
LOAD
READ
READQ
```

Use of ADDRESS registers replaces the need to define BLL (Base Locator for Linkage) cells to hold addresses of items in the Linkage Section. The methods for using ADDRESS described in Chapter 7, such as the linked list processing, are particularly suitable to programs on CICS systems.

10.6.4   Establishing Addressability

Before you can refer to an item in your program, you must have addressability to it. You have addressability to items in Working Storage at all times. For Linkage Section items, you can establish addressability to an area by any of the following methods:

- issue a CICS GETMAIN with SET
- issue a CICS READ with SET
- issue a CICS ADDRESS with SET or USING
- issue a CICS LOAD with SET
- receive item passed as Commarea
- receive passed as a parameter in CALL statement
- receive a pointer passed by any of the above, and use SET ADDRESS TO . . .

The example programs in Listing 10-4 illustrate all these methods.

Calling Program:

```
ID DIVISION.
PROGRAM-ID. PROG1.
ENVIRONMENT DIVISION.
DATA DIVISION.
WORKING-STORAGE SECTION.
01  PR2-COMMAREA.
    02  USER-ADDRESS            POINTER.
    02  RECORD-ADDRESS          POINTER.
01  PR3-COMMAREA.
    02  CWA-ADDRESS             POINTER
    02  CURRENCY-ADDRESS        POINTER.

LINKAGE SECTION.
01  USER-AREA                   PIC X(2000).
01  RECORD-AREA                 PIC X(1000).
01  CWA-AREA                    PIC X(4000).
01  CURRENCY-TABLE              PIC X(5000).

PROCEDURE DIVISION.
    EXEC CICS
        GETMAIN
            SET (ADDRESS OF USER-AREA)
            LENGTH (LENGTH OF USER-AREA)
    END-EXEC

    EXEC CICS
        READ
            DATASET ('MASFILE')
            RIDFLD  (MAS-KEY)
            SET (ADDRESS OF RECORD-AREA)
    END-EXEC

    EXEC CICS
        ADDRESS
            CWA (ADDRESS OF CWA-AREA)
    END-EXEC

    EXEC CICS
        LOAD
            PROGRAM ('CURRTAB')
            SET     (ADDRESS OF CUREENCY-TABLE)
            HOLD
    END-EXEC

    EXEC CICS
        LINK
            PROGRAM ('PROG2')
```

Listing 10-4   Establishing Addressability. (Continued)

```
                    COMMAREA (PR2-COMMAREA)
          END-EXEC

          CALL 'PROG3' USING DFHEIBLK,
                             PR3-COMMAREA

          GOBACK.
```

First Called Program:

```
          ID DIVISION.
          PROGRAM-ID. PROG2.
          ENVIRONMENT DIVISION.
          DATA DIVISION.
          LINKAGE SECTION.
          01  PR2-COMMAREA.
              02  USER-ADDRESS          POINTER.
              02  RECORD-ADDRESS        POINTER.
          01  USER-AREA                 PIC X(2000).
          01  RECORD-AREA               PIC X(1000).


          PROCEDURE DIVISION.
              SET ADDRESS OF USER-AREA TO USER-ADDRESS
              SET ADDRESS OF RECORD-AREA TO RECORD-ADDRESS
              ...
     *** -- DO THINGS WITH USER-AREA AND RECORD-AREA
              ...
              GOBACK.
```

Second Called Program:

```
          ID DIVISION.
          PROGRAM-ID. PROG3.
          ENVIRONMENT DIVISION.
          DATA DIVISION.
          LINKAGE SECTION.
          01  PR3-COMMAREA.
              02  CWA-ADDRESS           POINTER
              02  CURRENCY-ADDRESS      POINTER.
          01  CWA-AREA                  PIC X(4000).
          01  CURRENCY-TABLE            PIC X(5000).


          PROCEDURE DIVISION.
              SET ADDRESS OF CWA-AREA TO CWA-ADDRESS
              SET ADDRESS OF CURRENCY-TABLE TO CURRENCY-ADDRESS
              ...
     *** -- DO THINGS WITH CWA-AREA AND CURRENCY-TABLE
              ...
              GOBACK.
```

Listing 10-4   Establishing Addressability.

10.6.5   When an Address Is Out of Scope

A pointer or an ADDRESS register has to point to something. Since addressability has to be positively established to any area in the Linkage Section, it is possible to try to address these areas before this is achieved or after it is lost. This leads to storage violations. These may cause immediate failure of the program or more subtle effects such as performance problems or sporadic failures of other program codes. Listing 10-5 shows examples of ways to produce a storage violation using pointers which are not pointing to anything.

10.7   THE LENGTH SPECIAL REGISTER

The CICS preprocessor program uses the LENGTH special register to make it unnecessary for the programmer to code a LENGTH option in most CICS commands. All the following options on CICS commands can now be omitted and will then default to the length of the data-item named in the FROM or INTO option:

```
DESTIDLENGTH

FLENGTH

FROMLENGTH

LENGTH

MAXLENGTH

MAXFLENGTH

VOLUMELENGTH
```

You now only need to code one of these LENGTH items if you need to pass CICS a LENGTH different from the data area you have defined.

If you are using the SET option rather than INTO, you must code the appropriate length option, but you can use the LENGTH register rather than coding it explicitly. Examples of the use of LENGTH will be found in Chapter 5.

In the example in Listing 10-6, in the GETMAIN statement, which allocates storage dynamically, you can code "LENGTH OF" rather than hard-coding the value. In the "WRITE" statement, which writes to a VSAM file, the LENGTH is not given but generated by the CICS preprocessor for you.

One warning: Remember the difference between LENGTH and FLENGTH. FLENGTH stands for FULLWORD length and is re-

```
      ID DIVISION.
      PROGRAM-ID. PROG1.
      ENVIRONMENT DIVISION.
      DATA DIVISION.
      WORKING-STORAGE SECTION.
      LINKAGE SECTION.
      01  PR1-COMMAREA.
           02  CWA-ADDRESS          POINTER.
      01  USER-AREA                PIC X(2000).
      01  CWA-AREA                        PIC X(4000).
      01  CURRENCY-TABLE                  PIC X(5000).


      PROCEDURE DIVISION.
    * -- THE FOLLOWING TWO STATEMENTS CAUSE STORAGE VIOLATIONS
    * -- BECAUSE ADDRESSABILITY IS NOT ESTABLISHED
           MOVE 'XXXX' TO USER-AREA
           MOVE 'XXXX' TO CWA-AREA

           EXEC CICS
                GETMAIN
                         SET (ADDRESS OF USER-AREA)
                         LENGTH (LENGTH OF USER-AREA)
           END-EXEC

           SET ADDRESS OF CWA-AREA TO CWA-ADDRESS

    * -- THE FOLLOWING TWO STATEMENTS EXECUTE CORRECTLY
    * -- BECAUSE ADDRESSABILITY WAS ESTABLISHED
           MOVE 'XXXX' TO USER-AREA
           MOVE 'XXXX' TO CWA-AREA

           EXEC CICS
                FREEMAIN
                         DATA (USER-AREA)
           END-EXEC

    * -- THE FOLLOWING STATEMENT CAUSES A STORAGE VIOLATION
    * -- BECAUSE ADDRESSABILITY WAS LOST AFTER THE FREEMAIN
           MOVE 'XXXX' TO USER-AREA

           GOBACK.
```

Listing 10-5   Storage Violations.

quired to pass values greater than 32,767 (32K), which will not fit in
the halfword LENGTH field. Check that the length is not greater
than 32K (32,767). If it is, you must use FLENGTH to avoid a run-
time error caused by overflowing the halfword CICS length field.

```
DATA DIVISION.
WORKING-STORAGE SECTION.
01  MISCFILE-LENGTH          PIC S9(08) COMP VALUE 200.

01  MISC-KEY                 PIC X(20).
01  MISC-FILE.
    02  ......
    02  LAST-REAL-FIELD      PIC X.
    02  FILLER               PIC X(75).
LINKAGE SECTION.
01  WORK-AREA                PIC X(1000).
01  HUGE-AREA                PIC X(50000).

PROCEDURE DIVISION.
EXEC CICS
    GETMAIN
        SET    (ADDRESS OF WORK-AREA)
        LENGTH(LENGTH OF WORK-AREA)
END-EXEC

EXEC CICS
    GETMAIN
        SET    (ADDRESS OF HUGE-AREA)
        FLENGTH(LENGTH OF HUGE-AREA)
END-EXEC

EXEC CICS
    WRITE
        DATASET ('MISCFILE')
        FROM    (MISC-FILE)
        RIDFLD  (MISC-KEY)
END-EXEC.
```

Listing 10-6   LENGTH Special Register.

10.8   FORBIDDEN OPTIONS

10.8.1   Compiler Options

These options are forbidden for CICS programs:

```
DYNAM
NORENT
NORES
NOLIB
TRUNC
```

The TRUNC option causes truncation of binary fields to the maximum decimal value defined for them. For instance, a PIC S9(04) COMP field can hold values up to 32,767 but would be truncated to 9999. Since CICS addresses and length fields are binary numbers which can range up to the highest value, this option may cause the alteration of these values. In addition, it is best to avoid arithmetic on such CICS fields because truncation can occur anyway.

The other options are disallowed because CICS requires the opposite values NODYNAM, RENT, RES, LIB for efficient storage management. To generate a CICS COBOL II program, you specify the option COBOL2 to the CICS preprocessor. This then generates a CBL statement with these required options for the compiler.

10.8.2 Macro Level CICS

The VS COBOL II compiler does not support CICS Macro Level calls. CICS macros will not compile and will not execute in COBOL II programs. For years now, IBM has been clearly stating its intention to leave Macro Level behind. The COBOL II library functions are written using Command Level CICS. One of the costs of conversion to COBOL II for old applications, then, will be that of converting to Command Level, for those who have not yet done so.

10.9 SUMMARY: CHANGES TO CICS

COBOL II introduces many changes for the better. The single biggest improvement is the removal of virtual storage constraint. Many applications should be reviewed to determine whether they should be tuned to exploit the new memory available. There is a considerable effort involved in converting older programs, particularly those using BLL cells or with extensive string handling. On the other hand, it is simpler to write new programs and there is now less difference between CICS and batch programs. The key simplifications are:

• BLL cells are no longer referred to
• LENGTH is not explicitly coded
• 4096-byte limitations are removed
• SERVICE RELOAD is not coded
• EXEC CICS RETURN is not needed

To summarize this, Listing 10-7 below shows the same small program in OS COBOL and COBOL II.

OS COBOL:

```
LINKAGE SECTION.
01  BLL-CELLS.
        02  FILLER      PIC 9(9) COMP.
        02  MAP-PTR     PIC 9(9) COMP.

        02  REC-PTR     PIC 9(9) COMP.
        02  REC-PTR2    PIC 9(9) COMP.
01  MAP-LAYOUT.
01  RECORD-LAYOUT.
PROCEDURE DIVISION.
        EXEC CICS
                GETMAIN
                        SET (MAP-PTR)
                        LENGTH (972)
        END-EXEC
        SERVICE RELOAD MAP-LAYOUT

        EXEC CICS
                READ
                        DATASET ('THE-FILE')
                        RIDFLD (THE-KEY)
                        SET (REC-PTR)
        END-EXEC
        SERVICE RELOAD RECORD-LAYOUT
        COMPUTE REC-PTR2 = REC-PTR + 4096.

        EXEC CICS
                RETURN
        END-EXEC

        GOBACK.
```

COBOL II:

```
        DATA DIVISION.
        LINKAGE SECTION.
        01  MAP-LAYOUT.
        01  RECORD-LAYOUT.

        PROCEDURE DIVISION.
```

Listing 10-7   Changes from OS COBOL. (Continued)

```
EXEC CICS
        GETMAIN
                SET (ADDRESS OF MAP-LAYOUT)
                LENGTH (LENGTH OF MAP-LAYOUT)
END-EXEC

EXEC CICS
        READ
                DATASET ('THE-FILE')
                RIDFLD (THE-KEY)
END-EXEC

GOBACK.
```

Listing 10-7   Changes from OS COBOL.

11

VSAM and Database Programming

This chapter includes some miscellaneous changes introduced in COBOL II in the interface to VSAM and database data management. None of these changes has any effect on existing programs or a significant effect on new programming.

11.1 CODING FOR VSAM EXTENDED RETURN CODES

With COBOL II, the COBOL programmer has access to extended VSAM return codes that were previously only available to Assembler programmers. To get this access, which is optional, you code a second file status field in the FILE STATUS clause of the FD statement. This field is 6 characters long and contains three separate fields with VSAM return codes. The first is the Register 15 return code from the VSAM access routine. The second is a function code which indicates two things: the function being attempted when the error occurred and whether the alternate-index upgrade set is correct following the error. If the alternate-index upgrade set is not correct, the alternate index must be rebuilt to ensure file integrity. The third field in the extended file status area is a feedback code indicating the

```
DATA DIVISION.
FILE SECTION.
FD  VSAM-FILE
    ASSIGN TO VSAMFILE
    ORGANIZATION IS INDEXED
    ACCESS MODE IS DYNAMIC
    RECORD KEY IS VSAM-KEY
    FILE STATUS IS COBOL-STATUS
                 VSAM-STATUS.

WORKING-STORAGE SECTION.
01  COBOL-STATUS                     PIC X(02).
01  VSAM-STATUS.
    02  VSAM-RETURN-CODE             PIC 9(4) COMP.
    02  VSAM-FUNCTION-CODE           PIC 9(4) COMP.
    02  VSAM-FEEDBACK-CODE           PIC 9(4) COMP.
```

Listing 11-1   File Status Example.

reason for the error. There is a separate set of values in this field for logical and physical errors.

Listing 11-1 shows the coding necessary to include the extended VSAM status code in a program.

11.2   EXTENDED RETURN CODE VALUES

The meanings of the VSAM extended codes are given in the following tables. Table 11-1 shows the original COBOL file status values. These should be sufficient for control of program flow in almost all cases.

Table 11-2 shows the VSAM return-code values. If this code is 8 or 12, the feedback code will have meaning. The feedback code should not be referenced if the return code is not 8 or 12, as its contents will be unpredictable.

Table 11-3 shows the VSAM function being executed and whether the upgrade set is guaranteed to be in a correct status after the error.

Tables 11-4 and 11-5 contain the feedback codes for physical and logical errors, respectively. This is more information than you are likely to need; some of the errors listed in Table 11-5 cannot occur from a COBOL program because they refer to types of processing

Table 11-1   VSAM File Status Values.

Value	Meaning
00	Successful
02	Successful, duplicate key on alternate index
10	At End
20	Invalid Key
21	Invalid Key, Sequence error
22	Invalid Key, Duplicate
23	Invalid Key, Not found
24	Invalid Key, Out of space on KSDS/RRDS file
30	I/O Error
34	I/O Error, Out of space on sequential file
90	Other Error
91	Other Error, Password failure
92	Other Error, Logic failure
93	Other Error, resource not available
94	Other Error, not positioned for read next
95	Other Error, bad file information
96	Other Error, no DD information
97	Successful, implicit verify performed

that can only be coded in Assembly language. This table is also likely to become out of date. Further information can be found, if necessary, in the VSAM Programmers Guide and VSAM Administrators Guide.

Table 11-2   VSAM Return-Code Values.

Value	Meaning
0	Successful
4	Another request active (does not apply to COBOL)
8	Logical error—see feedback Table 9-4
12	Physical error—see feedback Table 9-5

Table 11-3   VSAM Function Code Values.

Value	Function	Upgrade Set Status
0	Accessing base cluster	OK
1	Accessing base cluster	May be bad
2	Accessing alternate index	OK
3	Accessing alternate index	May be bad
4	Upgrade processing	OK
5	Upgrade processing	May be bad

An application program could display this information as part of an error routine to support later diagnosis. Such a program is included later in the chapter.

11.3   REVIEW OF COBOL/VSAM CODING

The program in Listing 11-2 is a complete program for VSAM file handling, using a key-sequenced (KSDS) file. It declares an extended status code, which is passed to the program in Listing 11-3. This second program serves as a skeleton example of an error-handling routine, which simply displays some messages on SYSOUT.

Table 11-4   VSAM Feedback Code Values: Physical Errors.

Value	Function
4	Read error: data set
8	Read error: index set
12	Read error: sequence set
16	Write error: data set
20	Write error: index set
24	Write error: sequence set

Table 11-5   VSAM Feedback Code Values: Logical Errors.

Value	Meaning
4	Past End of File
8	Duplicate Key
12	Key Sequence Error
16	Not Found
20	Control Interval held by another requester
24	Volume cannot be mounted
28	Cannot extend dataset
32	RBA doesn't exist
36	Key not in a defined key range
40	Not enough memory (virtual storage) available
44	Work area too small
64	All available strings in use
68	Attempted processing not specified on OPEN
72	Tried keyed access to an ESDS or RRDS
76	Attempted insert to wrong type of dataset
80	Attempted deletion from ESDS
84	OPTCD=LOC for a PUT request
88	No positioning established
92	PUT without GET for update
96	Tried to change the primary key
100	Tried to change the record length
104	Invalid or conflicting RPL options
108	Invalid record length
112	Invalid key length
116	Violation of LOAD MODE restrictions
120	Wrong task submitted request
132	Tried to get spanned record in locate mode
136	Tried to get spanned record by address in KSDS
140	Inconsistent spanned record
144	Alt index pointer with no matching base record
148	Exceeded mamimum pointers in alt index record
152	Not enough buffers available
156	Invalid control interval
192	Invalid relative record number
196	Tried addressed request to RRDS
200	Tried invalid access through a path
204	Tried PUT in backward mode
208	Invalid ENDREQ macro

```
000100 IDENTIFICATION DIVISION.
000200 PROGRAM-ID. VSAMREAD.
000300* DISPLAY SCHOOL LOCATION FILE.
000400 ENVIRONMENT DIVISION.
000500 INPUT-OUTPUT SECTION.
000600 FILE-CONTROL.
000700     SELECT LOC-FILE   ASSIGN TO LOCFILE
000800                       ORGANIZATION IS INDEXED
000900                       ACCESS MODE IS DYNAMIC
001000                       RECORD KEY IS SCH-LOC-CODE
001100                       FILE STATUS IS LOC-STATUS-1
001200                                      LOC-STATUS-2.
001300     SELECT PRINT-FILE ASSIGN TO PRINTER.
001400 DATA DIVISION.
001500 FILE SECTION.
001600 FD  LOC-FILE
001700     RECORD CONTAINS 80 CHARACTERS
001800     BLOCK CONTAINS 0 RECORDS
001900     DATA RECORD IS SCH-RECORD
002000     LABEL RECORDS ARE STANDARD.
002100
002200 01  SCH-RECORD.
002300* * * * * * * * * * * * * * * * * * * * * * * * * * * * *
002400*   THIS IS THE SCHOOL LOCATION RECORD DESCRIPTION        *
002500*   KEY IS SCH-LOC-CODE                                   *
002600*   LRECL IS 100                                          *
002700* * * * * * * * * * * * * * * * * * * * * * * * * * * * *
002800     02  SCH-LOC-CODE       PIC X(04).
002900     02  SCH-NAME           PIC X(30).
003000     02  SCH-ADDR-STR       PIC X(22).
003100     02  SCH-ADDR-CITY      PIC X(18).
003200     02  SCH-ADDR-ST-ZIP    PIC X(11).
003300     02  FILLER             PIC X(15).
003400
003500 FD  PRINT-FILE
003600     RECORD CONTAINS 133 CHARACTERS
003700     RECORDING MODE F
003800     LABEL RECORDS ARE STANDARD.
003900
004000 01  PRINT-LINE.
004100     02  PR-SKIP-CHAR       PIC X(01).
004200     02  FILLER             PIC X(02).
004300     02  PR-LOC-CODE        PIC X(04).
004400     02  FILLER             PIC X(02).
004500     02  PR-NAME            PIC X(30).
004600     02  FILLER             PIC X(02).
```

Listing 11-2   Example of COBOL II and VSAM Processing. (Continued)

```
004700      02  PR-ADDR-STR          PIC X(22).
004800      02  FILLER               PIC X(02).
004900      02  PR-ADDR-CITY         PIC X(18).
005000      02  FILLER               PIC X(02).
005100      02  PR-ADDR-ST-ZIP       PIC X(11).
005200      02  FILLER               PIC X(37).
005300
005400 WORKING-STORAGE SECTION.
005500 01  END-OF-FILE-SW            PIC X VALUE ZERO.
005600     88  END-OF-FILE                VALUE '1'.
005700 01  W-ACTION                  PIC X(06).
005800 01  LOC-STATUS-1              PIC X(02).
005900 01  LOC-STATUS-2              PIC X(06).
006000
006100 PROCEDURE DIVISION.
006200
006300 P000-MAIN SECTION.
006400      OPEN INPUT   LOC-FILE
006500      IF LOC-STATUS-1 NOT = '00'
006600         MOVE 'OPEN' TO W-ACTION
006700         PERFORM VSAM-ERROR
006800         GOBACK
006900      END-IF
007000
007100      OPEN OUTPUT PRINT-FILE
007200
007300      PERFORM READ-LOC
007400
007500      PERFORM UNTIL END-OF-FILE
007600          PERFORM DISPLAY-OUTPUT
007700          PERFORM READ-LOC
007800      END-PERFORM
007900
008000      CLOSE LOC-FILE
008100      CLOSE PRINT-FILE
008200      GOBACK.
008300
008400 READ-LOC.
008500      READ LOC-FILE
008600
008700      EVALUATE LOC-STATUS-1
008800      WHEN '10'
008900          SET END-OF-FILE TO TRUE
009000      WHEN '00'
009100          CONTINUE
009200      WHEN OTHER
```

Listing 11-2   Example of COBOL II and VSAM Processing. (Continued)

```
009300          MOVE 'READ' TO W-ACTION
009400          PERFORM VSAM-ERROR
009500          GOBACK
009600      END-EVALUATE.
009700
009800 DISPLAY-OUTPUT SECTION.
009900      MOVE SPACES                TO PRINT-LINE
010000
010100      MOVE SCH-LOC-CODE          TO PR-LOC-CODE
010200      MOVE SCH-NAME              TO PR-NAME
010300      MOVE SCH-ADDR-STR          TO PR-ADDR-STR
010400      MOVE SCH-ADDR-CITY         TO PR-ADDR-CITY
010500      MOVE SCH-ADDR-ST-ZIP       TO PR-ADDR-ST-ZIP
010600
010700      WRITE PRINT-LINE.
010800
010900 VSAM-ERROR SECTION.
011000* * * * * * * * * * * * * * * * * * * * * * * * * * * * * *
011100*  STANDARD ERROR FOR SCHOOL FILE
011200* * * * * * * * * * * * * * * * * * * * * * * * * * * * * *
011300      CALL 'VSAMERR' USING BY CONTENT 'LOC4      ',
011400                           BY CONTENT 'LOCFILE ',
011500                           BY CONTENT LOC-STATUS-1,
011600                           BY CONTENT LOC-STATUS-2,
011700                           BY CONTENT W-ACTION,
011800                           BY CONTENT SCH-LOC-CODE.
```

Listing 11-2   Example of COBOL II and VSAM Processing.

11.4   DATABASE CONSIDERATIONS

All the database considerations below apply to the older hierarchical
database products DL/I and IMS. There are no special considerations
for using VS COBOL II with DB2 and SQL/DS.

11.4.1   Using Literals in DL/I Calls

It is now possible to code literals in calls to DL/I, which can make
the program easier to read. Any call can contain literals preceded by
the phrase BY CONTENT, as discussed in Chapter 7. Listing 11-4 is
an example of a DL/I call using BY CONTENT to pass literals to
DL/I.

```
       IDENTIFICATION DIVISION.
       PROGRAM-ID. VSAMERR.
     * DISPLAY ERROR MESSAGE
       ENVIRONMENT DIVISION.
       INPUT-OUTPUT SECTION.
       FILE-CONTROL.
       DATA DIVISION.
       FILE SECTION.
       WORKING-STORAGE SECTION.

       LINKAGE SECTION.
       01  EP-PROGRAM-NAME          PIC X(08).
       01  EP-FILENAME              PIC X(08).
       01  EP-STATUS-1              PIC X(02).
       01  EP-STATUS-2.
           02  EP-RETURN-CODE       PIC 9(4) COMP.
           02  EP-FUNCTION-CODE     PIC 9(4) COMP.
           02  EP-FEEDBACK-CODE     PIC 9(4) COMP.
       01  EP-ACTION                PIC X(06).
       01  EP-KEY                   PIC X(30).


       PROCEDURE DIVISION USING EP-PROGRAM-NAME
                                EP-FILENAME
                                EP-STATUS-1
                                EP-STATUS-2
                                EP-ACTION
                                EP-KEY.
       MAIN SECTION.

           DISPLAY 'Program          ' EP-PROGRAM-NAME
           DISPLAY 'Accessing File' EP-FILENAME
           DISPLAY 'Current Action' EP-ACTION
           DISPLAY 'Key Value        ' EP-KEY

           DISPLAY 'File Status of' EP-STATUS-1

           IF EP-RETURN-CODE = 8
               DISPLAY 'Logical Error'
               DISPLAY 'Function Code ' EP-FUNCTION-CODE
               DISPLAY 'Feedback Code ' EP-FEEDBACK-CODE
           END-IF

           IF EP-RETURN-CODE = 12
               DISPLAY 'Physical Error'
               DISPLAY 'Function Code ' EP-FUNCTION-CODE
               DISPLAY 'Feedback Code ' EP-FEEDBACK-CODE
           END-IF

           GOBACK.
```

Listing 11-3   Program to Process VSAM Error Codes.

```
CALL 'CBLTDLI' USING
   BY CONTENT 'GU',
              DB-PCB,
              I-O-AREA,
   BY CONTENT 'LIMITS(LOCATION = NY)'
```

Listing 11-4   Calling DL/I from COBOL II.

11.4.2   Preloading Programs with IMS

With IMS/DC, programs can be preloaded. This means they remain resident in storage and do not have to be loaded with each request. IMS/DC programs in OS COBOL are generally linked REUS and coded to be serially reusable, that is, one program can follow another in the same piece of code without needing a fresh load. With VS COBOL II, programs which are to be preloaded must be reentrant and use the Library Management Facility; that is, they should be compiled with the RENT and RES options.

11.4.3   DL/I Is Below the Line

The DL/I code runs below the line, so calls to DL/I must ensure that all the data areas they refer to are below the line also. The simple way to do this is with the compiler option DATA(24), which keeps all of the program data below the line. An alternative approach is discussed in Chapter 10. You only have to ensure that data areas passed to DL/I are below the line. Under CICS, this can be done by acquiring all storage for these areas with user getmains of less than 4K. If this is difficult to do, you can isolate DL/I calls in one or a few modules compiled with DATA(24) and call them dynamically from modules which are above the line.

11.4.4   Coding Restrictions with IMS

The following verbs are not allowed in VS COBOL II programs running under IMS/DC:

```
ACCEPT
CLOSE
DISPLAY
OPEN
READ
RECEIVE
REWRITE
SEND
STOP RUN
WRITE
```

12

Calling the Sort Program

This chapter covers the changes introduced in the interface between COBOL and DFSORT, which is the IBM-supplied sort program. A lot of installations use sort programs from a third-party vendor, like SYNCSORT and CA-SORT, instead of the IBM sort. If you work at one of these sites, you are free to ignore this chapter and refer to the documentation of that product instead.

There is no change in the syntax of the SORT statement between OS COBOL and COBOL II.

12.1 THE FASTSRT OPTION

When you invoke the FASTSRT option, the IBM DFSORT program attempts to perform the I/O on any sequential input and output files named in SORT . . . USING and GIVING statements. It has no effect on files used with input or output procedures. The advantage of this option is that the sort program has been specially designed to optimize I/O in large blocks to and from sequential files and will perform this more quickly without having to go through the COBOL library, which is written to perform a more general-purpose set of functions.

Since FASTSRT is faster precisely because it only allows a limited set of possibilities, there are a number of conditions to be met for FASTSRT to work. These are listed below under three categories: sort, QSAM, and VSAM restrictions.

12.1.1   General Sort Restrictions with FASTSRT

You may not use the DFSORT options SORTIN and SORTOUT, which reformat the sort records, with FASTSRT. Only one input file can be used. All sort work files must be on disk, not tape.

12.1.2   QSAM File Restrictions with FASTSRT

QSAM files used with FASTSRT must have a format of F, V, or S. LABEL and ERROR/EXCEPTION declaratives cannot be applied. The LINAGE clause cannot be specified for output.

If you want to use the same QSAM file for input and output, you must take care to define it in two separate FDs and two JCL statements. The example in Listing 12-3 given later in this chapter illustrates this.

12.1.3   VSAM File Restrictions with FASTSRT

VSAM files used with FASTSRT will be processed sequentially, so they must be specified as ACCESS IS SEQUENTIAL. They must not be password-protected. The sort program is doing the I-O, so any file status variable will be ignored. The same VSAM file cannot be named in both USING and GIVING statements in the same program. A VSAM file in use with FASTSRT can be accessed with a normal OPEN in the same program, but not until the sort is complete.

12.1.4   FASTSRT Information Messages

DFSORT issues messages which may help improve performance. If any of the conditions for FASTSRT were not met, the program will run as if the option had not been requested. In other words, COBOL will perform all the I/O.

12.2   PASSING INFORMATION TO DFSORT

There are now six sort special registers. Five are retained from OS COBOL and operate in a similar fashion. The sixth, the SORT-CONTROL register, is introduced in COBOL II. In COBOL II, the

Table 12-1   Sort Special Registers.

Register	*Function*
SORT-CONTROL	Indicates the name of a dataset from which the sort control values are to be taken
SORT-RETURN	Returns 0 to the program if the sort was successful, 16 if the sort fails
SORT-CORE-SIZE	Indicates the required amount of main memory
SORT-FILE-SIZE	Indicates the number of records to be sorted
SORT-MESSAGE	Changes the default message file from SYSOUT
SORT-MODE-SIZE	Indicates the commonest record length in a variable-length file

sort values can be set in a control file, which overrides the other special registers. SORT-CONTROL contains the name of that control file.

Early versions of COBOL II deleted the registers CORE-SIZE, FILE-SIZE, MESSAGE, and MODE-SIZE. It was then necessary to use the control file to pass information. These registers are restored in Release 2. Table 12-1 indicates the purpose of each register.

12.2.1 The Sort Control File

If control values are supplied to DFSORT in a sequential dataset, this should either be named in SORT-CONTROL, or be given the default name, which is IGZSRTCD. If there is no SORT-CONTROL, DFSORT will attempt to open the default file. The sort control file should have the characteristics:

```
(RECFM=FB,LRECL=80,BLKSIZE=400)
```

If the file is not found, the sort will still proceed, but a message will be issued on SYSOUT as follows:

```
IGZ027I THE SORT-CONTROL DATA SET CANNOT BE OPENED
```

```
IEC130I IGZSRTCD DD SATATEMENT MISSING
```

The control file is preferred to the special registers, and a W-level warning message is issued for each special register that is set.

Table 12-2   Sort Control File Values.

Control Statement	Equivalent Register	Meaning
MAINSIZE=	SORT-CORE-SIZE=+...	Amount of memory to use
RESINV=	SORT-CORE-SIZE=-...	Amount of memory to reserve
MAINSIZE=MAX	SORT-CORE-SIZE=+999999	Use maximum memory
FILSZ=	SORT-FILE-SIZE	Estimated number of records
MSGDDN=	SORT-MESSAGE	DDNAME to use instead of SYSOUT
SMS=	SORT-MODE-SIZE	Most common record length in variable-length file
EQUALS		Preserve sequence of records with the same key

Table 12-2 lists the acceptable values for the sort registers and the sort control file.

12.3 CHANGES TO SORT LIMITATIONS

Certain compiler limits on the sort have been relaxed. There is now no limit on the number of sort keys. The limit under OS COBOL was 12. The total length of all sort keys can now total 4092 bytes (or 4088 with the EQUALS option), rather than 256 as in OS COBOL.

12.4 REVIEW OF INTERNAL SORT CODING

Three short examples of COBOL II programs with internal sorts are given in Listings 12-1, 12-2, and 12-3. All of these programs qualify for the FASTSRT option. Each program performs the same simple job, reformatting a file of names and addresses and sorting it by ZIP code. The program in Listing 12-1 illustrates an input procedure with GIVING. The program in Listing 12-2 has USING with an output procedure, while the program in Listing 12-3 contains a sort with USING and GIVING, then reopens the same file for processing. These programs are essentially skeletons; the problem solved here does not need COBOL but could be coded with DFSORT alone.

```
000100 IDENTIFICATION DIVISION.
000200 PROGRAM-ID. FASTSRT1.
000300* SORT A FILE OF NAMES BY ZIP USING INPUT PROCEDURE / GIV-
       ING
000400 ENVIRONMENT DIVISION.
000500 INPUT-OUTPUT SECTION.
000600 FILE-CONTROL.
000700     SELECT INPUT-FILE  ASSIGN TO INPFILE.
001300     SELECT SORT-FILE   ASSIGN TO SORTFILE.
001300     SELECT OUTPUT-FILE ASSIGN TO OUTFILE.
001400 DATA DIVISION.
001500 FILE SECTION.
001600 SD  SORT-FILE
001700     RECORD CONTAINS 100 CHARACTERS.

001800 01  SORT-RECORD.
004300     02  SORT-KEY-1            PIC X(04).
004400     02  FILLER               PIC X(82).
005100     02  SORT-KEY-2           PIC X(11).
005200     02  FILLER               PIC X(03).
002100
001600 FD  INPUT-FILE
001700     RECORD CONTAINS 100 CHARACTERS
001800     BLOCK CONTAINS 0 RECORDS.
002100
002200 01  INP-RECORD.
002800     02  INP-LOC-CODE         PIC X(04).
002900     02  INP-NAME             PIC X(30).
003000     02  INP-ADDR-STR         PIC X(22).
003100     02  INP-ADDR-CITY        PIC X(18).
003200     02  INP-ADDR-ST-ZIP      PIC X(11).
003300     02  FILLER               PIC X(15).
003400
003500 FD  OUTPUT-FILE
003600     RECORD CONTAINS 100 CHARACTERS
003700     RECORDING MODE F.
003900
004000 01  OUTPUT-LINE              PIC X(100).
005300
005400 WORKING-STORAGE SECTION.
005500 01  END-OF-FILE-SW           PIC X VALUE ZERO.
005600     88  END-OF-FILE              VALUE '1'.
006000
       01  OUT-FORMAT.
004300     02  OUT-LOC-CODE         PIC X(04).
004400     02  FILLER               PIC X(03).
```

Listing 12-1   Sort with Input Procedure and GIVING. (Continued)

```
004500      02  OUT-NAME              PIC X(30).
004600      02  FILLER               PIC X(03).
004700      02  OUT-ADDR-STR         PIC X(22).
004800      02  FILLER               PIC X(03).
004900      02  OUT-ADDR-CITY        PIC X(18).
005000      02  FILLER               PIC X(03).
005100      02  OUT-ADDR-ST-ZIP      PIC X(11).
005200      02  FILLER               PIC X(03).


006100 PROCEDURE DIVISION.
006200
006300 P000-MAIN SECTION.
006400      OPEN INPUT  INPUT-FILE
007100      OPEN OUTPUT OUTPUT-FILE
007200
            SORT SORT-FILE
            ON ASCENDING KEY SORT-KEY-2
            INPUT PROCEDURE P100-INPUT
            GIVING OUTPUT-FILE
007400
008000      CLOSE INPUT-FILE
008100      CLOSE OUTPUT-FILE
008200      GOBACK.
008300
008400 P100-INPUT SECTION.
008500      READ INPUT-FILE
008600      AT END
008900          SET END-OF-FILE TO TRUE
009600      END-READ
009700
            PERFORM UNTIL END-OF-FILE
               PERFORM P200-FORMAT
010700            RELEASE SORT-RECORD FROM OUT-FORMAT
008500            READ INPUT-FILE
008600            AT END
008900               SET END-OF-FILE TO TRUE
009600            END-READ
            END-PERFORM.

       P200-FORMAT SECTION.
009900      MOVE SPACES           TO OUT-FORMAT
010100      MOVE INP-LOC-CODE     TO OUT-LOC-CODE
010200      MOVE INP-NAME         TO OUT-NAME
010300      MOVE INP-ADDR-STR     TO OUT-ADDR-STR
010400      MOVE INP-ADDR-CITY    TO OUT-ADDR-CITY
010500      MOVE INP-ADDR-ST-ZIP  TO OUT-ADDR-ST-ZIP.
```

Listing 12-1   Sort with Input Procedure and GIVING.

```
000100 IDENTIFICATION DIVISION.
000200 PROGRAM-ID. FASTSRT2.
000300* SORT A FILE OF NAMES BY ZIP with OUTPUT PROCEDURE / GIV-
ING
000400 ENVIRONMENT DIVISION.
000500 INPUT-OUTPUT SECTION.
000600 FILE-CONTROL.
000700     SELECT INPUT-FILE  ASSIGN TO INPFILE.
001300     SELECT SORT-FILE   ASSIGN TO SORTFILE.
001300     SELECT OUTPUT-FILE ASSIGN TO OUTFILE.
001400 DATA DIVISION.
001500 FILE SECTION.
001600 SD  SORT-FILE
001700     RECORD CONTAINS 100 CHARACTERS.

001800 01  SORT-RECORD.
004300     02  SORT-KEY-1          PIC X(04).
004400     02  FILLER             PIC X(70).
005100     02  SORT-KEY-2          PIC X(11).
005200     02  FILLER             PIC X(15).
002100
001600 FD  INPUT-FILE
001700     RECORD CONTAINS 100 CHARACTERS
001800     BLOCK CONTAINS 0 RECORDS.
002100
002200 01  INP-RECORD.
002800     02  INP-LOC-CODE        PIC X(04).
002900     02  INP-NAME            PIC X(30).
003000     02  INP-ADDR-STR        PIC X(22).
003100     02  INP-ADDR-CITY       PIC X(18).
003200     02  INP-ADDR-ST-ZIP     PIC X(11).
003300     02  FILLER             PIC X(15).
003400
003500 FD  OUTPUT-FILE
003600     RECORD CONTAINS 100 CHARACTERS
003700     RECORDING MODE F.
003900
004000 01  OUTPUT-LINE             PIC X(100).
005300
005400 WORKING-STORAGE SECTION.
005500 01  END-OF-FILE-SW          PIC X VALUE ZERO.
005600     88  END-OF-FILE             VALUE '1'.
006000
       01  OUT-FORMAT.
004300     02  OUT-LOC-CODE        PIC X(04).
004400     02  FILLER             PIC X(03).
```

Listing 12-2   Sort with Output Procedure and USING. (Continued)

```
004500          02  OUT-NAME                PIC X(30).
004600          02  FILLER                  PIC X(03).
004700          02  OUT-ADDR-STR            PIC X(22).
004800          02  FILLER                  PIC X(03).
004900          02  OUT-ADDR-CITY           PIC X(18).
005000          02  FILLER                  PIC X(03).
005100          02  OUT-ADDR-ST-ZIP         PIC X(11).
005200          02  FILLER                  PIC X(03).


006100 PROCEDURE DIVISION.
006200
006300 P000-MAIN SECTION.
006400     OPEN INPUT   INPUT-FILE
007100     OPEN OUTPUT OUTPUT-FILE
007200
           SORT SORT-FILE
           ON ASCENDING KEY SORT-KEY-2
           USING INPUT-FILE
           OUTPUT PROCEDURE P100-OUTPUT
007400
008000     CLOSE INPUT-FILE
008100     CLOSE OUTPUT-FILE
008200     GOBACK.
008300
008400 P100-OUTPUT SECTION.
008500     RETURN SORT-FILE
008600     AT END
008900        SET END-OF-FILE TO TRUE
009600     END-RETURN
009700
           PERFORM UNTIL END-OF-FILE
             PERFORM P200-FORMAT
010700        WRITE OUTPUT-LINE FROM OUT-FORMAT
008500        RETURN SORT-FILE
008600        AT END
008900           SET END-OF-FILE TO TRUE
009600           END-RETURN
           END-PERFORM.

       P200-FORMAT SECTION.
009900     MOVE SPACES            TO OUT-FORMAT
010100     MOVE INP-LOC-CODE      TO OUT-LOC-CODE
010200     MOVE INP-NAME          TO OUT-NAME
010300     MOVE INP-ADDR-STR      TO OUT-ADDR-STR
010400     MOVE INP-ADDR-CITY     TO OUT-ADDR-CITY
010500     MOVE INP-ADDR-ST-ZIP   TO OUT-ADDR-ST-ZIP.
```

Listing 12-2   Sort with Output Procedure and USING.

```
000100 IDENTIFICATION DIVISION.
000200 PROGRAM-ID. FASTSRT3.
000300* SORT A FILE OF NAMES BY ZIP, THEN OPEN AND PROCESS
000400 ENVIRONMENT DIVISION.
000500 INPUT-OUTPUT SECTION.
000600 FILE-CONTROL.
000700     SELECT INPUT-FILE   ASSIGN TO INPFILE.
000700     SELECT INPUT-FILE-2 ASSIGN TO INPFILE2.
001300     SELECT SORT-FILE    ASSIGN TO SORTFILE.
001300     SELECT OUTPUT-FILE  ASSIGN TO OUTFILE.
001400 DATA DIVISION.
001500 FILE SECTION.
001600 SD  SORT-FILE
001700     RECORD CONTAINS 100 CHARACTERS.

001800 01  SORT-RECORD.
004300     02  SORT-KEY-1          PIC X(04).
004400     02  FILLER              PIC X(70).
005100     02  SORT-KEY-2          PIC X(11).
005200     02  FILLER              PIC X(15).
002100
001600 FD  INPUT-FILE-2
001700     RECORD CONTAINS 100 CHARACTERS
001800     BLOCK CONTAINS 0 RECORDS.
002100
002200 01  INP-RECORD-2            PIC X(100).
002100
001600 FD  INPUT-FILE
001700     RECORD CONTAINS 100 CHARACTERS
001800     BLOCK CONTAINS 0 RECORDS.
002100
002200 01  INP-RECORD.
002800     02  INP-LOC-CODE        PIC X(04).
002900     02  INP-NAME            PIC X(30).
003000     02  INP-ADDR-STR        PIC X(22).
003100     02  INP-ADDR-CITY       PIC X(18).
003200     02  INP-ADDR-ST-ZIP     PIC X(11).
003300     02  FILLER              PIC X(15).
003400
003500 FD  OUTPUT-FILE
003600     RECORD CONTAINS 100 CHARACTERS
003700     RECORDING MODE F.
003900
004000 01  OUTPUT-LINE             PIC X(100).
005300
005400 WORKING-STORAGE SECTION.
```

Listing 12-3   Sort Followed by File Open. (Continued)

```
005500 01  END-OF-FILE-SW          PIC X VALUE ZERO.
005600     88  END-OF-FILE             VALUE '1'.
006000
       01  OUT-FORMAT.
004300     02  OUT-LOC-CODE        PIC X(04).
004400     02  FILLER              PIC X(03).
004500     02  OUT-NAME            PIC X(30).
004600     02  FILLER              PIC X(03).
004700     02  OUT-ADDR-STR        PIC X(22).
004800     02  FILLER              PIC X(03).
004900     02  OUT-ADDR-CITY       PIC X(18).
005000     02  FILLER              PIC X(03).
005100     02  OUT-ADDR-ST-ZIP     PIC X(11).
005200     02  FILLER              PIC X(03).


006100 PROCEDURE DIVISION.
006200
006300 P000-MAIN SECTION.
           SORT SORT-FILE
           ON ASCENDING KEY SORT-KEY-2
           USING   INPUT-FILE-2
           GIVING INPUT-FILE

006400     OPEN INPUT   INPUT-FILE
007100     OPEN OUTPUT OUTPUT-FILE
007200
           PERFORM P100-PROCESS
007400
008000     CLOSE INPUT-FILE
008100     CLOSE OUTPUT-FILE
008200     GOBACK.
008300
008400 P100-PROCESS SECTION.
008500     READ INPUT-FILE
008600     AT END
008900        SET END-OF-FILE TO TRUE
009600     END-READ
009700
           PERFORM UNTIL END-OF-FILE
             PERFORM P200-FORMAT
010700        WRITE OUTPUT-LINE FROM OUT-FORMAT
008500        READ INPUT-FILE
008600        AT END
008900           SET END-OF-FILE TO TRUE
009600        END-READ
           END-PERFORM.
```

Listing 12-3   Sort Followed by File Open. (Continued)

```
        P200-FORMAT SECTION.
009900      MOVE SPACES              TO OUT-FORMAT
010100      MOVE INP-LOC-CODE        TO OUT-LOC-CODE
010200      MOVE INP-NAME            TO OUT-NAME
010300      MOVE INP-ADDR-STR        TO OUT-ADDR-STR
010400      MOVE INP-ADDR-CITY       TO OUT-ADDR-CITY
010500      MOVE INP-ADDR-ST-ZIP     TO OUT-ADDR-ST-ZIP.
```

Listing 12-3   Sort Followed by File Open.

Listing 12-4 contains the JCL necessary to run the example programs. Notice that for FSORT3, two DD statements refer to the same file. I will mention two other points, although they are unchanged from OS COBOL. There is no DD statement for SORTFILE, and there is no need to supply DD statements for SORTWK files.

12.5 SUMMARY OF SORT CHANGES

It is not normally necessary to change the sort default values using special registers or a control file. Most programs will be unaffected by the changes introduced here, but FASTSRT will produce a performance improvement for programs that meet its limitations.

```
//          JOB
//          EXEC PGM=FSORT1
//INPFILE   DD   DSN=TEST.NAMES1,DISP=SHR
//OUTFILE   DD   DSN=TEST.NAMES2,DISP=SHR
//          EXEC PGM=FSORT2
//INPFILE   DD   DSN=TEST.NAMES1,DISP=SHR
//OUTFILE   DD   DSN=TEST.NAMES2,DISP=SHR
//          EXEC PGM=FSORT3
//INPFILE2  DD   DSN=TEST.NAMES1,DISP=SHR
//INPFILE   DD   DSN=TEST.NAMES1,DISP=SHR
//OUTFILE   DD   DSN=TEST.NAMES2,DISP=SHR
```

Listing 12-4   Job Control Language for Sort Programs.

13

MVS/XA and MVS/ESA Support

One of the principal reasons for the initial release of COBOL II was its support for extended addressing. Programs compiled with the VS COBOL II compiler can execute in the 31-bit addressing mode of MVS/XA and MVS/ESA, which allows them to use much more memory. No changes are necessary in program code to take advantage of this, and, in fact, a COBOL program is unaware of whether data areas that it refers to are below or above the line.

Although it is not necessary to change the programs, some applications will benefit from a rewrite which exploits the expanded limits now available. Programs that need to address arrays of greater than 32K, or that need to allocate storage dynamically, may particularly benefit. A full list of the expanded compiler limits available is included in Appendix B.

13.1 MVS/XA AND 31-BIT ADDRESSING

The /XA in MVS/XA stands for Extended Architecture. MVS/XA (and MVS/ESA) are the newest versions of the operating system for large IBM processors. Earlier versions of these processors used a series of operating systems, of which the newest was OS/VS2 System Product (referred to here as MVS/370). In all the versions before MVS/XA, the processor used 24 bits to determine memory addresses. Table 13-1 lists all the powers of two. As this table shows, with 24 bits

Table 13-1   Powers of Two.

n	2^n	n	2^n	n	2^n	n	2^n
0	1	10	1K	20	1M	30	1G
1	2	11	2K	21	2M	31	2G
2	4	12	4K	22	4M		
3	8	13	8K	23	8M		
4	16	14	16K	24	16M		
5	32	15	32K	25	32M		
6	64	16	64K	26	64M		
7	128	17	128K	27	128M		
8	256	18	256K	28	256M		
9	512	19	512K	29	512M		
10	1024	20	1024K	30	1024M		

approximately 16 million different addresses can be specified. This is the architectural limit of 16 megabytes in MVS/370.

The System/370 architecture was developed in the early 1960s. At that time, the limit of 16 megabytes was very high. A typical business mainframe installation of that time might have 16K to 64K of memory, and the limit was two to three orders of magnitude higher than this. By the early 1980s, the architecture was 20 years old and had been successful beyond its creators' wildest dreams. Memory prices in the intervening decades have dropped by an order of magnitude every four or five years (see Figure 13-1), and applications have been written to exploit this memory. The 16-megabyte limit was becoming a ceiling against which users were bumping. Figure 13-2 shows that large mainframes were finding this limit restrictive in the early 1980s, and by 1989 even some desktop machines need more than 16 megabytes.

13.1.1   Real Storage Limits

There were two particular consequences of this architectural limit that proved to be serious problems to large mainframe users. The first was the limit on real storage per processor. MVS/370 restricted users of IBM mainframe computers to 16 megabytes of main memory per processor. Many were willing, even desperate, to purchase more. IBM did find a means of raising this limit to 32 Mb for MVS/370, but that was as far as it went. A processor can only address this limited

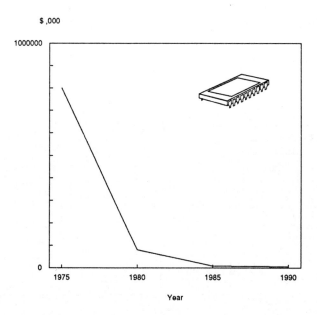

Figure 13-1   Approximate Cost of 16 Mb of Memory Chips.

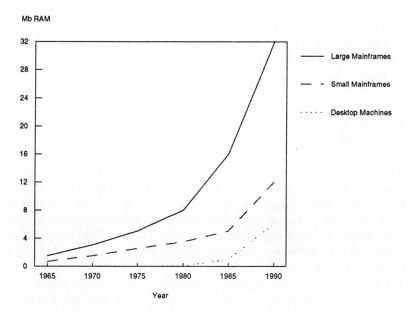

Figure 13-2   Average RAM Memory Installed.

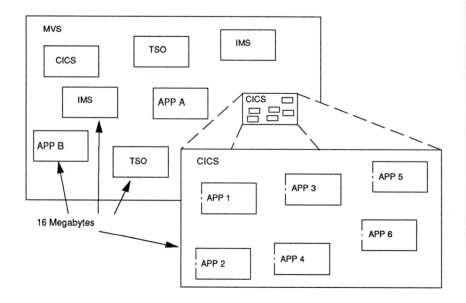

Figure 13-3   MVS Address Spaces.

amount of real memory. It is true that there is no limit on virtual storage, but in practice there is a constraint on the amount of virtual storage which a system can have without excessive paging. All applications access the virtual storage through the same real storage "window."

13.1.2   Virtual Storage Limits

The second consequence of the MVS/370 architecture was a 16-megabyte limit on the amount of virtual storage per task. The first place where this storage constraint arose as a serious problem was CICS, because of one of its design features. Normally, each program in an MVS environment runs in its own 16-Mb address space. Any batch, TSO, or IMS/DC programs is able to use most of that 16-Mb address space for itself. However, all the programs in one CICS region run in that single address space, as illustrated in Figure 13-3. They must all fit in with the operating system and the CICS code itself. This usually leaves a space of about 5 or 6 megabytes for all the application programs and work areas. This problem is known to

Memory in Megabytes

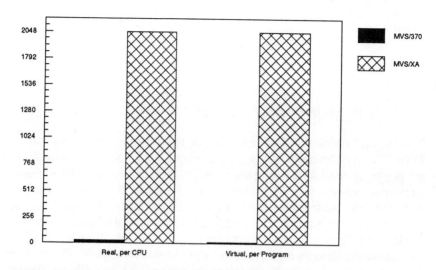

Figure 13-4   MVS/XA Memory vs. MVS/370 Memory.

CICS shops as Virtual Storage Constraint. It has been a major goal of CICS tuners and designers for some time now to limit this problem.

In the 31-bit addressing introduced with MVS/XA, the processor can address up to approximately two billion bytes (2 gigabytes). This means that more memory can be attached to IBM processors running MVS/XA. It also means that programs can address larger areas. Figure 13-4 shows the increase in real and virtual memory constraints under MVS/XA.

Since almost every instruction in the System/370 instruction set contains address references, the object code for MVS/XA is different from that of MVS/370. MVS/XA systems can run 24-bit code, but MVS/370 systems cannot execute 31-bit code. New assemblers and compilers to generate this object code had to be introduced. Initially, only an assembler was available, and only Assembly language programs could take advantage of 31-bit addressing. Many IBM products are written in Assembly language (although this is often an intermediary), and the first programs to take advantage of extended addressing were IBM program products such as CICS, VSAM, and CSP.

IBM followed with new MVS compilers for the standard high-level languages such as COBOL and PL/I. Whereas the PL/I compiler

(Release 5.1) was simply updated to support MVS/XA, the COBOL compiler was totally rewritten. There is no plan to enhance OS COBOL in any way now, so any COBOL shop that plans to take advantage of extended addressing in its COBOL programs will have to convert to COBOL II.

13.2   THE 16-MEGABYTE LINE

The terms "above the line" and "below the line" are often used in an MVS/XA environment. As we said above, MVS/XA can run 24-bit programs as well as 31-bit programs. In fact, the reason the architecture was expanded to 31 rather than 32 bits is because the first bit indicates the addressing mode in use. Since under MVS/XA an address space much larger than 16 Mb is available, and programs compiled in 24-bit mode can only address up to 16 Mb, they can be said to behave as though an invisible "line" kept them back. There is no line, of course, but it is occasionally convenient to talk as though there were. A program in 24-bit mode is always below the line. A program in 31-bit mode can be above or below, and will not generally know or care.

13.2.1   Communicating Across the Line

A single module must be linked as either 24 bit or 31 bit. However, modules with different addressing modes can communicate with dynamic calls or CICS links. A 24-bit program can freely call a 31-bit program. Unfortunately, some care is needed when going the other way. The 24-bit program will abend if given a 31-bit address that happens to be above the line, and it is generally difficult to predict whether this could be the case in a 31-bit program. For this reason, an option is available whereby a program can execute in 31-bit mode but ensure that the data it contains has been defined below the line.

13.3   COMPILE AND LINK OPTIONS FOR 24/31-BIT SUPPORT

MVS/XA programs have two important attributes that refer to their storage addressing. These are AMODE and RMODE. AMODE stands for Addressing Mode, and refers to the type of addressing (24 or 31

Table 13-2   RMODE/AMODE Combinations.

AMODE	RMODE	Result
ANY	ANY	Best general case. Program takes full advantage of MVS/XA extended addressing.
24	24	Program resides below line and addresses below line, like an OS COBOL program. Can be linked with OS COBOL programs.
ANY	24	Program resides below the line, so its data is below the line. Can address data above the line. Useful for dynamic linking with below-the-line code such as OS COBOL programs or DL/I.

bit) used by the program. AMODE sets the addressing bit in the Program Status Word (PSW). RMODE stands for Residence Mode, and refers to where in storage the program can be loaded. AMODE can have the values 24, 31, or ANY. RMODE can have the values 24 or ANY. Table 13-2 shows the possible combinations.

It is not necessary to code AMODE and RMODE. The compiler generates default values based on the reentrancy and residency options shown in Table 13-3.

It follows from the discussion and these two tables that programs which will run above the line should be specified as RENT and RES. They are then eligible for inclusion in the MVS Link Pack Area (LPA) or Extended Link Pack Area (ELPA).

Programs which are compiled RENT and RES can execute on MVS/370 or MVS/XA without recompiling and will take advantage of XA. In other words, they never have to go above the line.

Table 13-3   Default AMODE and RMODE.

Res / Rent	AMODE	RMODE
RENT, RES	ANY	ANY
NORENT,NORES	24	24
NORENT,RES	ANY	24

14

Using FDUMP to Get Formatted Dumps

In COBOL II, you can request that, if an abnormal termination occurs, a formatted dump be produced. This dump is formatted so that it is easier to read the items most likely to be of interest to the COBOL programmer. A program which will produce a formatted dump must be compiled with a special option. The compiler saves source information in the object file so that machine addresses in the dump can be translated into line numbers and data names.

14.1 GETTING A FORMATTED DUMP

To obtain a formatted dump, the program must be compiled with the FDUMP option. The TEST option must not be used, since this suppresses FDUMP. Of course, if the TEST option is used, there are other facilities within COBTEST for obtaining a storage dump. These are discussed in the next chapter. If neither FDUMP nor TEST is coded and an abnormal termination occurs, a normal system dump will still be produced.

For batch programs, the formatted dump output is produced on SYSDBOUT. A DD line for this file should be included for any program compiled with FDUMP, or the output will be lost. For CICS programs, the output is produced on the Temporary Storage queue

CEBRtttt, where tttt is the terminal id of the task producing the dump.

The run-time option STAE should be in effect. This option allows the COBOL II abend handler to take control. This is the default run-time option, so you usually shouldn't have to do anything. If these steps are followed, and an abnormal termination occurs, a formatted storage dump should appear on SYSDBOUT.

14.2 USING A FORMATTED DUMP FOR DEBUGGING

A formatted dump is printed, if requested, for the program which abended. A separate data division dump is printed for any separate programs in the run unit that called the failing program, directly or indirectly.

Using the formatted dump, you can see:

• the program that was running
• the abend code
• the PSW (program status word)
• the line number and verb number of the statement that failed
• the contents of the registers
• the name, level number, and contents of every data item

14.2.1 Abend Code, PSW, and Registers

These three items are present in a system dump (as in OS COBOL) as well as a formatted dump. The completion code, or abend code, can be a system error (S....) or a user error (U....). The common system errors for COBOL programs are, of course, 0C4 (protection exception, or attempt to address storage not owned by the program) and 0C7 (data exception). "User" errors in COBOL programs will be errors inserted by the compiler or COBOL run-time modules. Examples are 1037 (fell off the end of the program) and 1090/1091 (CICS GETMAIN error often caused by above/below-line problems). User errors can be generated by other software you are using, such as the sort program.

The registers will be useful to you if you are prepared to follow through all the addresses in the dump, using maps to the storage blocks.

The program status word (PSW) can be used to determine the exact machine code statement that failed. The address of the next instruction to be executed is contained in the last 4 bytes of the PSW.

14.2.2 The Program Executing

If there were several programs linked together in the run unit, it is useful to know which one failed. In a COBOL II formatted dump, this is the first piece of information in the output. In a system dump, as under OS COBOL, this has to be determined by looking into the Save Area Trace to find the calling sequence.

14.2.3 The Statement Executing

Immediately under the completion code and PSW in the formatted dump, you see the line number and verb number of the statement which failed. This replaces the STATE option of OS COBOL, which has been deleted. Unfortunately, if the OPTIMIZE compiler option was used, the line and verb numbers cannot be given. An offset from the start of the program is given instead. You will have to use the LIST or OFFSET compiler option to determine the source line that corresponds to the problem statement.

14.2.4 Values of Data Items

Below the line number that failed in the dump are the contents of the 16 general-purpose registers. Below these are laid out all the Data Division data items, including File Section and Linkage Section items. For each item, the following are displayed:

- source code statement number
- level number
- name, in the form *program-name.name*
- data type (picture)
- contents at time of abend
- if appropriate, the message "INVALID DATA FOR THIS DATA TYPE"

```
Source Code:

001240 01  W-RECORD.
001250 01  FILLER REDEFINES W-RECORD.
001260     02  WR-CHAR            PIC X(06).
001270     02  WR-NUM             PIC 9(4)V99.
001280     02  WR-PACKED          PIC S9(5) COMP-3.

Dump Format:

001240 01  RECORD-1           AN
                         BEAMON4032.00

001250 01  FILLER             AN-GR

001260 02  WR-CHAR            AN                   BEAMON

001270 02  WR-NUM             ND                   4032.00

001280 02  WR-PACKED          NP-S                     +5
```

Listing 14-1   Example of Data Display in a Formatted Dump Layout.

Listing 14-1 is an example of part of a COBOL II formatted dump, showing the formatted display of a small record area. Each field is listed, including the group field, with its contents.

14.3 UNFORMATTED DUMPS

A normal system dump will be produced if a program abends and a dataset SYSUDUMP, SYSMDUMP, or SYSABEND has been allocated. This can be in addition to a formatted dump, or instead of it. The system dump is laid out in the same way as with OS COBOL, of course. There are differences in detail because of the manner in which the reentrant and resident options are implemented, but it is not the purpose of this book to cover debugging using system dumps.

14.4 THE COBOL RUN-TIME LIBRARY

When a program is compiled, the source code is translated into Assembly language code. Most of this code will be "in-line," but some COBOL verbs are translated into a call to a library subroutine. Ta-

Table 14-1   Verbs That Are Subroutines.

Verb	Subroutine
ACCEPT	CACP
ALTER	CGDR
CALL	CLNK
CANCEL	CLNK
CLOSE - QSAM	EQOC
CLOSE - VSAM	EVOC
DELETE - VSAM	EVIO
DISPLAY	CDSP
DIVIDE	CXDI
GO TO	CGDR
INSPECT	CINS
MOVE	CSMV or CVMO
MULTIPLY	CXMU
OPEN - QSAM	EQOC
OPEN - VSAM	EVOC
READ - QSAM	EQBL
READ - VSAM	EVIO
REWRITE - QSAM	EQBL
REWRITE - VSAM	EVIO
SEARCH ALL	CSCH
START - VSAM	EVIO
STOP	CACP
STRING	CSTG
UNSTRING	CUST
WRITE - QSAM	EQBL
WRITE - VSAM	EVIO

bles 14-1 and 14-2 list these verbs and the subroutines which implement them. The full name of each subroutine is IGZxxxx, where xxxx is the short name entered in this table. If a program fails in one of these subroutines, you can trace it by finding the pointer to COBVEC in COBCOM and looking up the address of the subroutine by name.

14.4.1   Effect of Options RES, RENT

If the compiler option NORES was used, all of the run-time routines are included in the load module of the program at link time. If RES was used, the routines are loaded at run-time as needed. A flag indicates which option was used.

Table 14-2   Subroutines Which Contain Verbs.

Subroutine	*Verb*
CACP	ACCEPT
	STOP
CDSP	DISPLAY
CGDR	GO TO
	ALTER
CINS	INSPECT
CLNK	CANCEL
	CALL
CSCH	SEARCH ALL
CSMV	MOVE
CSTG	STRING
CUST	UNSTRING
CVMO	MOVE
CXDI	DIVIDE
CXMU	MULTIPLY
EQBL	WRITE - QSAM
	REWRITE - QSAM
	READ - QSAM
EQOC	CLOSE - QSAM
	OPEN - QSAM
EVIO	DELETE - VSAM
	WRITE - VSAM
	REWRITE - VSAM
	READ - VSAM
	START - VSAM
EVOC	OPEN - VSAM
	CLOSE - VSAM

If the RENT option was used, the TGT and Working Storage for the task will be found in dynamic storage. The copies in the load module were not used except to initialize values in the dynamic area. If the NORENT option were used, the TGT and Working Storage are contained in the load module.

14.5 SUMMARY: DEBUGGING WITH DUMPS

The FDUMP option makes dump reading a little easier. It works with CICS and batch programs. Unfortunately, it does make the programs larger so many sites will not use it in production. Also, when programs are optimized, FDUMP no longer tells you the failing statement. For most debugging during development, the symbolic debugger covered in the next chapter will be the tool of choice. Debugging using system dumps has not changed in principle, but some details are altered owing to changes in the run-time organization of COBOL programs.

15

COBTEST: Debugging in the Development Environment

IBM introduced the symbolic debugger COBTEST with COBOL II. If you have not used this kind of tool before, you may well find this to be one of the major benefits of the new compiler. A similar product called IBM OS COBOL Interactive Debug (TESTCOB) has been available for use with OS COBOL programs for many years now. If you have used the TESTCOB command before, you will be able to use the new product immediately, since COBTEST is a considerably enhanced product based on TESTCOB. You should read the paragraph "Differences from TESTCOB" and the instructions on setting up for your environment.

If you have access to a third-party symbolic debugger, such as Intertest or Xpediter, you may not be concerned with COBTEST. You may want to consider, though, that COBTEST is available in all environments at every VS COBOL II installation. Third-party products are generally less widespread, and many are available only for CICS.

After discussing the differences from TESTCOB, we will consider how to prepare for and invoke COBTEST in various environments— ISPF full-screen, MVS batch, CICS batch, and TSO interactive. Then we will cover the use of the product from the TSO command-line. Then we will look at some differences in usage in the batch and full-screen situations. Finally, there is a reference of all the COBTEST commands.

15.1   DIFFERENCES FROM TESTCOB

The following paragraphs summarize the chief differences between the debugger included with VS COBOL II and the TESTCOB debugger. This should be of value to programmers who have used the TESTCOB product.

COBTEST is bundled with the VS COBOL II compiler, whereas TESTCOB is an optional, extra-cost product to add on to OS COBOL. While many installations did not use TESTCOB, they will all have COBTEST available.

COBTEST works in all of the IBM mainframe environments; CICS as well as batch, TSO, CMS, and IMS/DC. TESTCOB was only available under TSO and CMS. In CICS and batch programs, you create a file of debugger commands for the program to execute, then view the output in another file after the run.

The first two points imply that every programmer writing a VS COBOL II program has access to the COBTEST debugger. Since COBTEST is certain to be available, it was not necessary for IBM to include debugging options in source code or compiler options. It is also another step in reducing the difference between batch and CICS programming. Any programmer who learns the COBTEST debugger for batch programs can use it to debug CICS programs also.

COBTEST can run as a full-screen product under ISPF. This provides a friendly, easy-to-use interface which improves on the command-line interface previously available.

COBTEST supports several new commands. These include;

FREQ and LISTFREQ, which enable you to count the number of times each statement in the program was executed

LINK and PROC, which allow the simulation of calling and called programs so that incomplete code can be tested

COMMENT, which allows insertion of comments into batches of debugging commands

STEP, which allows execution of a series of statements

RESTART, which deletes and reloads a clean copy of the program, but retains all the breakpoints

The last part of this chapter contains a complete summary of COBTEST commands.

15.2   PREPARING FOR COBTEST

In order for you to use COBTEST on a program it must have been compiled with the TEST option. You should not specify WITH DEBUGGING MODE, which disables the TEST option. (You should never specify this, anyway. It is an obsolete usage.) Once you have successfully compiled and linked a program using TEST, you are ready to use COBTEST.

15.3   INVOKING COBTEST IN FULL-SCREEN ISPF MODE

To invoke COBTEST in full-screen mode under ISPF, you select the "FOREGROUND" panel (usually option 4) of ISPF/PDF. From this panel, select "VS COBOL II Debug." From this panel, enter the name of your program on the line "DATASET NAME." You will now see the full-screen debug panel. The top line of the screen should look like this:

```
COBTEST QUALIFY:  GFPBDOC    WHERE:    GFPBDOC.197.1
```

If this is not available, you should still be able to use the TSO command-line mode. The full-screen option requires installation by tailoring of ISPF/PDF, and not all installations do this. Section 15.3.1 explains the installation briefly.

15.3.1   Installation of Full-Screen ISPF

If ISPF full-screen support has not been installed, you may be able to tailor your personal ISPF environment. To do this, you will need some knowledge of TSO and the ISPF Dialog Manager. The modification involves two steps.

A. Modify the ISPF/PDF CLIST

Your PDF invocation CLIST should be modified by concatenating the necessary COBTEST libraries to those already there as follows:

```
ALLOC DD(SYSPROC) DSN(add: 'SYS1.COB2CLIB')
ALLOC DD(ISPMLIB) DSN(add: 'SYS1.COB2MLIB')
ALLOC DD(ISPPLIB) DSN(add: 'SYS1.COB2PLIB')
ALLOC DD(ISPLLIB) DSN(add: 'SYS1.COB2LIB')
```

You may have to change the format of these datasets because of problems stemming from the MVS rules for file concatenation. The CLIST library is distributed with format FB, whereas many sites use VB CLIST libraries.

B. Modify the ISPF Panels

The ISPF Foreground panel needs to be modified to allow selection of COBTEST. This is stored as panel ISRFPA in the ISPF/PDF library ISRPLIB. The code to invoke the debugger is:

```
'PGM(ISRFPR) PARM(IGZTPIN2) NEWAPPL(DPA)'
```

The associated tutorial panels should be modified also. The panel is ISR40000. The debugger tutorial panel is IGZTMTU1.

15.4   INVOKING COBTEST IN TSO COMMAND-LINE MODE

To run COBTEST under TSO, the library SYS1.COB2LIB should be included as a STEPLIB (DISP=SHR) in the TSO logon procedure.

To invoke COBTEST in line mode under TSO, you should be in TSO native mode or in the ISPF TSO Command panel (usually option 6).

Enter COBTEST *program-name* or COBTEST LOAD(*program-name:loadlib*). If the load library containing your program is allocated in your TSO logon, use the first form, otherwise the second. The response from COBTEST should look like this:

```
PP - 5668-958 VS COBOL II DEBUG FACILITY -- REL 2.0
GFPBDOC.197.1
COBTEST
```

```
JCL:

//SYSOUT    DD   SYSOUT=A
//PRINTER   DD   DSN=USR.TEST.PRINT,DISP=OLD
//INPUT     DD   DSN=USR.TEST.INPUT,DISP=SHR

CLIST:

ALLOC         DD(SYSOUT)   SYSOUT(A)
ALLOC OLD     DD(PRINTER)  DSN(TEST.PRINT)
ALLOC SHR     DD(INPUT)    DSN('USR.TEST.INPUT')
```

Listing 15-1   JCL and CLIST.

15.4.1   Allocating Files for COBTEST

It is necessary to allocate any files that a program will be using. In batch programs, this is done with JCL, but to run under TSO another mechanism is required. Files are allocated under TSO with the ALLOC command. Listing 15-1 translates a few lines of JCL to the equivalent TSO ALLOC statements.

15.5   INVOKING COBTEST FROM MVS JCL

To invoke COBTEST in batch mode under MVS, you run a job with COBDBG as the main program and the COBTEST commands in the file SYSDBIN. Listing 15-2 contains a skeleton example. Of course, any files needed by the program must be included.

15.6   INVOKING COBTEST FROM CICS

To invoke COBTEST in batch mode under CICS, you place all the debug commands in a temporary storage queue called CSCO*tttt*, where *tttt* is the terminal id of the terminal you will be using. One way to create such a queue is to use a series of CECI commands like this:

```
CECI WRITEQ TS QUEUE(CSCOtrm1) FROM('....................')
```

```
//          JOB
//          EXEC PGM=COBDBG
//SYSOUT   DD    SYSOUT=*
//SYSDBOUT DD    SYSOUT=*
...
          include any files used by GFPBDOC
...
//SYSDBIN  DD    *
COBTEST GFPBDOC
RECORD
QUALIFY GFPBDOC
TRACE NAME
/*
```

Listing 15-2 Invoking COBTEST with JCL.

Listing 15-3 contains an example of such a queue. Then, initiate the transaction, for instance by typing its transaction id from the terminal. Output will go to the temporary storage queue CEBR*tttt*. Successive runs will add to this queue, rather than overwriting it.

15.7 USING COBTEST FOR INTERACTIVE DEBUGGING

First I will discuss the general method of using COBTEST, then some individual commands.

15.7.1 What the Debugger Can Do

If you do not have a symbolic debugger available, you trace the flow of a program with READY TRACE. You can examine variables with DISPLAY statements. With the debugger, you can easily do the equivalent of these things without needing to recompile. In addition,

```
CECI WRITEQ TS QUEUE(CSCOTRM1) FROM('COBTEST GFPBDOC')
CECI WRITEQ TS QUEUE(CSCOTRM1) FROM('RECORD')
CECI WRITEQ TS QUEUE(CSCOTRM1) FROM('QUALIFY GFPBDOC')
CECI WRITEQ TS QUEUE(CSCOTRM1) FROM('TRACE NAME')
```

Listing 15-3 Invoking COBTEST from CICS.

```
000244   SALARY-TEST.
000245      IF SALARY > 40000 MOVE 'E' TO TYPE-CODE.

AT 245
AT SALARY-TEST
AT 245.1
AT 245.2
AT SALARY.245.1
```

Listing 15-4   COBTEST Example.

you can set breakpoints anywhere in the program. At these break-points, you can examine or change any variable in the program, or change the flow of control by going to another point in the procedure division. A conditional breakpoint can be set by specifying a conditional expression. The program will then stop when that condition is true.

15.7.2 Specifying Names

To specify a data item in COBTEST, you use its name. If you are going to use it often, you can also define an alias to save typing. To specify a point in the procedure division, you use its line number. The full specification is "program-name.line-number.verb-number," but program-name defaults to the current program and verb-number to 1. If you want to put a breakpoint in another program, you can specify the program name. If there is more than one verb on a line where you wish to set a breakpoint (which is poor style), you can specify the number of the verb. Also, if the statement is the first line of a procedure (a section or a paragraph), you can use the procedure name. I will illustrate this using the AT command, which we will meet in a minute. In Listing 15-4 are a source code line and several valid AT commands.

15.7.3 Sample COBTEST Session

Now that we know how to specify names to COBTEST, we can introduce some basic commands with a sample session. In this session we will set breakpoints, examine variables, step through the program, and produce a trace.

First we need a program to debug. Listing 15-5 contains a short COBOL II program which we can debug in this session. A recording of the session is given in Listing 15-6. The output from TESTCOB is on the left in uppercase, and the prgrammer-entered input on the right in lowercase. The purpose of each command issued in the session is explained below.

COBTEST CM93	starts debugging the program CM93.
LINK(LS-DATE-EXT . . .)	prepares a linkage section with three variables.
SET LS-DATE-EXT . . .	moves a value to the variable LS-DATE-EXT.
AT 5900	sets a breakpoint at which execution will stop.
GO	goes to the next breakpoint.
LIST LS-DATE-EXT . . .	shows the value of the group variable LS-DATE-EXT.
OFF 5900	removes the breakpoint at line 5900.
WHEN LPO LEAP=0	sets a conditional breakpoint called LPO to the condition LEAP=0. We will stop whenever this condition becomes true, that is, LEAP becomes 0.
GO	goes to the next breakpoint.
LIST YR	shows the value of the variable YR.
OFFWN LPO	removes the conditional breakpoint LPO.
STEP	goes forward one statement, from 6200 to 6300.
TRACE NAME	lists all paragraphs or lines as they execute.
AT 7800	sets a breakpoint at line 7800.
GO	goes to the next breakpoint.
LIST LS-DATE-NUM	shows the value of the variable LS-DATE-NUM.
RUN	executes, ingnoring all breakpoints, until the normal or abnormal end of the program.
QUIT	exits the debugger.

```
000100 IDENTIFICATION DIVISION.
000200 PROGRAM-ID.    CM93.
000300*** DATE PROCESSING ***
000400 ENVIRONMENT DIVISION.
000500 DATA DIVISION.
000600 WORKING-STORAGE SECTION.
000700 01   YR            PIC 9999 COMP.
000800 01   MN            PIC 9999 COMP.
000900 01   YEAR-DAYS     PIC 9999 COMP.
001000 01   LEAP          PIC 9999 COMP.
001010 01   WORK1         PIC 9999 COMP.
001100 01   MONTH-TABLE.
001200      02   JAN  PIC 9999 COMP VALUE 31.
001300      02   FEB  PIC 9999 COMP VALUE 28.
001400      02   MAR  PIC 9999 COMP VALUE 31.
001500      02   APR  PIC 9999 COMP VALUE 30.
001600      02   MAY  PIC 9999 COMP VALUE 31.
001700      02   JUN  PIC 9999 COMP VALUE 30.
001800      02   JUL  PIC 9999 COMP VALUE 31.
001900      02   AUG  PIC 9999 COMP VALUE 31.
002000      02   SEP  PIC 9999 COMP VALUE 30.
002100      02   OCT  PIC 9999 COMP VALUE 31.
002200      02   NOV  PIC 9999 COMP VALUE 30.
002300      02   DEC  PIC 9999 COMP VALUE 31.
002400 01   FILLER REDEFINES MONTH-TABLE.
002500      02   MONTH-DAYS PIC 9999 COMP OCCURS 12.
002600 LINKAGE SECTION.
002700 01   LS-DATE-EXT.
002800      02 MONTH        PIC 99.
002900      02 L-DAY        PIC 99.
003000      02 YEAR         PIC 99.
003100 01   LS-DATE-NUM     PIC 9999 COMP.
003200 01   LS-RETURN       PIC X(02).
003300 PROCEDURE DIVISION USING LS-DATE-EXT,
003400                         LS-DATE-NUM,
003500                         LS-RETURN.
003600 P000-MAIN.
003700      MOVE '00' TO LS-RETURN
003900
004000      IF MONTH NOT NUMERIC
004100      OR YEAR  NOT NUMERIC
004200      OR L-DAY NOT NUMERIC
004300         MOVE '10' TO LS-RETURN
004400         GOBACK
004500      ENDIF
004600
004700      IF MONTH < 01 OR > 12
004800         MOVE '20' TO LS-RETURN
004900         GOBACK
```

Listing 15-5   Date Edit Program for TESTCOB Example. (Continued)

```
005000      ENDIF
005100
005200      IF L-DAY > MONTH-DAYS (MONTH)
005300         MOVE '30' TO LS-RETURN
005400         GOBACK
005500      ENDIF
005600
005700      MOVE 0 TO LS-DATE-NUM
005800
005900      PERFORM VARYING YR FROM 85 BY 1
006000      UNTIL YR NOT < YEAR
006100         DIVIDE 4 INTO YR GIVING WORK1 REMAINDER LEAP
006200         IF LEAP = 0
006300            MOVE 366 TO YEAR-DAYS
006400            MOVE 29 TO FEB
006500         ELSE
006600            MOVE 365 TO YEAR-DAYS
006700            MOVE 28 TO FEB
006800         ENDIF
006900         COMPUTE LS-DATE-NUM = LS-DATE-NUM + YEAR-DAYS
007000      END PERFORM
007100 P000-MONTHS.
007200      PERFORM VARYING MN FROM 1 BY 1
007300      UNTIL MN NOT < MONTH
007400         COMPUTE LS-DATE-NUM = LS-DATE-NUM + MONTH-DAYS (MN)

007500      END PERFORM
007600 P000-EXIT.
007700      ADD L-DAY TO LS-DATE-NUM
007800      GOBACK.
```

Listing 15-5   Date Edit Program for TESTCOB Example.

15.8   USING COBTEST IN BATCH MODE

In batch mode, there is no possibility of interacting with the debugger from the terminal. It is necessary to develop the complete script before the program is run. While this takes more thought, it does allow the reuse of debugging scripts.

The line-mode commands HELP, RESTART, and SYSCMD are not available in batch mode because they would not make sense in that context.

Comments may be placed in batch files. Any text after an asterisk on a line is treated as a comment. You can create either complete comment lines or put comments on the same line as the commands.

Debugger Output	Programmer Input
	cobtest cm93
CM93.003800.1	
COBTEST	link(ls-date-ext,ls-date-num,ls-return)
COBTEST	set ls-date-ext = '081753'
COBTEST	at 5900
COBTEST	go
CM93.005900.1	
COBTEST	list ls-date-ext group
002700 01 LS-DATE-EXT X006	
DISP ===>081753	
COBTEST	off 5900
COBTEST	when lpo leap = 0
COBTEST	go
CM93.006200.1	
COBTEST	list yr
000700 01 YR N	
53	
COBTEST	offwn lpo
COBTEST	step
CM93.006300.1	
COBTEST	trace name
COSBTEST	at 7800
COBTEST	go
TRACING	
P000-MONTHS.	
P000-EXIT.	
CM93.007800.1	
COBTEST	list ls-date-num
003100 01 LS-DATE-NUM N	
9370	
COBTEST	run
PROGRAM UNDER COBTEST ENDED NORMALLY	
	quit

Listing 15-6   Example of COBTEST Dialog.

15.9 USING COBTEST IN FULL-SCREEN MODE

The following commands are only available in full-screen mode:

AUTO

COLOR

LISTINGS

MOVECURS

```
PEEK
POSITION
PREVDISP
PROFILE
RESTORE
SEARCH
SELECT
SOURCE
SUFFIX
VTRACE
```

15.10   QUICK COMMAND REFERENCE

Remember that in line or full-screen mode, you can issue HELP *command* to get reference pages for any command.

AT

The AT command sets breakpoints at a verb or verbs in the program. A list of breakpoints can be set in a single command, or a range of breakpoints can be defined with a start and end point. A count can be specified so that the break occurs on the first or every 10th time, for instance. At a breakpoint, execution stops temporarily. A prompt can be issued, and a list of commands can be executed. This list can include a GO, RUN, or STEP command, so that execution continues without halting. If there is no such command, execution waits for commands issued from the terminal.

Examples:

```
AT 1100
```

Stop at statement 1100 and issue a prompt.

```
AT 1100:1150 (LIST CHAR-INDEX; LIST CHAR1 (CHAR-INDEX); GO)
```

Stop at all statements between 1100 and 1150. Display the two variables named, then continue.

```
AT 1120, 1150 (LIST RECORD-KEY; GO) COUNT (1, 10, 1000) NONOTIFY
```

Stop at statements 1120 and 1150 on the first and every 10th time until the 1000th (about 100 times on each statement). List the field record-key and continue.

AUTO (Full-Screen)

The AUTO command enables automatic listing of variables in the auto monitoring area of the screen. AUTO LIST specifies a LIST command which names the variables to monitor, and AUTO ON and AUTO OFF turn the display on and off, respectively.
Examples:

```
AUTO LIST name,socsecno
AUTO ON
...
AUTO OFF
```

List the contents of the program variables name and socsecno in the monitoring area between the statements AUTO ON and AUTO OFF.

COLOR (Full-Screen)

The COLOR command allows you to set the attributes of the display.

DROP

The DROP command lets you delete synonyms established with the EQUATE command.
Examples:

```
DROP ms
DROP (ms, sum)
```

DUMP

The DUMP command ends the COBTEST session with a snap dump of the program storage areas. Output goes to MVS SYSABOUT or the CICS dump data set.
Example:

```
DUMP
```

EQUATE

The EQUATE command (abbreviated EQ) lets you define a short name as a synonym for another name in a program, in order to save typing effort.
Examples:

```
EQUATE ms MASTER-SUMMARY-FILE
EQ sum MS-SUMMARY-TOTAL
```

FLOW

The FLOW command (abbreviated FL) collects information on the control flow of the program and maintains a table containing the last 255 verbs where control could have changed. This is displayed or printed on request—note that there is no difference between display and print in batch mode.
Examples:

```
FLOW ON
...
FLOW (10)
FL (200) PRINT
FL OFF
```

In this example, the FLOW is turned on. Subsequently, the last 10 verbs are displayed on the terminal. The last 200 are displayed on MVS SYSDBOUT. Then the flow is turned off.

FREQ

The FREQ command (abbreviated FR) maintans a count of the frequency of execution of each verb in the program or programs.
Examples:

```
FREQ
...
FREQ OFF
```

This example sets frequency checking on and off for all programs executed between the two points.

GO

The GO command starts or restarts execution of the program. This will continue until the next breakpoint is reached, or until the end of the program. Execution can resume from the current point, or a new point to begin from can be specified. If a new point is specified, this will alter the flow of the program logic.
  Examples:

```
GO
GO 1120
```

The first example restarts from the current breakpoint. The second restarts from statement 1120.

HELP

The HELP command (abbreviated H) gives information about the use of the debugger.
  Examples:

```
HELP HELP
HELP
HELP AT
HELP AT FUNCTION
HELP AT SYNTAX
HELP AT OPERANDS (COUNT)
```

The first example gets help on the HELP command. The second gets a list of all commands. The other four give the differing levels of help available for a command, in this case AT. HELP AT will give all information for the AT command.

IF

The IF command (abbreviated I) causes a debugger command to be executed if the specified condition is true. IF is useful in command lists, as it can evaluate expressions and halt execution when some condition occurs. IF is preferable to WHEN, if possible, on efficiency grounds. An IF is only executed at a specific breakpoint, and a WHEN is executed after every COBOL statement. WHEN is more powerful because of this.

Examples:

```
AT 1100 (IF (sum GT 99999) HALT)
AT 2125 (IF (name1 EQ name2) (LIST name1; LIST name2); GO)
```

In the first case, the IF statement will cause execution to stop if the variable sum goes over 99999 before the execution of statement 1100. In the second case, the two variables name1 and name2 will be listed on occasions that they are equal. Execution will continue.

LINK

The LINK command is used when a calling program is not available. You issue a LINK command naming any variables in the linkage section that will not be passed because the program is not there. These are then allocated by COBTEST. You can then use the SET command in the normal way to assign values to these variables.
Example:

```
LINKAGE SECTION.
01  RATE        PIC S9(05)V99.
01  TERM        PIC S999.
01  AMOUNT      PIC S9(15)V99.
PROCEDURE DIVISION.
LINK (RATE, TERM, AMOUNT)
SET RATE = 12.5
SET TERM = 60
SET AMOUNT = 5000000
```

In this example, the three input parameters to a program are simulated using LINK and SET.

LIST

The LIST command (abbreviated L) is used to display the values or addresses of program variables. These can be group, subscripted, or indexed items. They can be displayed in normal or hexadecimal form, or both, on the terminal or the MVS SYSDBOUT file.
Examples:

```
LIST sum
LIST payroll-record RECORD
```

```
LIST ALL BOTH
LIST @sum HEX
```

The first instance lists the contents of the variable sum. The second lists all the fields in payroll-record. The third lists the contents of all variables in the program, in both display and hex. The fourth lists the address of the variable sum.

LISTBRKS

The LISTBRKS command (abbreviated LISTB) lists all breakpoints set by AT, NEXT, or WHEN commands.
Examples:

```
LISTBRKS
LISTB PRINT
```

LISTEQ

The LISTEQ command lists all synonyms set by EQ commands.
Examples:

```
LISTEQ
LISTEQ PRINT
```

LISTFREQ

The LISTFREQ command (abbreviated LISTF) lists the frequency of execution of verbs in programs turned on by use of the FREQ command. You can optionally request only those statements which have not been executed at all.
Examples:

```
LISTFREQ ALL
LISTFREQ ALL PRINT ZEROFREQ
```

LISTINGS (Full-Screen)

The LISTINGS command calls up the source listing panel.

MOVECURS (Full-Screen)

The MOVECURS command jumps the cursor between source or monitoring areas and the command line. It is generally defined as PF12.

NEXT

The NEXT command (abbreviated N) causes execution to continue for one COBOL statement. This is primarily useful in interactive mode.
Examples:

```
NEXT
N
```

OFF

The OFF command turns off breakpoints set with the AT command. A list or range of statements can be specified.
Examples:

```
OFF 1200
OFF (1100:1250)
OFF
```

The first example removes one breakpoint, the second removes all breakpoints in a range, and the third removes all breakpoints in the current program.

OFFWN

The OFFWN command turns off breakpoints set with the WHEN command. A list of statements can be specified.
Examples:

```
OFFWN toob
OFFWN (toob,matc)
```

ONABEND

The ONABEND command specifies the action to take when an abend occurs. This could be return of control to the terminal or execution of a list of COBTEST commands.
    Examples:

```
ONABEND
ONABEND (FLOW PRINT; LIST ALL PRINT)
```

The first example causes control to return to the terminal on an abend. The second will print a flow and a list of all variables.

PEEK (Full-Screen)

The PEEK command displays an obscured line number.

POSITION (Full-Screen)

The POSITION command specifies the line number to display in the source code, monitor, or log area.

PREVDISP (Full-Screen)

The PREVDISP command requests display of a previous panel displayed by an application program written to use ISPF Dialog Manager services.

PRINTDD

The PRINTDD command redirects output from SYSDBOUT to a dataset of your choice. It has no meaning under CICS.
    Example:

```
PRINTDD PRNTFILE
```

PROC

The PROC command is used when a called program is not available. When you use this command, calls to an absent program are trapped and you are given the opportunity to enter the values which would have been returned by using the SET command in the normal way to assign values to these variables.

Example:

```
WORKING-STORAGE SECTION.
01  RATE        PIC S9(05)V99.
01  TERM        PIC S999.
01  AMOUNT      PIC S9(15)V99.
PROCEDURE DIVISION.
CALL NPV USING RATE, TERM, AMOUNT.
------------------------------
PROC NPV (SET RATE = 12.5; SET TERM = 60; SET AMOUNT = 5000000)
```

In this example, the three parameters returned from a program are simulated using PROC.

PROFILE (Full-Screen)

The PROFILE command calls up the profile panel, where optional parameters can be set.

QUALIFY

The QUALIFY command (abbreviated Q) changes the default program name to a specified program. It is an alternative to specifying the program-name on each statement. QUALIFY is not needed if you have a single module.
Example:

```
QUALIFY program1
```

RECORD

The RECORD and NORECORD (abbreviated RE and NORE) turn session logging on and off. The log is recorded on SYSDBOUT under MVS.

RESTART

The RESTART command deletes and reloads a clean copy of the program being debugged, but retains any breakpoints and session parameters.

RESTORE (Full-Screen)

The RESTORE command restores the position in the source screen to the last-executed statement.

RUN

The RUN command (abbreviated R) turns off debugging commands for a program and causes the program to run to completion. As with GO, you can specify a point from which to start.
Examples:

```
RUN
RUN 1150
```

SEARCH (Full-Screen)

The SEARCH command is used to search for text in the source listing.

SELECT (Full-Screen)

The SELECT command specifies the verb on a line for which the frequency count is to be displayed.

SET

The SET command changes the value of variables in the program. These variables can be indexed or subscripted. The data is moved according to COBOL MOVE rules.
Examples:

```
SET date = '12/01/89'
SET name = old-name
```

SOURCE (Full-Screen)

The SOURCE command controls the size and appearance of the source listing panel.

STEP

The STEP command causes the execution of one or a number of verbs.
Examples:

```
STEP
STEP 20
```

SUFFIX (Full-Screen)

The SUFFIX command opens or closes a suffix area for displaying the results of the FREQ command.

SYSCMD

The SYSCMD command allows execution of CMS commands. It has no meaning under other operating systems.

TRACE

The TRACE command (abbreviated T) turns on or off a display of the flow of program execution on the terminal or on SYSDBOUT. Line numbers or numbers and names can be displayed.
Examples:

```
TRACE
TRACE NAME PRINT
TRACE OFF
```

VTRACE (Full-Screen)

The VTRACE command allows you to view an animation of the program. It is similar to a continuous use of the STEP command.

WHEN

The WHEN command sets a conditional breakpoint. Before the execution of each verb in the program, COBTEST checks to see if the condition is true. If it is, control is returned to the terminal or the command list is executed. The WHEN command is very powerful, and may slow program execution dramatically.

Examples:

```
WHEN toob (sum > 999999)(LIST sum; WHERE)
WHEN matc (name1 = name2)
```

WHERE

The WHERE statement displays the current line number. This is useful interactively after an attention interrupt, and in batch mode after execution of a WHEN statement.

15.11   CONVERSION TO PRODUCTION

You will not want to use TESTCOB in production, or incur the overhead which its use entails. You will, therefore, want to recompile programs for production with the NOTEST option. Other options, such as SSRANGE (see Chapter 16), may need alteration also at this point.

16

Other Debugging Changes

In addition to the new symbolic debugger and formatted dump described in the previous two chapters, there are other changes to the practice of debugging introduced with COBOL II. Some of the Procedure Division debugging statements and some of the compiler options for debugging have been removed. An option for range checking of tables and variable-length records has been introduced.

16.1 SSRANGE: ARRAY BOUNDARY CHECKING

The SSRANGE option generates a test before every reference to a subscripted or indexed variable to see if the reference is within the bounds of the table. If the SSRANGE option is set, the array boundary is checked on every reference to a table. This works on fixed or variable length tables. Each subscript, index, or Occurs Depending On clause is checked whenever it is referred to in the program. If the target field is out of bounds, the program will print an error message on SYSPRINT, or the CEBR temporary storage queue under CICS, and terminate.

16.1.1   Limitations of SSRANGE

The SSRANGE option is a very useful new feature. It will correctly find most errors in table handling. There are two cases where it can mislead. In the first case, it will report errors which are not really problems. In the second, it will fail to find bugs in certain tables. These two points are not errors in the SSRANGE option, but simply reflect that one new feature cannot solve every problem.

Certain programs may have problems with the SSRANGE option, although they do not really have bugs that would cause data integrity problems. Programs are sometimes written to treat the immediate boundaries of tables as special cases. This is particularly common with the zero element of a table. Listing 16-1 shows examples of this technique. In the first case, a terminating period is placed after the table so that the scan will always stop. This saves an additional test comparing the index to the table size. This code was taken from the innner loop of a program, where it was executed millions of times a day. The saved test was really worth it. In the second case, a low sentinel value is placed before the first element of the table. Again, this allows a test against the table size to be omitted from the inner loop of the code. Coding in this way can generally be avoided, unless efficiency is very important. However, if this type of coding is necessary, you will have to disable subscript range checking.

There is one type of subscript range error that the SSRANGE option will not find, because of the way it works. SSRANGE operates by ensuring that the storage address to be referenced is within the range of valid storage addresses for that table. This means that for two- and three-dimensional tables, the individual indexes or subscripts may be in error without being detected. This is illustrated in Listing 16-2. In this program, the indexes have been confused so that invalid values of TR-IX greater than 10 will be used. The data in the table is corrupted. However, no attempt is made to address past the end of the table, so SSRANGE will not report the problem.

16.1.2   When to Use SSRANGE

As a general rule, all programs that use tables should be tested with SSRANGE set. Almost every program has some table-handling, and those programs with no table-handling code are not damaged by the SSRANGE option. Your installation may want to make the use of

A: Sentinel at end of table

```
DATA DIVISION.
01  TARGET-AREA.
    02  TARGET-FACT.
        03  TARGET-CHAR           PIC X OCCURS 10
                                      INDEXED BY C1-IX.
    02  TARGET-SENTINEL           PIC X VALUE '.'.

01  COPY-AREA.
    02  COPY-FACT.
        03  COPY-CHAR             PIC X OCCURS 11
                                      INDEXED BY C2-IX.


    PROCEDURE DIVISION.
        MOVE SPACES TO COPY-AREA

    *** -- IF TARGET-FACT CONTAINS A PERIOD, COPY CHARACTERS
    *** -- UP TO AND INCLUDING THE PERIOD. OTHERWISE COPY
    *** -- ALL THE CHARACTERS AND APPEND A PERIOD.
        PERFORM WITH TEST AFTER
    VARYING C1-IX FROM 1 BY 1 UNTIL TARGET-CHAR (C1-IX) = '.'
            MOVE TARGET-CHAR (C1-IX) TO COPY-CHAR (C1-IX)
        END-PERFORM.
```

B: Sentinel at beginning of table

```
DATA DIVISION.
01  SORT-AREA.
    02  SORT-SENTINEL             PIC X(12) VALUE LOW-VALUES.

    02  SORT-ITEM                 PIC X(12) OCCURS 100
                                      INDEXED BY X1 X2.
    02  CURRENT-ITEM              PIC X(12).

PROCEDURE DIVISION.
INSERTION-SORT.
    PERFORM VARYING X1 FROM 2 BY 1 UNTIL X1 > 100
        MOVE SORT-ITEM (X1) TO CURRENT-ITEM
        PERFORM VARYING X2 FROM X1 BY -1
        UNTIL SORT-ITEM (X2 - 1) NOT > CURRENT-ITEM
            MOVE SORT-ITEM (X2) TO SORT-ITEM (X2 - 1)
        END-PERFORM
        MOVE CURRENT-ITEM TO SORT-ITEM (X2)
    END-PERFORM.
```

Listing 16-1   Using Sentinel Values.

```
DATA DIVISION.
01  TEST-TABLE.
    02  TABLE-COLUMN         OCCURS 20 INDEXED BY TC-IX.
        03  TABLE-ROW        OCCURS 10 INDEXED BY TR-IX.
            04  TABLE-ITEM   PIC X(30).


PROCEDURE DIVISION.
*** THIS CODE IS IN ERROR, BUT WILL NOT BE DETECTED BY SSRANGE
    PERFORM VARYING TC-IX FROM 1 BY 1 UNTIL TC-IX > 10
        PERFORM VARYING TR-IX FROM 1 BY 1 UNTIL TR-IX > 20
            COMPUTE TABLE-ITEM (TC-IX, TR-IX) = TC-IX * TR-IX
        END-PERFORM
    END-PERFORM.
```

Listing 16-2   Multiple Subscripts.

SSRANGE a standard in their development area by making it the default compiler option. The errors this will discover can be a type that is difficult to debug in the conventional manner. For instance, CICS programs that exceed table boundaries can cause invalid data or program crashes in other parts of the CICS region. It may not be easy to discover which program is the guilty party.

16.1.3   Removing SSRANGE for Production

This option should not be used for production because it can have a very serious impact on performance. Programs can take a hundred times as long to execute. To remove the SSRANGE check, you can either recompile the program with NOSSRANGE or run it with the run-time option NOSSRANGE. The run-time option has slightly inferior performance. Since there are other options that change between test and production situations, and many shops have a standard of recompiling for production, you will usually recompile rather than use the run-time option. You might leave the error-checking code in, using the run-time option to disable it, if you anticipate possible errors in a situation where you cannot easily recompile. One example would be code distributed to a remote site. If an error was reported, you could call by phone and request the users to add a PARM state-

ment to the JCL and rerun the job. That PARM statement is
'/NOSSRANGE' as in the example below:

```
//        EXEC PGM=YOURPROG,PARM='/NOSSRANGE'
```

16.2 MISSING DEBUGGING FEATURES

Several debugging features which were present in OS COBOL have
been removed. The Procedure Division statements READY TRACE,
RESET TRACE, EXHIBIT, and ON and the compiler options
COUNT, FLOW, and STATE are missing and must be replaced by
use of similar features in COBTEST. Use of COBTEST is covered in
Chapter 14. Once COBTEST is installed and its use is mastered, the
loss of these features will be of no concern.

16.2.1 READY and RESET TRACE

The statements READY TRACE and RESET TRACE are accepted by
the compiler, but have no effect. To obtain a trace, it is now necessary to compile the program with the TEST option and run it under
COBTEST, which has a TRACE command.

16.2.2 EXHIBIT

The EXHIBIT statement is no longer available, and is not accepted
by the compiler. Some uses of EXHIBIT can be replaced by DIS-
PLAY. For instance, the following two statements are approximately
equivalent:

```
EXHIBIT NAMED FIELD-A
DISPLAY 'FIELD-A ' FIELD-A
```

Use of EXHIBIT CHANGED must be replaced by user-written
code, or by compiling the program with the TEST option, running it
under COBTEST, and using suitable combinations of AT, WHEN,
and LIST. There is no exact equivalent to EXHIBIT CHANGED, but
the available debugging environment is so much more powerful that
this should not be a problem.

```
OS COBOL:

    DATA DIVISION.
    ...
    PROCEDURE DIVISION.
        ON 1 PERFORM INITIAL-ROUTINE
        ...
        ON 1 AND EVERY 60 PERFORM PAGE-BREAK
        ...

COBOL II:

    DATA DIVISION.

    01  FIRST-TIME-SW          PIC X VALUE '1'.
        02  FIRST-TIME             VALUE '1'.
        02  NOT-FIRST-TIME         VALUE '0'.

    01  LINE-CTR              PIC S9(09) COMP VALUE +99.
    ...
    PROCEDURE DIVISION.

        IF FIRST-TIME
            SET NOT-FIRST-TIME TO TRUE
            PERFORM INITIAL-ROUTINE
        END-IF
        ...
        IF LINE-CTR > 60
            PERFORM PAGE-BREAK
            MOVE ZERO TO LINE-CTR
        END-IF
        ...
```

Listing 16-3   Replacing ON.

16.2.3   ON

The ON statement is no longer available, and is not accepted by the
compiler. Use of the ON statement for debugging can be replaced by
compiling the program with the test option, running it under
COBTEST, and using the command AT . . . COUNT (i, j, k). Unfortunately, although the ON statement was intended for debugging, it
has often been used in production programs, generally in its simplest
form—ON 1. It must be replaced here by a user-programmed counter
or switch. Listing 16-3 has two examples of the replacement of the
ON statement by user-written code.

Table 16-1   Default Run-Time Options.

Option	Default
AIXBLD	NOAIXBLD
DEBUG	DEBUG
LIBKEEP	NOLIBKEEP
RTEREUS	NORTEREUS
SPOUT	NOSPOUT
SSRANGE	SSRANGE
STAE	STAE
UPSI	UPSI(00000000)

16.2.4   COUNT, FLOW, and STATE

The compiler options COUNT, FLOW, and STATE have been removed. Use of the COUNT option can be replaced by appropriate use of the COBTEST FREQ and LISTFREQ commands. The STATE option is superceded by FDUMP, which includes that information at the front of the dump, or by use of COBTEST, which will stop at the statement in error automatically. Use of the FLOW option can be replaced by the FLOW command of COBTEST.

16.3   RUN-TIME OPTIONS

A number of run-time options are available with COBOL II. These allow certain changes to be made in program behavior without any need for recompiling or relinking. This is usually done for debugging. These options can be specified on the PARM parameter of the EXEC statement in a batch environment. Table 16-1 lists these options and their default values. Note that DEBUG, SSRANGE, and STAE default to ON, so only their negations NODEBUG, NOSSRANGE, and NOSTAE have any meaning as run-time options.

Run-time options are coded following the last slash in the PARM field. Listing 16-4 shows some valid examples of the coding of run-time options. Slashes can be included in the user parameter data, so long as the last one introduces the run-time options.

```
EXEC PROG1,PARM='89-02-01/NOSSRANGE'

EXEC PROG2,PARM='/NODEBUG,NOSSRANGE'

EXEC PROG3,PARM='89/02/01/NODEBUG'

EXEC PROG4,PARM='89/02/01/'
```

Listing 16-4   Run-Time Options.

16.3.1   AIXBLD

This option invokes the VSAM IDCAMS (Access Method Services) program to define components of a newly created VSAM file.

16.3.2   DEBUG

Coding NODEBUG suppresses the debugging features of a program compiled WITH DEBUGGING MODE. It has no effect if the program was not so compiled.

16.3.3   LIBKEEP

This option is present for performance reasons. If the main program in a run unit is not COBOL II, so that COBOL II programs are being called by non-COBOL programs, the COBOL libraries may be continually loaded and released. This option will retain the libraries until the task ends.

16.3.4   RTEREUS

This option cannot be specified on the PARM statement. It sets up the run-time environment for reusability.

16.3.5   SPOUT

The SPOUT option prints an explanation of the storage used by COBOL space management. This can be used in performance tuning.

16.3.6 SSRANGE

NOSSRANGE can be coded to turn off the SSRANGE option. The compiler SSRANGE option can seriously degrade performance, but is useful in debugging. By combining the SSRANGE compile option with the NOSSRANGE run-time option, almost all this performance degradation is recovered, but the debugging support can still be switched on without recompiling or linking. This option has no effect if the compiler option NOSSRANGE was specified.

16.3.7 STAE

NOSTAE can be coded to prevent the run-time environment from trapping abends.

16.3.8 UPSI Switches

The eight UPSI bit-switches can be set on or off.

16.3.9 Run-Time Options in CICS

In a CICS system, AIXBLD and STAE have no meaning, but the other options can be controlled by linking-in the IBM-supplied module IGZEOPT as the first program in the run unit. This module can be tailored as required.

Compiler-Directing Changes

When IBM wrote the VS COBOL II compiler, they reviewed the compiler options carefully. As well as introducing new options, many of the old ones have been renamed or operate slightly differently. This chapter will explain the significant changes and new compiler options, with examples where appropriate. Appendix D contains a complete alphabetical reference of compiler options. First, we will summarize the major changes which have been introduced.

17.1 MAJOR CHANGES INTRODUCED

Some compile options can now be placed in the COBOL source code, using the CONTROL and PROCESS statements.

With the WORD option, an installation can define their own reserved words, and disable statements they do not wish to support.

With the FLAG option, compiler error messages can be embedded in the output listing next to the statement in error.

The new option DATA(24) allows above-the-line programs to pass data to those below. FASTSRT allows the sort program to be invoked more efficiently. FDUMP creates dumps which are easier to read. PFDSGN changes the sign handling of certain numeric fields. RENT creates truly reentrant programs. SSRANGE enables a feature which checks on table handling to make sure that subscripts and indexes do not go out of bounds.

The LISTER options have been removed, mostly because these features were incorporated into other compiler options. Many option names were changed, as explained in this chapter.

17.2 COMPILER-DIRECTING STATEMENTS

The following compiler-directing statements are retained from OS COBOL:

```
BASIS
COPY
DELETE
EJECT
ENTER
INSERT
SERVICE LABEL
SKIP1
SKIP2
SKIP3
TITLE
USE
```

COBOL II introduces two new compiler-directing statements.

```
*CONTROL    or    *CBL
PROCESS     or    CBL
```

17.2.1 *CONTROL

*CONTROL, or its synonym *CBL, controls the printing of compiler listings. The statement is placed with one or more options in the source code beginning at column 7. The options available are SOURCE/NOSOURCE, MAP/NOMAP, and LIST/NOLIST. Each of these three parameters turns on or off the printing of the related compiler output from that point in the source. This can only have any effect if that output was requested as a compile option. Listing 17-1 shows two examples. The first case is an example of turning off all output for a file layout which might be a common piece of code. In the second case, the object code listing for one routine is desired.

```
    DATA DIVISION.
*CONTROL NOSOURCE NOMAP NOLIST
    COPY MASTFILE.
*CONTROL SOURCE MAP LIST

-----------------------------------------

    ID DIVISION.
*CONTROL NOLIST
    ...
    PROCEDURE DIVISION.
    ...
*CONTROL LIST
    5000-RATE-CALCULATION.
    ...
*CONTROL NOLIST
```

Listing 17-1   Using *CONTROL.

17.2.2 PROCESS

Compiler options may be coded in the source code using the PROCESS statement, or its synonym CBL. Any PROCESS statements must be coded at the beginning of the program before the Identification Division statement. The PROCESS statement does not use standard COBOL syntax, but appears more like JCL. The word PROCESS can appear anywhere in columns 1-72, possibly preceded by a COBOL sequence number. It must be followed by at least one space. Options can be separated by commas or blanks, but can have no embedded spaces. It is possible for an installation to disable the PROCESS statement. Listing 17-2 has an example of the PROCESS statement.

17.3 RULES FOR USE OF COMPILER OPTIONS

An installation will have default compiler options set. These may be the same as those IBM supply, or they may have been tailored at your site. Some of these defaults may be fixed, so that you cannot override them. Others can be overridden with the PARM statement in JCL or TSO, or with the PROCESS statement discussed above. The process statement overrides the PARM options.

In addition, certain options force others, as indicated below.

```
PROCESS LIST,MAP,FLAG(4,4)
     ID DIVISION.
     ...
```

Listing 17-2 PROCESS.

DYNAM   implies   RES

OFFSET   implies   NOLIST

RENT   implies   RES

TEST   implies   NOFDUMP
                          OBJECT
                          NOOPTIMIZE
                          RES

NOCOMPILE   implies   NODECK
                          NOFDUMP
                          NOLIST
                          NOOBJECT
                          NOOFFSET
                          NOOPTIMIZE
                          NOSSRANGE
                          NOTEST

17.4 RECOMMENDED COMPILER OPTIONS

The IBM default options are listed for each option in Appendix D. The following are recommendations for changes in those options, with justification. Of course, they will need review to compare with the needs and limitations of your site.

NOC(E)   Default is NOC(S), but E-level errors are sufficiently serious that they should all be corrected.

DYN   Use for batch and IMS programs, but not for CICS.

FDU   Use for production if you don't mind a slight performance degradation. Use for noninteractive testing.

FLAG(I, E)   Use this to get embedded error messages in the source listing. This is a useful feature once you get used to it, and really comes "for free"—it has little effect on listing size or compile time.

LIB   You may well want COPY statements.

MAP   You will want to use MAP on any compiles that are stored for reference, at a minimum.

OFF   You will want a condensed listing on compiles which are stored for reference.

OPT   Always use this.

RES   Always use this.

RENT   Always use this.

SSR   Use for development, but not for production.

NOSEQ   Unnecessary; sequence number checking is a holdover from card deck days.

TEST   Use for development, not production when using the COBTEST debugger.

NOTRU   This is generally safer.

X   A useful option on compiles that are stored for reference.

An alphabetic reference of all options is contained in Appendix D.

17.5   COMPILER OUTPUT

17.5.1   Compiler Message Codes

Compiler errors come in five categories: I, W, E, S, and U. See Table 17-1 for a description of these errors. You can use FLAG to control which of these messages you see.

Table 17-1   Compiler Errors.

Error Code	Return Code	Meaning
I Information	0	A hint or comment, not an error.
W Warning	4	Assumptions were made, or punctuation missing. Program may be correct.
E Error	8	Error Found. Compiler attempted to correct, but program is probably incorrect.
S Serious	12	Serious Error. Program is incorrect.
U Unrecoverable	16	Unrecoverable error. Compiler stopped.

17.5.2   Compiler Error Messages

You can create a list of all compiler error messages by compiling a program with the name ERRMSG. The program in Listing 17-3 is an example.

17.6   APPEARANCE OF OUTPUT OPTIONS

Figure 17-1 shows the first page of VS COBOL II compiler output. On this page, the compiler prints the options in effect. You may want to check this page against the options you set, since sometimes, owing to the way different methods of setting options interrelate, you may not get what you expect. The options chosen on this page are those which I generally use, except that I will turn on SSRANGE and TEST during debugging.

```
ID DIVISION.
PROGRAM-ID. ERRMSG.
ENVIRONMENT DIVISION.
DATA DIVISION.
PROCEDURE DIVISION.
    GOBACK.
```

Listing 17-3   Getting a Printout of All Error Messages.

```
*OPTIONS IN EFFECT*
  ADV
  APOST
  BUFSIZE(4096)
  NOCOMPILE(E)
  DATA(31)
  NODECK
  NODUMP
  DYNAM
  FASTSRT
  FDUMP
  FLAG(I,E)
  LIB
  LINECOUNT(60)
  NOLIST
  MAP
  NUMBER
  OBJECT
  OFFSET
  OPTIMIZE
  OUTDD(SYSOUX  )
  NOPFDSON
  RENT
  RESIDENT
  NOSEQUENCE
  SIZE(MAX)
  SOURCE
  SPACE(1)
  NOSSRANGE
  NOTERM
  NOTEST
  NOTRUNC
  NOVBREF
  NOWORD
  XREF
  ZWB
```

Figure 17-1   Compiler Options List.

17.6.1   VBREF Output

Figure 17-2 shows a page from the Verb cross-reference listing produced by the VBREF option. This is an alphabetic listing of the COBOL verbs used. On the left is a count of how many times each was used. On the right are the line number references for each verb.

```
COUNT   CROSS-REFERENCE OF VERBS        REFERENCES

   9    ADD. . . . . . . . . . . . . .  361 362 413 438 690 727 755 907 929
   2    CLOSE. . . . . . . . . . . . .  246 247
   4    DISPLAY. . . . . . . . . . . .  204 210 216 698
   1    EVALUATE . . . . . . . . . . .  886
   4    GOBACK . . . . . . . . . . . .  205 211 217 249
  57    IF . . . . . . . . . . . . . .  203 209 215 255 260 281 283 288 292 294 309 313 321 323 353 355 360 364 371 377
                                        384 395 399 400 417 422 423 437 449 453 457 488 501 503 521 532 543 552 572 628
                                        670 687 691 704 741 747 754 761 771 786 802 891 892 909 918 931 942
   1    INITIALIZE . . . . . . . . . .  679
   2    INSPECT. . . . . . . . . . . .  282 354
 143    MOVE . . . . . . . . . . . . .  225 226 227 231 232 233 234 235 236 257 258 264 265 267 269 284 289 290 306 310
                                        311 315 318 319 334 335 336 337 342 343 344 356 367 368 369 374 375 391 392 401
                                        405 414 419 426 430 439 442 450 454 465 466 467 472 473 489 490 491 504 505 512
                                        517 545 550 555 561 573 574 575 584 586 588 590 593 595 598 600 603 609 611 613
                                        617 618 629 630 631 640 641 643 645 648 658 659 661 663 666 680 681 694 717 722
                                        730 739 763 766 768 773 777 779 784 797 801 825 827 829 834 836 839 842 844 847
                                        851 855 856 862 866 867 872 874 882 888 894 898 902 903 906 911 919 922 926 928
                                        933 936 937
   2    OPEN . . . . . . . . . . . . .  197 198
 112    PERFORM. . . . . . . . . . . .  200 202 208 214 220 222 239 240 241 242 243 244 254 259 262 263 266 268 270 273
                                        280 285 291 293 300 308 312 314 320 322 328 365 370 372 376 378 385 387 389 394 399 407 415
                                        421 425 435 441 458 484 486 500 520 540 544 553 567 571 585 587 589 594 599 604
                                        608 610 612 614 615 619 624 627 642 644 646 652 660 662 664 668 672 682 686 688
                                        692 700 702 705 719 721 736 758 759 767 769 776 778 785 826 828 830 832 835 837
                                        838 843 848 852 853 857 863 864 868 873 876 884
   1    READ . . . . . . . . . . . . .  943
   2    SEARCH . . . . . . . . . . . .  650 696
  85    SET. . . . . . . . . . . . . .  228 229 230 237 261 295 307 316 324 338 339 340 341 345 346 347 351 357 396 420
                                        424 428 440 443 461 462 463 464 475 476 477 483 485 487 494 497 498 499 502 508
                                        511 518 519 522 523 525 526 527 528 533 542 546 551 556 557 569 570 577 625 626
                                        635 649 671 683 684 695 703 707 715 716 723 724 726 731 732 742 746 748 850 858
                                        861 869 875 885 945
  12    STRING . . . . . . . . . . . .  591 596 601 787 791 798 804 810 815 840 845 920
   1    SUBTRACT . . . . . . . . . . .  740
   2    UNSTRING . . . . . . . . . . .  402 469
   5    WRITE. . . . . . . . . . . . .  762 904 910 925 932
```

Figure 17-2   Verb Cross-Reference List.

```
◆N "M" PRECEDING A DATA-NAME REFERENCE INDICATES THAT THE DATA-NAME IS MODIFIED BY THIS REFERENCE.
DEFINED   CROSS-REFERENCE OF DATA NAMES   REFERENCES
  000083   BOX-LINE . . . . . . . . . .   000766 000768 000777 M000784 000787 M000787 000791 M000791 000798 000815 M000815
  000078   CAN-OET-NEW-LINE . . . . . .   M000420 M000424 M000440 000543
  000077   CAN-OET-NEW-LINE-SW. . . . .   M000414 M000561
  000166   CL-IX. . . . . . . . . . . .   000225 M000229 000232 000234 M000339 000356 M000357 000449 000450 M000463
                                          000466 000475 M000850 000853 000855 M000858
  000030   COBOL-COL-7. . . . . . . . .   000255 000281 000309 000353
  000032   COBOL-COL-8. . . . . . . . .   000255 000288 000364
  000021   COBOL-FILE . . . . . . . . .   000197 000246 000943
  000031   COBOL-REC-DATA . . . . . . .   000034 M000282 000283 000284 M000354 000355 000356 000360 000402 000469
  000028   COBOL-RECORD
  000167   COMMENT-DATA . . . . . . . .   M000232 M000356 M000466 000855
  000168   COMMENT-DELIM. . . . . . . .   M000225 M000234 M000450 000853
  000166   COMMENT-LINE
  000165   COMMENT-SPACE. . . . . . . .   M000335
  000072   COP-AX . . . . . . . . . . .   M000624 000624 000625 000628 000630 000631
  000072   COP-BX . . . . . . . . . . .   M000625 M000626 000627 000628 000629 000630 M000633
  000072   COP-IX . . . . . . . . . . .   M000307 000315 M000316 M000615 000615 000615 000617 000624 000627
  000071   COPY-ITEM. . . . . . . . . .   M000315 000615 000617 000628 000628 000629 000630 M000630 M000631
  000070   COPYBOOK-LIST. . . . . . . .   M000306
  000035   CR-IX. . . . . . . . . . . .   M000518 000520 000521 M000522 M000525 M000527 000540 M000542 000543 M000546
                                          000552 000553 000553 000555 M000557
  000035   CR-LETTER. . . . . . . . . .   000521 000540 000553 000555
  000065   DATA-DIV-FOUND . . . . . . .   000280 M000295
  000064   DATA-DIV-FOUND-SW
  000131   DISPLAY-NUMBER . . . . . . .   M000590 000591 M000595 000596 M000600 000601 M000839 000840 M000844 000845
  000179   EL-IX. . . . . . . . . . . .   000227 M000230 000233 000236 M000341 000347 000439 M000443 000453 000454
                                          M000464 000467 000477 M000861 000864 000866 M000869
  000076   END-OF-FILE. . . . . . . . .   000203 000209 000215 000222 000254 000280 000308 000543 000942 M000945
  000075   END-OF-FILE-SW
  000068   FIRST-PARA . . . . . . . . .   000400
  000066   FIRST-PARA-NAME. . . . . . .   M000402 000405 000650
  000067   FIRST-PARA-SW. . . . . . . .   M000401
  000002   OFPBDOC
  000130   HIGH-PL-IX . . . . . . . . .   M000237 000716 000731 M000732
  000122   INDENT-AMOUNT. . . . . . . .   M000265 M000593 M000598 M000603 M000618 M000842 M000847 M000856 M000867 000918
                                          000920 M000937
  000088   INDENT-LINE. . . . . . . . .   M000919 M000920 000922
  000121   INDENT-PIC . . . . . . . . .   000920
  000089   INDENT-PIC-TABLE . . . . . .   000120
  000141   LEVEL. . . . . . . . . . . .   M000680 000684 000686 M000690 000691 000694 000707 000736 000739 M000740 000741
                                          000742 000747 000748 000773 000785 000802
  000140   LEVEL-X
  000129   LINE-CTR . . . . . . . . . .   M000641 M000659 000761 M000763 M000907 000909 M000911 M000929 000931 M000933
  000172   LO-PARA
  000157   LOW-PROC
  000085   LP-CHAR. . . . . . . . . . .   000886 000892 000892
  000085   LP-IX. . . . . . . . . . . .   M000885 000886 000891 000891 000892 000892
  000084   LP-LINE. . . . . . . . . . .   M000766 M000777 M000926
  000086   LP-SUB . . . . . . . . . . .   M000884 000884 000885 000888 000894 000898
  000137   M-EXECS. . . . . . . . . . .   M000438 000595
  000136   M-LINES. . . . . . . . . . .   M000361 000590
  000138   M-PERFS. . . . . . . . . . .   M000413 000600
  000053   MAX-LEVEL. . . . . . . . . .   M000648 M000666 000691 000754 M000874
  000135   METRICS
```

Figure 17-3   XREF of Data Division Listing.

A glance at this page can indicate whether any verb has been used
in the program that is not according to installation standards. Also,
some people like to use metrics to determine a program's complexity
or style, and they may be able to use these numbers for that purpose. The page reproduced here has 112 PERFORMs and no GO
TOs. This may tell somebody something. Of course, for programs
with a preprocessor, like CICS, you are counting the code generated
by the preprocessor in these numbers.

17.6.2   XREF Output

Figure 17-3 shows a page from the Data Division cross-reference produced by the XREF option. This is a sorted cross-reference of data
names. On the left is the line number where the data-name is defined. On the right is every line number where it is referenced. If
this reference modifies the item (for example by moving data to it), it
is marked with an M.

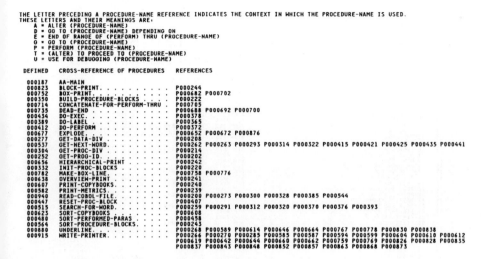

```
THE LETTER PRECEDING A PROCEDURE-NAME REFERENCE INDICATES THE CONTEXT IN WHICH THE PROCEDURE-NAME IS USED.
THESE LETTERS AND THEIR MEANINGS ARE:
     A = ALTER (PROCEDURE-NAME)
     D = GO TO (PROCEDURE-NAME) DEPENDING ON
     E = END OF RANGE OF (PERFORM) THRU (PROCEDURE-NAME)
     G = GO TO (PROCEDURE-NAME)
     P = PERFORM (PROCEDURE-NAME)
     T = (ALTER) TO PROCEED TO (PROCEDURE-NAME)
     U = USE FOR DEBUGGING (PROCEDURE-NAME)

DEFINED    CROSS-REFERENCE OF PROCEDURES    REFERENCES

  000187   AA-MAIN
  000823   BLOCK-PRINT. . . . . . . . .  P000244
  000752   BOX-PRINT. . . . . . . . . .  P000682 P000702
  000350   BUILD-PROCEDURE-BLOCKS . . .  P000222
  000714   CONCATENATE-FOR-PERFORM-THRU  P000705
  000735   DEAD-END . . . . . . . . . .  P000688 P000692 P000700
  000434   DO-EXEC. . . . . . . . . . .  P000378
  000389   DO-LABEL . . . . . . . . . .  P000365
  000412   DO-PERFORM . . . . . . . . .  P000372
  000677   EXPLODE. . . . . . . . . . .  P000652 P000672 P000876
  000277   GET-DATA-DIV . . . . . . . .  P000208
  000537   GET-NEXT-WORD. . . . . . . .  P000262 P000263 P000293 P000314 P000322 P000415 P000421 P000425 P000435 P000441
  000304   GET-PROC-DIV . . . . . . . .  P000214
  000252   GET-PROG-ID. . . . . . . . .  P000202
  000656   HIERARCHICAL-PRINT . . . . .  P000242
  000332   INIT-PROC-BLOCKS . . . . . .  P000220
  000782   MAKE-BOX-LINE. . . . . . . .  P000758 P000776
  000638   OVERVIEW-PRINT . . . . . . .  P000241
  000607   PRINT-COPYBOOKS. . . . . . .  P000240
  000582   PRINT-METRICS. . . . . . . .  P000239
  000940   READ-COBOL-FILE. . . . . . .  P000200 P000273 P000300 P000328 P000385 P000544
  000447   RESET-PROC-BLOCK . . . . . .  P000407
  000515   SEARCH-FOR-WORD. . . . . . .  P000259 P000291 P000312 P000320 P000370 P000376 P000393
  000623   SORT-COPYBOOKS . . . . . . .  P000608
  000564   SORT-PERFORMED-PARAS . . . .  P000458
  000356   SORT-PROCEDURE-BLOCKS. . . .  P000243
  000880   UNDERLINE. . . . . . . . . .  P000268 P000589 P000614 P000646 P000664 P000767 P000778 P000830 P000838
  000915   WRITE-PRINTER. . . . . . . .  P000266 P000270 P000285 P000585 P000587 P000594 P000599 P000604 P000610 P000612
                                         P000619 P000642 P000644 P000660 P000662 P000759 P000769 P000826 P000828 P000835
                                         P000837 P000843 P000848 P000852 P000857 P000863 P000868 P000873
```

Figure 17-4   XREF of Procedure Division Listing.

Figure 17-4 shows a page from the Procedure Division cross-reference, also produced by the XREF option. This has a similar layout to the Data Division cross-reference. It is a sorted cross-reference of procedure names (sections and paragraphs). On the left is the line number where the procedure name is defined. On the right is every line number where it is referenced. This number is tagged to indicate the type of reference. The meaning of these tags is printed at the top of the page. The most common are P, meaning it was the target of a PERFORM statement, and G, meaning it was the target of a GO TO. In the example printed, all the numbers are tagged P, which is a consequence of the style rules the program follows. These rules forbid the use of Alter, Go To Depending, Perform Thru, Go To, and Use for Debugging.

17.6.3   MAP Output

Figure 17-5 shows a page from the Data Division map. This is a rather complicated display. The location and properties of each item in the Data Division are listed in the order in which they were declared. From left to right, the page shows:

```
DATA DIVISION MAP
LINE     LEVEL NUMBER AND SOURCE NAME                    BASE      DISPL  STRCT DISP  DEFINITION   USAGE        R O D F
  21     FD COBOL-FILE. . . . . . . . . . . . . . . .              001                             QSAM              FB
  28     01 COBOL-RECORD. . . . . . . . . . . . . .     BLF=0000   000               DS 0CL80      GROUP
  29        02 FILLER. . . . . . . . . . . . . . .      BLF=0000   000    0 000 000  DS 6C         DISPLAY
  30        02 COBOL-COL-7 . . . . . . . . . . . .      BLF=0000   006    0 000 006  DS 1C         DISPLAY
  31        02 COBOL-REC-DATA. . . . . . . . . . .      BLF=0000   007    0 000 007  DS 0CL65      GROUP
  32           03 COBOL-COL-8 . . . . . . . . . .       BLF=0000   007    0 000 007  DS 1C         DISPLAY
  33           03 FILLER. . . . . . . . . . . . .       BLF=0000   008    0 000 008  DS 64C        DISPLAY
  34        02 FILLER. . . . . . . . . . . . . . .      BLF=0000   007    0 000 007  DS 0CL65      GROUP        R
  35           03 CR-LETTER . . . . . . . . . . .       BLF=0000   007    0 000 007  DS 1C         DISPLAY      O
  35              CR-IX . . . . . . . . . . . . .       IDX=0001   000                             INDEX-NAME
  36        02 FILLER. . . . . . . . . . . . . . .      BLF=0000   048    0 000 048  DS 8C         DISPLAY
  38     FD PRINT-FILE. . . . . . . . . . . . . . .                001                             QSAM              F
  43     01 PRINT-LINE. . . . . . . . . . . . . . .     BLF=0001   000               DS 0CL133     GROUP
  44        02 SKIP-CHAR . . . . . . . . . . . . .      BLF=0001   000    0 000 000  DS 1C         DISPLAY
  45        02 PRINT-DATA. . . . . . . . . . . . .      BLF=0001   001    0 000 001  DS 132C       DISPLAY
  48     01 PA-SIZE . . . . . . . . . . . . . . . .     BLW=0000   000               DS 4C         COMP
  49     01 W-PERFORM-AREA. . . . . . . . . . . . .     BLW=0000   008               DS 66C        DISPLAY
  50     01 PATTERN-ARRAY . . . . . . . . . . . . .     BLW=0000   050               DS 0CL10      GROUP
  51        02 PA-LETTER . . . . . . . . . . . . .      BLW=0000   050    0 000 000  DS 1C         DISPLAY      O
  51           PA-IX . . . . . . . . . . . . . . .      IDX=0002   000                             INDEX-NAME
  53     01 MAX-LEVEL . . . . . . . . . . . . . . .     BLW=0000   060               DS 2C         DISP-NUM
  54     01 READ-NEW-LINE-SW. . . . . . . . . . . .     BLW=0000   068               DS 1C         DISPLAY
  55        88 READ-NEW-LINE. . . . . . . . . . . .     BLW=0000   068    0 000 068
  56     01 WORD-FOUND-SW . . . . . . . . . . . . .     BLW=0000   070               DS 1C         DISPLAY
  57        88 WORD-FOUND. . . . . . . . . . . . .      BLW=0000   070    0 000 070
  58     01 PROG-ID-FOUND-SW. . . . . . . . . . . .     BLW=0000   078               DS 1C         DISPLAY
  59        88 PROG-ID-FOUND. . . . . . . . . . . .     BLW=0000   078    0 000 078
  60     01 SECTION-FOUND-SW. . . . . . . . . . . .     BLW=0000   080               DS 1C         DISPLAY
  61        88 SECTION-FOUND. . . . . . . . . . . .     BLW=0000   080    0 000 080
  62     01 PROC-DIV-FOUND-SW . . . . . . . . . . .     BLW=0000   088               DS 1C         DISPLAY
  63        88 PROC-DIV-FOUND. . . . . . . . . . .      BLW=0000   088    0 000 088
  64     01 DATA-DIV-FOUND-SW . . . . . . . . . . .     BLW=0000   090               DS 1C         DISPLAY
  65        88 DATA-DIV-FOUND. . . . . . . . . . .      BLW=0000   090    0 000 090
  66     01 FIRST-PARA-NAME . . . . . . . . . . . .     BLW=0000   098               DS 30C        DISPLAY
  67     01 FIRST-PARA-SW . . . . . . . . . . . . .     BLW=0000   0B8               DS 1C         DISPLAY
  68        88 FIRST-PARA. . . . . . . . . . . . .      BLW=0000   0B8    0 000 000
  70     01 COPYBOOK-LIST . . . . . . . . . . . . .     BLW=0000   0C0               DS 0CL800     GROUP
  71        02 COPY-ITEM . . . . . . . . . . . . .      BLW=0000   0C0    0 000 000  DS 8C         DISPLAY      O
  72           COP-IX. . . . . . . . . . . . . . .      IDX=0003   000                             INDEX-NAME
  72           COP-AX. . . . . . . . . . . . . . .      IDX=0004   000                             INDEX-NAME
  72           COP-BX. . . . . . . . . . . . . . .      IDX=0005   000                             INDEX-NAME
  73     01 NEXT-WORD . . . . . . . . . . . . . . .     BLW=0000   3E0               DS 0CL70      GROUP
  74        02 NEXT-LETTER . . . . . . . . . . . .      BLW=0000   3E0    0 000 000  DS 1C         DISPLAY      O
  74           NL-IX . . . . . . . . . . . . . . .      IDX=0006   000                             INDEX-NAME
  75     01 END-OF-FILE-SW. . . . . . . . . . . . .     BLW=0000   428               DS 1C         DISPLAY
  76        88 END-OF-FILE . . . . . . . . . . . .      BLW=0000   428    0 000 428
  77     01 CAN-GET-NEW-LINE-SW . . . . . . . . . .     BLW=0000   430               DS 1C         DISPLAY
  78        88 CAN-GET-NEW-LINE. . . . . . . . . . .    BLW=0000   430    0 000 430
  79     01 THREE-DASHES. . . . . . . . . . . . . .     BLW=0000   438               DS 3C         DISPLAY
  80     01 UL-CHARACTER. . . . . . . . . . . . . .     BLW=0000   440               DS 1C         DISPLAY
  81     01 UL-LINE . . . . . . . . . . . . . . . .     BLW=0000   448               DS 0CL133     GROUP
  82        02 UL-CHAR . . . . . . . . . . . . . .      BLW=0000   448    0 000 000  DS 1C         DISPLAY      O
  82           UL-IX . . . . . . . . . . . . . . .      IDX=0007   000                             INDEX-NAME
  83     01 BOX-LINE. . . . . . . . . . . . . . . .     BLW=0000   4D0               DS 132C       DISPLAY
  84     01 LP-LINE . . . . . . . . . . . . . . . .     BLW=0000   558               DS 0CL133     GROUP
  85        02 LP-CHAR . . . . . . . . . . . . . .      BLW=0000   558    0 000 000  DS 1C         DISPLAY      O
```

Figure 17-5   Data Division Map Listing.

LINE: The line number in the source code where the item is defined. This line number was not printed with OS COBOL, which showed an internal data-name in this place which was of no use.

LEVEL NUMBER AND SOURCE NAME: The level number and name of the item. The level number is not the same as that in the source code, but is normalized. If the source uses levels 01-05-10, this page will show 01-02-03. The level number is indented to make it easier to read, unlike OS COBOL.

BASE: The base locator, from which the displacement is calculated. This will often, but not always correspond to a register. BLF is a base locator for the File Section, BLW for Working Storage, and BLL for Linkage. Every 4K of storage needs another base locator. In OS COBOL terminology, these items were termed DCB, BL, and BLL, respectively.

DISPL: This is the displacement from the base of this data item, in hexadecimal.

STRCT DISP: The structure displacement. This is the displacement of the data item from the beginning of the structure in which it is contained (the 01 level). This information was not available in the OS COBOL DMAP listing.

DEFINITION: This is an Assembly language description of the data item. It has the same format as the definition field in the OS COBOL DMAP listing.

USAGE: This is a one-word description of the item loosely based on the COBOL USAGE value, extended to include a description for items like file names and group fields which do not have a USAGE.

Possible values are:

```
COMP
COMP-3
DISPLAY
DISP-NUM
GROUP
INDEX-NAME
QSAM
VSAM
```

R O D F: These fields indicate certain special cases. R flags items which are redefined. O is for items which have OCCURS clauses. D is for OCCURS DEPENDING ON items, and F gives the file attributes.

17.6.4   OFFSET Output

Figure 17-6 and 17-7 show two pages of the output generated by the OFFSET option. The first page includes the literal pool. At the very bottom of the page is the beginning of the offset listing, which represents the object code. It contains three values.

LINE #: This is the original line number from the source code.

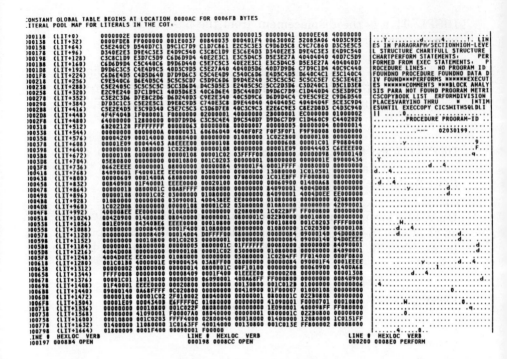

Figure 17-6   OFFSET Listing with Literal Pool. (Page 1 of 2)

HEXLOC: This is the object code address, in hexadecimal.

VERB: This is the first verb on that line.

The page is formatted in three columns. It should be read from left to right first, then down. An optimized program will have all line numbers in sequence, as they were in OS COBOL. The example page shows the effect of the optimizer on the object code. Performed paragraphs have been brought into line in the code, so that the line numbers are not sequential.

17.6.5   LIST Output

Figure 17-8 shows the first and last pages of the output generated by the LIST option for a small program. As the page numbers show,

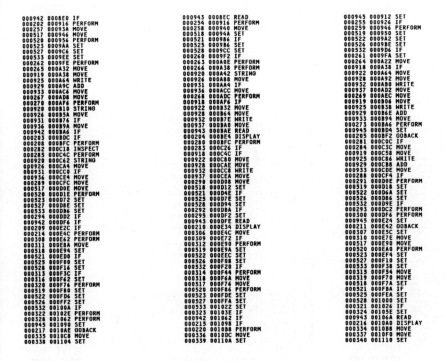

Figure 17-7   OFFSET Listing with Literal Pool. (Page 2 of 2)

there were 59 pages of output. The COBOL program listing was 14 pages long, so LIST output can get unmanageable very quickly.

17.6.6   Error Messages and Statistics

Figure 17-9 shows an example of the last page of a COBOL II listing, with error messages and program statistics. Error messages are identified by a source code line number and a Message Code, which includes a number and level. A table of these levels appears earlier in this chapter. The messages in this example are I and W level and are not reporting errors but giving information. The W level messages in this case are produced by the optimizer. It is common to get additional messages when this option is on.

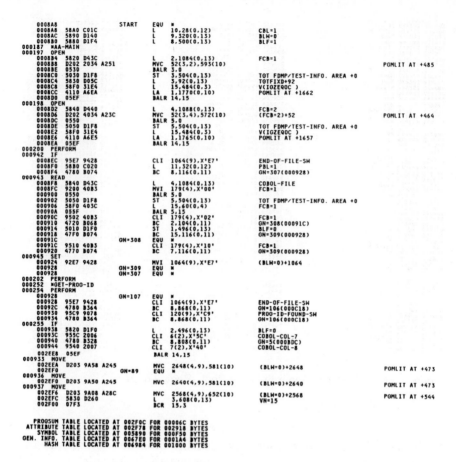

```
                            START  EQU  *
         0008A8  58A0 C01C          L    10,28(0,12)           CBL=1
         0008AC  5890 D140          L    9,320(0,13)           BLW=0
         0008B0  5880 D1F4          L    8,500(0,13)           BLF=1
000187   *AA-MAIN
000197   OPEN
         0008B4  5820 D43C          L    2,1084(0,13)          FCB=1
         0008B8  D202 2034 A251     MVC  52(3,2),593(10)                        PGMLIT AT +485
         0008BE  0530               BALR 3,0
         0008C0  5050 D1F8          ST   5,504(0,13)           TGT FDMP/TEST-INFO. AREA +0
         0008C4  5830 D05C          L    3,92(0,13)            TGTFIXD+92
         0008C8  58F0 31E4          L    15,484(0,3)           V(IOZEQOC )
         0008CC  4110 A6EA          LA   1,1770(0,10)          PGMLIT AT +1662
         0008D0  05EF               BALR 14,15
000198   OPEN
         0008D2  5840 D440          L    4,1088(0,13)          FCB=2
         0008D6  D202 4034 A23C     MVC  52(3,4),572(10)       (FCB=2)+52                       PGMLIT AT +464
         0008DC  0550               BALR 5,0
         0008DE  5050 D1F8          ST   5,504(0,13)           TGT FDMP/TEST-INFO. AREA +0
         0008E2  58F0 31E4          L    15,484(0,3)           V(IGZEQOC )
         0008E6  4110 A6E5          LA   1,1765(0,10)          PGMLIT AT +1657
         0008EA  05EF               BALR 14,15
000200   IF
000942   IF
         0008EC  95E7 9428          CLI  1064(9),X'E7'         END-OF-FILE-SW
         0008F0  58B0 C020          L    11,32(0,12)           PBL=1
         0008F4  4780 B074          BC   8,116(0,11)           GN=307(000928)
000943   READ
         0008F8  5840 D43C          L    4,1084(0,13)          COBOL-FILE
         0008FC  9200 40B3          MVI  179(4),X'00'          FCB=1
         000900  0550               BALR 5,0
         000902  5050 D1F8          ST   5,504(0,13)           TGT FDMP/TEST-INFO. AREA +0
         000906  58F0 403C          L    15,60(0,4)            FCB=1
         00090A  05FF               BALR 5,15
         00090C  9502 40B3          CLI  179(4),X'02'          FCB=1
         000910  4720 B068          BC   2,104(0,11)           GN=308(00091C)
         000914  5010 D1F0          ST   1,496(0,13)           BLF=0
         000918  47F0 B074          BC   15,116(0,11)          GN=309(000928)
         00091C        GN=308       EQU  *
         00091C  9510 40B3          CLI  179(4),X'10'          FCB=1
         000920  4770 B074          BC   7,116(0,11)           GN=309(000928)
000945   SET
         000924  92E7 9428          MVI  1064(9),X'E7'         (BLW=0)+1064
         000928        GN=309       EQU  *
         000928        GN=307       EQU  *
000202   PERFORM
000252   *GET-PROG-ID
000254   PERFORM
         000928        GN=107       EQU  *
         000928  95E7 9428          CLI  1064(9),X'E7'         END-OF-FILE-SW
         00092C  4780 B364          BC   8,868(0,11)           GN=106(000C18)
         000930  95C9 9078          CLI  120(9),X'C9'          PROG-ID-FOUND-SW
         000934  4780 B364          BC   8,868(0,11)           GN=106(000C18)
000255   IF
         000938  5820 D1F0          L    2,496(0,13)           BLF=0
         00093C  955C 2006          CLI  6(2),X'5C'            COBOL-COL-7
         000940  4780 B328          BC   8,808(0,11)           GN=5(000BDC)
         000944  9540 2007          CLI  7(2),X'40'            COBOL-COL-8
         002EE8  05EF               BALR 14,15
000933   MOVE
         002EEA  D203 9A58 A245     MVC  2648(4,9),581(10)     (BLW=0)+2648                     PGMLIT AT +473
         002EF0        GN=89        EQU  *
000936   MOVE
         002EF0  D203 9A50 A245     MVC  2640(4,9),581(10)     (BLW=0)+2640                     PGMLIT AT +473
000937   MOVE
         002EF6  D203 9A08 A28C     MVC  2568(4,9),652(10)     (BLW=0)+2568                     PGMLIT AT +544
         002EFC  5830 D260          L    3,608(0,13)           VN=15
         002F00  07F3               BCR  15,3

         PROGSUM TABLE LOCATED AT 002F0C FOR 00006C BYTES
       ATTRIBUTE TABLE LOCATED AT 002F78 FOR 002918 BYTES
          SYMBOL TABLE LOCATED AT 005890 FOR 000F50 BYTES
     GEN. INFO. TABLE LOCATED AT 0067E0 FOR 0001A4 BYTES
            HASH TABLE LOCATED AT 006984 FOR 001000 BYTES
```

Figure 17-8   LIST Option Listing.

```
LINEID  MESSAGE CODE   MESSAGE TEXT ( IMBEDDED MESSAGES MAY BE IDENTIFIED BY THE <*> PRECEDING THE MESSAGE CODE )

        IGYDS0015-I    DIAGNOSTIC MESSAGES WERE ISSUED DURING PROCESSING OF COMPILER OPTIONS. THESE MESSAGES ARE LOCATED AT THE
                       BEGINNING OF THE LISTING.

  919   IGYOP3115-W    WHEN COPIED IN-LINE FOR THE PERFORM STATEMENT AT < LINE 587.01 >, CODE FROM < "MOVE" (LINE 919.01) > TO <
                       "MOVE" (LINE 922.01) > WAS FOUND TO BE UNREACHABLE IN THAT CONTEXT AND WAS DELETED.

  919   IGYOP3115-W    WHEN COPIED IN-LINE FOR THE PERFORM STATEMENT AT < LINE 612.01 >, CODE FROM < "MOVE" (LINE 919.01) > TO <
                       "MOVE" (LINE 922.01) > WAS FOUND TO BE UNREACHABLE IN THAT CONTEXT AND WAS DELETED.


TOTAL MESSAGES    INFORMATIONAL    WARNING    ERROR    SEVERE    TERMINATING
      5                 2             2          0        0           0

* STATISTICS FOR COBOL PROGRAM GFPBDOC :
*    SOURCE RECORDS = 947
*    DATA DIVISION STATEMENTS = 97
*    PROCEDURE DIVISION STATEMENTS = 445
```

Figure 17-9   Errors and Statistics Listing.

18

Optimizing and Performance

In this chapter, we discuss some factors that impinge on the performance of programs. Several changes introduced in COBOL II have a bearing on this area, but bear in mind that high performance is not a simple thing to design. There is usually a set of desirable things wanted from a system. Examples of legitimate goals include:

- low response time
- high throughput
- rapid restart
- minimum impact on other systems
- low resource utilization
- low cost

Often (but not always) there is a trade-off between these goals. For example, logging all transactions will slow down a system but give better data integrity. Converting a batch system to on-line improves response time but consumes more system resources. Some code optimizations reflect these trade-offs; bringing performed paragraphs in-line may decrease the run time of a program but increase its size. Other optimizations, on the other hand, may have no trade-offs. Making a file smaller will both save on disk speed and make programs run faster. Taking constant expressions out of a loop speeds up a program with no ill effects.

18.1   IMPROVING PROGRAM PERFORMANCE

The improvements that the optimizer can make may bring speed gains of as much as 20–30%. This is in line with that achieved by third-party optimizer products with OS COBOL. To get really big improvements in run-time, you have to do something more basic, such as:

• change the basic algorithm of the program
• change the I/O strategy
• recode critical pieces in Assembly language

A simple example of changing a basic algorithm is replacing a linear search with a binary search (SEARCH ALL). This has a surprisingly large result. It is usually worth taking the trouble to order a table so that a binary search can be applied. The shell sort algorithm in Chapter 5 is another example of an improved algorithm—this runs orders of magnitude faster than the common bubble sort.

MVS/XA has changed the availability of memory. Any design trade-off involving memory should be reconsidered during conversion to COBOL II. You may be able to speed up some applications dramatically by using memory to cut out I/O, for instance. VSAM buffers could be enlarged, or files replaced by in-core areas.

When you measure programs with a performance monitor to determine where they spend their time, you generally find a few hot spots where nearly all the time is spent. These are often inside loops. The code in these spots can sometimes be speeded up after careful inspection, as in Listing 18-1, which shows a piece of code taken out of a loop. Such spots may even be candidates for tuning in Assembly language code. However, such steps are very drastic and should not be taken without obtaining timing figures to discover which areas of the program are taking the time. It is not fruitful to guess at this.

18.2   USING THE OPTIMIZER

Compared with the OS COBOL compiler, more code optimization is automatic with this compiler, including the code for table-handling and other addressing. To invoke the full optimization, use the OPTIMIZE (or OPT) compiler option. You will notice that most programs run with the optimizer will produce several warning messages. This is normal.

Before:

```
MOVE ZERO TO TOTAL
PERFORM VARYING I FROM 1 BY 1 UNTIL I > 10
   COMPUTE TOTAL = TOTAL + ITEM (I) * DISCOUNT
END-PERFORM
```

After Removing Multiply Code from Loop:

```
MOVE ZERO TO TOTAL
PERFORM VARYING I FROM 1 BY 1 UNTIL I > 10
   COMPUTE TOTAL = TOTAL + ITEM (I)
END-PERFORM
COMPUTE TOTAL = TOTAL * DISCOUNT
```

Listing 18-1   Removing Code from a Loop.

18.3 WHAT THE OPTIMIZER DOES

The optimizer eliminates unnecessary branches. These are not necessarily "GO TO"s and such which you coded, but assembler branches in the generated code. After each statement has been translated into assembler, there are often redundancies in the object code. The optimizer also simplifies code for a PERFORM statement. In OS COBOL, each PERFORM statement generated a lot of code to call and return from the subroutine. The optimizer is often able to bring the code for a performed paragraph in-line. In other cases, it can reduce the amount of code needed to call and return from the procedure to a couple of instructions.

The optimizer recognizes redundant calculations and eliminates them by saving the result of the first one and reusing it. It eliminates the evaluation of constants by doing them at compile-time. Constants are recognized if they are initialized with a VALUE clause and never updated in the program. It is often able to merge a series of contiguous move statements into a single assembler character move.

The optimizer can also recognize unreachable code and eliminate it, with a warning message. Sometimes such code is the result of repeated maintenance changes in old code, but this unreachable code does not have to be a mistake by the programmer. Code can be made unexecutable by earlier optimizations. Listing 18-2 shows an example of unreachable code. The optimizer has pulled the common subroutine "WRITE-PRINTER" in-line. In this context of PRINT-METRICS the branch in lines 919-922 cannot occur, because

```
000581**
000582**    PRINT-METRICS SECTION.                                          05690000
000583**    *  PRINT THE COUNTS                                             05700000
000584**       MOVE SPACES TO PRINT-DATA                                    05710000
000585**       PERFORM WRITE-PRINTER                                        05720000
000586**       MOVE 'PROGRAM METRICS' TO PRINT-DATA                         05730000
000587**       PERFORM WRITE-PRINTER                                        05740000
000588**       MOVE '=' TO UL-CHARACTER                                     05750000
000589**       PERFORM UNDERLINE                                            05760000
000590**       MOVE M-LINES TO DISPLAY-NUMBER                               05770000
000591**       STRING 'PROCEDURE LINES: ' DISPLAY-NUMBER                    05780000
000592**       DELIMITED BY SIZE INTO PRINT-DATA                            05790000
000593**       MOVE 4 TO INDENT-AMOUNT                                      05800000
000594**       PERFORM WRITE-PRINTER                                        05810000
000595**       MOVE M-EXECS TO DISPLAY-NUMBER                               05820000
000596**       STRING 'EXEC STATEMENTS: ' DISPLAY-NUMBER                    05830000
000597**       DELIMITED BY SIZE INTO PRINT-DATA                            05840000
000598**       MOVE 4 TO INDENT-AMOUNT                                      05850000
000599**       PERFORM WRITE-PRINTER                                        05860000
000600**       MOVE M-PERFS TO DISPLAY-NUMBER                               05870000
000601**       STRING 'PERFORM STATEMENTS: ' DISPLAY-NUMBER                 05880000
000602**       DELIMITED BY SIZE INTO PRINT-DATA                            05890000
000603**       MOVE 4 TO INDENT-AMOUNT                                      05900000
000604**       PERFORM WRITE-PRINTER.                                       05910000
000605**                                                                    05920000
000606**                                                                    05930000
000607**    PRINT-COPYBOOKS SECTION.                                        05940000
000608**       PERFORM SORT-COPYBOOKS                                       05950000
000609**       MOVE SPACES TO PRINT-DATA                                    05960000
000610**       PERFORM WRITE-PRINTER                                        05970000
000611**       MOVE 'COPYBOOK LIST' TO PRINT-DATA                           05980000
000612**       PERFORM WRITE-PRINTER                                        05990000
000613**       MOVE '=' TO UL-CHARACTER                                     06000000
000614**       PERFORM UNDERLINE                                            06010000
000615**       PERFORM VARYING COP-IX FROM 1 BY 1                           06020000
000616**       UNTIL COPY-ITEM (COP-IX) = HIGH-VALUES OR COP-IX > 99        06030000
000617**          MOVE COPY-ITEM (COP-IX) TO PRINT-DATA                     06040000
000618**          MOVE 4 TO INDENT-AMOUNT                                   06050000
000619**          PERFORM WRITE-PRINTER                                     06060000
000620**       END-PERFORM.                                                 06070000
000621**                                                                    06080000
000622**                                                                    06090000
000623**    SORT-COPYBOOKS SECTION.                                         06100000
000624**       PERFORM VARYING COP-AX FROM 1 BY 1 UNTIL COP-AX > COP-IX     06110000
000625**          SET COP-BX TO COP-AX                                      06120000
000626**          SET COP-BX UP BY 1                                        06130000
000627**          PERFORM UNTIL COP-BX > COP-IX                             06140000
000628**             IF COPY-ITEM (COP-BX) < COPY-ITEM (COP-AX)             06150000
000629**                MOVE COPY-ITEM (COP-BX) TO SWAP-COPY                06160000
000630**                MOVE COPY-ITEM (COP-AX) TO COPY-ITEM (COP-BX)       06170000
000631**                MOVE SWAP-COPY          TO COPY-ITEM (COP-AX)       06180000
000632**             END-IF                                                 06190000
000633**             SET COP-BX UP BY 1                                     06200000
000634**          END-PERFORM                                              06210000
000635**       END-PERFORM.                                                 06220000
000636**                                                                    06230000
000637**                                                                    06240000
000638**    OVERVIEW-PRINT SECTION.                                         06250000
                                                                            06260000
```

Listing 18-2   Optimization Example. (Page 1 of 4)

INDENT-AMOUNT has been set to zero. This code is eliminated.
The power of optimization is the way these improvements can build
on each other.

18.4 THE OPTIMIZER AND
STRUCTURED PROGRAMMING

The presence of the optimizer frees you to write code which is structured for easy reading and maintenance. With OS COBOL, programmers were often concerned about the costs of perform linkage. Use of
subroutines could also reduce locality of reference and cause virtual-
storage paging problems. With COBOL II, these concerns can be ignored and subroutines can be freely used to express the problem at
hand.

The optimizer will work best when used on programs with a
straightforward structured control flow. EVALUATE and the in-line

```
000871**                                                                            08350000
000872**              MOVE '***PERFORMS ***' TO PRINT-DATA                           08360000
000873**              PERFORM WRITE-PRINTER                                          08370000
000874**              MOVE 2 TO MAX-LEVEL                                            08380000
000875**              SET P-IX TO P2-IX                                             08390000
000876**              PERFORM EXPLODE                                               08400000
000877**          END-PERFORM.                                                      08410000
000878**                                                                            08420000
000879**                                                                            08430000
000880**      UNDERLINE SECTION.                                                    08440000
000881**  *   PRINT DASHES UNDER A LINE OF TEXT, IGNORING SPECIAL CHARACTERS08450000
000882**          MOVE SPACES TO UL-LINE                                            08460000
000883**                                                                            08470000
000884**          PERFORM VARYING LP-SUB FROM 1 BY 1 UNTIL LP-SUB > 132             08480000
000885**              SET LP-IX TO LP-SUB                                           08490000
000886**              EVALUATE LP-CHAR (LP-IX)                                      08500000
000887**                  WHEN '|'                                                  08510000
000888**                      MOVE '|'            TO UL-CHAR (LP-SUB)               08520000
000889**                  WHEN SPACE                                                08530000
000890**                      IF (LP-IX > 1 AND LP-IX < 132)                        08540000
000891**                          IF (LP-CHAR (LP-IX - 1) NOT = SPACE AND '-'       08550000
000892**                          AND LP-CHAR (LP-IX + 1) NOT = SPACE AND '-')      08560000
000893**                              MOVE UL-CHARACTER TO UL-CHAR (LP-SUB)         08570000
000894**                          END-IF                                           08580000
000895**                      END-IF                                               08590000
000896**                  WHEN OTHER                                                08600000
000897**                      MOVE UL-CHARACTER TO UL-CHAR (LP-SUB)                 08610000
000898**              END-EVALUATE                                                  08620000
000899**          END-PERFORM                                                       08630000
000900**                                                                            08640000
000901**                                                                            08650000
000902**          MOVE '-' TO UL-CHARACTER                                          08660000
000904**          MOVE UL-LINE TO PRINT-DATA                                        08670000
000905**          WRITE PRINT-LINE AFTER ADVANCING 1 LINES                          08680000
000906**                                                                            08690000
000907**          MOVE SPACES TO PRINT-DATA                                         08700000
000908**          ADD 1 TO LINE-CTR                                                 08710000
000909**                                                                            08720000
000910**          IF LINE-CTR > +55                                                 08730000
000911**              WRITE PRINT-LINE AFTER ADVANCING PAGE                         08740000
000912**              MOVE 1 TO LINE-CTR                                            08750000
000913**          END-IF.                                                           08760000
000914**                                                                            08770000
000915**                                                                            08780000
000916**      WRITE-PRINTER SECTION.                                                08790000
000917**  *   LOW-LEVEL I/O ROUTINE                                                 08800000
000918**  *   PRINT A LINE OF TEXT, IDENTED BY A GIVEN AMOUNT                       08810000
000919**          IF INDENT-AMOUNT > ZERO                                           08820000
000920**              MOVE SPACES TO INDENT-LINE                                    08830000
000921**              STRING INDENT-PIC (INDENT-AMOUNT) DELIMITED BY '*'            08840000
000922**                     PRINT-DATA DELIMITED BY SIZE INTO INDENT-LINE          08850000
000923**              MOVE INDENT-LINE TO PRINT-DATA                                08860000
000924**          END-IF                                                            08870000
000925**                                                                            08880000
000926**          WRITE PRINT-LINE AFTER ADVANCING NUMBER-LINES LINES               08890000
000927**          MOVE PRINT-DATA TO LP-LINE                                        09000000
000928**                                                                            08910000
000928**          MOVE SPACES    TO PRINT-DATA                                      08920000
```

Listing 18-2   Optimization Example. (Page 2 of 4)

PERFORM are preferred to alternatives using IF and subroutines. Paragraph names should be eliminated where possible. The optimizer cannot work effectively across paragraph names since it cannot be sure where the code branched in from. Backward branches should be minimized. The ALTER statement should be avoided, of course.

```
000929**              ADD NUMBER-LINES TO LINE-CTR                                  08930000
000930**                                                                            08940000
000931**              IF LINE-CTR > +55                                             08950000
000932**                  WRITE PRINT-LINE AFTER ADVANCING PAGE                     08960000
000933**                  MOVE 1 TO LINE-CTR                                        08970000
000934**              END-IF                                                        08980000
000935**                                                                            08990000
000936**              MOVE 1 TO NUMBER-LINES                                        09000000
000937**              MOVE 0 TO INDENT-AMOUNT.                                      09010000
000938**                                                                            09020000
000939**                                                                            09030000
000940**      READ-COBOL-FILE SECTION.                                              09040000
000941**  *   LOW-LEVEL I/O ROUTINE                                                 09050000
000942**          IF NOT END-OF-FILE                                                09060000
000943**              READ COBOL-FILE                                               09070000
000944**                  AT END                                                    09080000
000945**                      SET END-OF-FILE TO TRUE                               09090000
000946**              END-READ                                                      09100000
000947**          END-IF.                                                           09110000
```

Listing 18-2   Optimization Example. (Page 3 of 4)

```
LINEID  MESSAGE CODE   MESSAGE TEXT ( IMBEDDED MESSAGES MAY BE IDENTIFIED BY THE <#> PRECEDING THE MESSAGE CODE )
        IGYDS0015-I    DIAGNOSTIC MESSAGES WERE ISSUED DURING PROCESSING OF COMPILER OPTIONS. THESE MESSAGES ARE LOCATED AT THE
                       BEGINNING OF THE LISTING.
  919   IGYOP3115-W    WHEN COPIED IN-LINE FOR THE PERFORM STATEMENT AT < LINE 587.01 >, CODE FROM < "MOVE" (LINE 919.01) > TO <
                       "MOVE" (LINE 922.01) > WAS FOUND TO BE UNREACHABLE IN THAT CONTEXT AND WAS DELETED.
  919   IGYOP3115-W    WHEN COPIED IN-LINE FOR THE PERFORM STATEMENT AT < LINE 612.01 >, CODE FROM < "MOVE" (LINE 919.01) > TO <
                       "MOVE" (LINE 922.01) > WAS FOUND TO BE UNREACHABLE IN THAT CONTEXT AND WAS DELETED.

TOTAL MESSAGES    INFORMATIONAL    WARNING    ERROR    SEVERE    TERMINATING
      4                 2             2

# STATISTICS FOR COBOL PROGRAM OFPBDOC :
#   SOURCE RECORDS = 947
#   DATA DIVISION STATEMENTS = 97
#   PROCEDURE DIVISION STATEMENTS = 445
```

Listing 18-2   Optimization Example. (Page 4 of 4)

To find out exactly what the optimizer does to your program, you can use the LIST option with and without OPT and compare the results.

18.5   WHEN TO USE THE OPTIMIZER

It is generally preferable to run the optimizer on all programs in production. You will not want to use it during initial testing, however. First, the TEST option inhibits the optimizer, so if you are planning to use COBTEST you cannot use it. Second, use of the optimizer alters the code in ways that can make dumps harder to read. Optimized code does not print the line number of the failing statement on the formatted dump. Third, the additional compile time needed to optimize the program may not be desired.

You will, of course, want to test with the optimizer before going to production. There is a chance, albeit slim, that its use creates a bug in the program. There is a higher chance that use of the optimizer will shift storage use around and bring to light a bug that was not found in unoptimized testing. Either way, you will want to use OPT when compiling for preproduction Quality Assurance.

18.6   COMPILER OPTIONS FOR PERFORMANCE

The following are the compiler options to achieve maximum run-time performance:

```
FASTSRT
NOFDUMP
```

```
OPTIMIZE
PFDSGN
NOSSRANGE
NOTEST
NOTRUNC
```

Use of the FASTSRT option speeds up I/O on programs which include internal sorts that meet its limitations, but otherwise it has no impact. FDUMP brings about a substantial increase on program size, but hardly affects speed. OPTIMIZE has a substantial effect, of course, and should always be selected unless its use causes program errors, which is very unlikely. PFDSGN generates slightly faster code, but you have to ensure that the program does no group moves to numeric display fields. SSRANGE will slow any program considerably and can slow programs with extensive table-handling a hundredfold. TEST generates much extra code and turns off optimization. TRUNC has a small effect because it adds code when COMP fields are updated.

The SPOUT compiler option can be used to see how COBOL performed storage management for the program. After reviewing the output from this command, it is possible to change space allocations to tune a program.

18.7 SUMMARY OF PERFORMANCE IMPROVEMENTS

The VS COBOL II compiler has introduced several performance improvements over OS COBOL. Sharing library code between programs saves storage, and the bulk loading of these routines improves execution time also. COBOL II no longer has a copy of working storage in the load module. This saves on virtual storage use, particularly in CICS where most modules are resident. Support for extended addressing has relieved virtual storage constraints and made possible a general expansion of storage limits. CALL statements in CICS bring a performance improvement over CICS LINK and XCTL statements. The optimizer speeds up program execution and allows a fuller use of structured programming by removing some efficiency considerations that used to discourage it.

19

Conversion Issues
and Missing Features

In this chapter I have assembled all the changes which will cause problems when converting programs from OS COBOL to COBOL II. These changes are covered by category throughout the book, but I have brought them together here to assist maintenance programmers who have this job. Most of the work is caused by the missing features which have to be replaced.

There is sufficient cost and risk in making this conversion to discourage it unless there is a good reason. At present, one good reason is the use of extended memory. Another might be standardization on the COBOL II language for a new system. Any old code might be converted to fit in.

Some aids to conversion are available from IBM, and I will briefly describe these.

19.1 ISAM AND BDAM FILES

We will review the acronyms for IBM access methods at this point, before discussing which types are supported under COBOL II. QSAM stands for Queued Sequential Access Method, which is the IBM access method used to read standard sequential files. BDAM (Basic Direct Access Method) refers to the use of a form of relative-record organization where fixed-length records are stored at absolute positions in a file. ISAM (Indexed Sequential Access Method) is a form of keyed file where an index associates key values with the address of the record. The use of BDAM and ISAM in application programs is obsolete, although some IBM products still use them internally. VSAM (Virtual Storage Access Method) is the current set of methods for reading more complex file types, replacing BDAM and ISAM. There are three types of VSAM dataset:

Entry-sequenced (ESDS): records are added sequentially. Can be accessed sequentially, by absolute address, or by alternate index.

Relative-record (RRDS): fixed-size records are stored and retrieved by record number. Usually needs an application mechanism, such as hashing, to derive the record numbers.

Key-sequenced (KSDS): records are stored and retrieved using an index which associates their address with a key value.

COBOL II only supports the IBM file types VSAM and QSAM. OS COBOL applications which use BDAM or ISAM files cannot be wholly converted to COBOL II unless the files are first converted to VSAM. ISAM files should be converted to VSAM KSDS, and BDAM files to VSAM RRDS, or occasionally ESDS. IBM no longer supports the use of ISAM and BDAM files for application programs, so scheduling this conversion would be a good idea. In the meantime, the shop with these files must continue to use OS COBOL programs with these old files. The NOMINAL KEY and TRACK-AREA options of the FD statement referred to ISAM files and are no longer supported.

19.2   REPORT WRITER MODULE

The Report Writer is not supported by the VS COBOL II compiler, Releases 1.0, 1.1, and 2.0. Since the report writer is one of the modules in the ANSI standard, it is possible that some future release will support it. At the moment, you can use the IBM Report Writer precompiler program offering. This converts programs written to use Report Writer to COBOL II. This product can be used as a one-time aid to conversion, after which you would cease to use Report Writer.

Alternatively, it could be retained permanently as a preprocessor in the compile/link JCL. In programs which will not use the Report Writer precompiler, all Report Writer features are unsupported. These include the REPORT clause of the FD statement, the entire Report Section, the PAGE-COUNTER special register, and the following Procedure Division statements:

```
INITIATE
GENERATE
TERMINATE
SUPPRESS
USE BEFORE REPORTING
```

19.3 COMMUNICATIONS MODULE

The VS COBOL II compiler, Releases 1.0, 1.1, and 2.0, does not support the ANSI Communications Module. Since this is one of the modules in the ANSI 1974 and 1985 standards, it is possible that some future release will support it. Fortunately, this module is very rarely used in COBOL programs written for IBM mainframes. All Communications features are unsupported in COBOL II. These include the entire Communication Section and the following Procedure Division statements:

```
ACCEPT MESSAGE COUNT
DISABLE
ENABLE
PURGE
RECEIVE
SEND
```

19.4 STRING-HANDLING

The two string-handling verbs EXAMINE and TRANSFORM have been deleted. Programs using EXAMINE and TRANSFORM will have to be re-written to use INSPECT instead. Unfortunately, in OS COBOL EXAMINE and TRANSFORM were preferred to INSPECT because they were more efficient and could be used under CICS. This change can lead to a lot of coding effort in programs which process text strings.

19.4.1 EXAMINE Deleted

The EXAMINE statement has been removed from COBOL II. It was not in the ANSI 1974 or 1985 standards, and can be easily replaced by INSPECT, which is in the standard. The INSPECT verb is much more powerful than EXAMINE, because it can search and replace strings as well as characters. The examples in Listing 19-1 show the replacement use of INSPECT for every possible case of EXAMINE. In the simplest and most common cases, substitution of the verb name is sufficient. Notice that when TALLYING options are used, EXAMINE replaces the contents of the special register TALLY. INSPECT adds to the contents of the user-defined variable *cnt*. You can use TALLY as this variable if you choose, but I wouldn't recommend it. TALLY is not in the ANSI standard, and was omitted from early releases of VS COBOL II. The INSPECT coding is more flexible, but relies on you to initialize the count variable.

19.4.2 TRANSFORM Deleted

The TRANSFORM statement has also been removed from COBOL II because it was not in the ANSI 1974 or 1985 standards. IBM recommends that, like EXAMINE, you replace it with INSPECT, as in Listing 19-2.

19.4.3 INSPECT and Release 3.0

Release 3.0 allows the INSPECT statement to name several characters to be replaced. It also supports a new format for INSPECT, which is:

```
INSPECT string CONVERTING chars-1 TO chars-2
```

If you are using Release 3.0, you can replace TRANSFORM statements with INSPECT . . . RPLACING or INSPECT . . . CONVERTING.

19.4.4 INSPECT Prior to Release 3.0

If you are using an earlier release of the compiler, the new formats of INSPECT are not yet available to you. There is no easy way to

```
EXAMINE source TALLYING UNTIL FIRST char-1

MOVE ZERO TO cnt
INSPECT source TALLYING cnt FOR CHARACTERS BEFORE INITIAL char-1

EXAMINE source TALLYING ALL char-1

MOVE ZERO TO cnt
INSPECT source TALLYING cnt FOR ALL char-1

EXAMINE source TALLYING LEADING char-1

MOVE ZERO TO cnt
INSPECT source TALLYING cnt FOR LEADING char-1

EXAMINE source TALLYING UNTIL FIRST char-1 REPLACING BY char-2

MOVE ZERO TO cnt
INSPECT source TALLYING cnt FOR CHARACTERS BEFORE INITIAL char-1
       REPLACING CHARACTERS BY char-2 BEFORE INITIAL char-1

EXAMINE source TALLYING ALL char-1 REPLACING BY char-2

MOVE ZERO TO cnt
INSPECT source TALLYING cnt FOR CHARACTERS
       REPLACING CHARACTERS BY char-2

EXAMINE source TALLYING LEADING char-1 REPLACING BY char-2

MOVE ZERO TO cnt
INSPECT source TALLYING cnt FOR LEADING char-1
       REPLACING LEADING char-1 BY char-2

EXAMINE source REPLACING ALL char-1 BY char-2

INSPECT source REPLACING ALL char-1 BY char-2

EXAMINE source REPLACING LEADING char-1 BY char-2

INSPECT source REPLACING LEADING char-1 BY char-2

EXAMINE source REPLACING FIRST char-1 BY char-2

INSPECT source REPLACING FIRST char-1 BY char-2

EXAMINE source REPLACING UNTIL FIRST char-1 BY char-2

INSPECT source REPLACING ALL char-1 BY char-2
       BEFORE INITIAL char-1
```

Listing 19-1   INSPECT and EXAMINE.

```
          TRANSFORM W-STRING FROM CHAR-1 TO CHAR-2
          INSPECT W-STRING REPLACING CHAR-1 BY CHAR-2
```

Listing 19-2   Single-Character TRANSFORM and INSPECT.

convert most TRANSFORM statements to an INSPECT statement. This is because TRANSFORM operated on a group of characters, translating them all, but INSPECT only works on one. You must code an INSPECT statement for each character, or write a loop as in Listing 19-3. In Listing 19-2, it is easy to replace a single-character TRANSFORM statement with an INSPECT statement. In

```
OS COBOL:

      DATA DIVISION.
      01  CHARS-1    PIC X(26) VALUE
'ABCDEFGHIJKLMNOPQRSTUVWXYZ'.
      01  CHARS-2    PIC X(26) VALUE
'ALGORITHMSBCDEFJKNPQUVWXYZ'.
      01  W-STRING          PIC X(500).


      PROCEDURE DIVISION.

          TRANSFORM W-STRING FROM CHARS-1 TO CHARS-2

COBOL II:

      DATA DIVISION.
      01  CHARS-1    PIC X(26) VALUE
'ABCDEFGHIJKLMNOPQRSTUVWXYZ'.
      01  FILLER REDEFINES CHARS-1.
        02  CHAR-1          PIC X OCCURS 26.
      01  CHARS-2    PIC X(26) VALUE
'ALGORITHMSBCDEFJKNPQUVWXYZ'.
      01  FILLER REDEFINES CHARS-2.
        02  CHAR-2          PIC X OCCURS 26.
      01  W-STRING          PIC X(500).


      PROCEDURE DIVISION.

          PERFORM VARYING CH-SUB FROM 1 BY 1
          UNTIL CH-SUB > LENGTH OF CHARS-1
              INSPECT W-STRING REPLACING ALL CHAR-1 (CH-SUB)
                          BY CHAR-2 (CH-SUB)
          END-PERFORM.
```

Listing 19-3   Multicharacter TRANSFORM and INSPECT.

```
OS COBOL:

    DATA DIVISION.
    01  IN-DATE  PIC X(08) VALUE '53/08/17'.
    01  OUT-DATE PIC X(08).


    PROCEDURE DIVISION.

        MOVE 'DA/MO/YR' TO OUT-DATE
        TRANSFORM OUT-DATE FROM 'YR/MO/DA' TO IN-DATE
        DISPLAY OUT-DATE.

COBOL II:

    DATA DIVISION.
    01  IN-DATE  PIC X(08) VALUE '53/08/17'.
    01  FILLER REDEFINES IN-DATE.
        02  YY        PIC X(02).
        02  S-1       PIC X.
        02  MM        PIC X(02).
        02  S-2       PIC X.
        02  DD        PIC X(02).
    01  OUT-DATE PIC X(08).
    01  FILLER REDEFINES OUT-DATE.
        02  MM        PIC X(02).
        02  S-1       PIC X.
        02  DD        PIC X(02).
        02  S-2       PIC X.
        02  YY        PIC X(02).


    PROCEDURE DIVISION.

        MOVE CORR IN-DATE TO OUT-DATE
        DISPLAY OUT-DATE.
```

Listing 19-4   Tricky Use of TRANSFORM.

Listing 19-3, a multicharacter TRANSFORM statement is replaced by an execution of INSPECT for each character in the string. Listing 19-3 works with all versions of COBOL II, but can be replaced by a single statement in Release 3.0.

Listing 19-4 contains a tricky use of TRANSFORM to reduce the amount of code in a date formatting routine. It illustrates that rather than replace the statement with a loop as in the previous example, it may be more appropriate to determine the intention of the program and rewrite it.

Table 19-1   Formats and Usage of Date and Time Fields.

Register	Picture	Format	Example
CURRENT-DATE	PIC X(8)	mm/dd/yy	12/25/89
TIME-OF-DAY	PIC 9(6)	hhmmss	123000
DATE	PIC 9(6)	yymmdd	891225
TIME	PIC 9(8)	hhmmssff	12300000

19.5 DATE AND TIME CHANGES

The special registers CURRENT-DATE and TIME-OF-DAY, which were IBM extensions, have been removed. Instead, you should use the ACCEPT verb with DATE and TIME. The implied formats of DATE and TIME are slightly different, however, as demonstrated in Table 19-1. There may be a need to rearrange the code as in Listing 19-5.

19.6 MISCELLANEOUS MISSING FEATURES

19.6.1 REMARKS

The REMARKS paragraph has been deleted. Simply replace this with asterisks in column 7. While you're at it, you could comment out everything else in the ID DIVISION except PROGRAM-ID. The ANSI committee has agreed that all of the comment paragraphs are obsolete, and will be deleted from COBOL at some later date. Your ID DIVISION would then look like Listing 19-6.

19.6.2 NOTE

The NOTE paragraph has been deleted. This statement was both unnecessary and dangerous, since it was easy to accidentally comment out executable code. You should simply comment out any NOTE paragraphs with asterisks in column 7.

```
OS COBOL:

    DATA DIVISION.
    01  W-DATE  PIC X(08).
    01  W-TIME  PIC 9(06).

    PROCEDURE DIVISION.

        MOVE CURRENT-DATE TO W-DATE
        MOVE TIME-OF-DAY  TO W-TIME.



COBOL II:

    DATA DIVISION.
    01  W-DATE  PIC X(08).
    01  W-TIME  PIC 9(06).
    01  INTERNAL-DATE.
        02  YY        PIC XX.
        02  MM        PIC XX.
        02  DD        PIC XX.

    01  INTERNAL-TIME.
        02  HH        PIC XX.
        02  MM        PIC XX.
        02  SS        PIC XX.
        02  FILLER    PIC XX.
    01  INTERNAL-TIME-9 REDEFINES INTERNAL-TIME PIC 9(08).

    01  EXTERNAL-DATE.
        02  MM        PIC XX.
        02  FILLER    PIC X VALUE '/'.
        02  DD        PIC XX.
        02  FILLER    PIC X VALUE '/'.
        02  YY        PIC XX.

    01  EXTERNAL-TIME  PIC X(06).

    PROCEDURE DIVISION.

        ACCEPT INTERNAL-DATE   FROM DATE
        MOVE CORR INTERNAL-DATE TO EXTERNAL-DATE

        ACCEPT INTERNAL-TIME-9 FROM TIME
        MOVE INTERNAL-TIME TO EXTERNAL-TIME.
```

Listing 19-5 Converting Dates.

```
ID DIVISION.
PROGRAM-ID.      ...
*AUTHOR.          ...
*INSTALLATION.    ...
*DATE-WRITTEN.    ...
*DATE-COMPILED.   ...
*SECURITY.        ...
```

Listing 19-6   Recommended ID DIVISION.

19.6.3   OTHERWISE

The OTHERWISE clause is no longer accepted on the IF statement. It should simply be replaced by ELSE.

19.6.4   POSITIONING

The AFTER POSITIONING option is no longer accepted on the WRITE statement. Use of AFTER POSITIONING must be replaced with AFTER ADVANCING. The positioning option has been removed because it was a nonstandard IBM extension. Also, its main purpose was to control printer channels, which are now obsolete.

The positioning option can be a little confusing. You could either code an integer value or the name of a one-character variable in the POSITIONING clause. If you coded an integer, 0 meant a new page and 1,2,3 meant advance one, two or three lines, respectively. If you coded a variable, you placed one from a quite different set of values in this variable. Table 19-2 summarizes the values used in the OS COBOL POSITIONING clause. You can convert the integer form of positioning by replacing the word POSITIONING with ADVANCING and any occurrence of 0 with PAGE, as in Table 19-3.

Conversion from the other form of the POSITIONING statement, using a character variable, is more complicated. This is because in COBOL II "WRITE AFTER PAGE" must be a separate statement from "WRITE AFTER 1." Also, any references to channels other than one must be converted by using SPECIAL-NAMES to define the channels. Such references probably need inspection to determine whether they have a meaning with the printers on the system where they will run.

Table 19-2   Values of WRITE AFTER POSITIONING.

-------- POSITIONING --------

Integer Value	Variable Value	Meaning
0	1	new page (skip to channel 1)
1	space	single-space
2	0	double-space
3	-	triple-space
	+	no space (over-strike)
	2-9,A,B,C	skip to channel 2 thru 12

19.6.5   Changing CICS Programs

To upgrade CICS programs to COBOL II you must, in addition to the COBOL changes already mentioned, change the addressing mechanism for Linkage Section items. Not all programs will require this—those programs which have nothing in the Linkage Section but "DFHCOMMAREA" may not be affected. Besides the changes which are required, there are other points you may wish to review while making the conversion.

The changes you must make to CICS programs are:

• Remove the entire record (the 01-level and all levels below it) defining BLL cells from the LINKAGE SECTION.
• Remove all SERVICE RELOAD statements.
• Change every CICS statement from SET(*bll-cell*) to SET(ADDRESS OF . . .).
• Remove all arithmetic for addressing involving multiples of 4096.

Table 19-3   Replacing POSITIONING Integer.

Replace	With
POSITIONING 0	ADVANCING PAGE
POSITIONING 1	ADVANCING 1
POSITIONING 2	ADVANCING 2
POSITIONING 3	ADVANCING 3

The changes which are optional but preferred are:

• Remove artificial assignments (e.g., MOVE LINE-COUNT TO LINE-COUNT) intended to fix Occurs Depending On.
• Review decisions on memory usage, such as using linkage or working storage for storage of map and file layouts.

Programs which work intimately with the CICS Base Locator for Linkage (BLL) mechanism, such as code dealing with chained storage, will need to be extensively rewritten. Fortunately, such programs are rare.

19.7   MISSING FEATURES IN EARLY VERSIONS

The early versions (1.0 and 1.1) of VS COBOL II were missing some features which were reintroduced in Release 2. This book assumes that you are using Release 2.0 or later, but if for some reason you have an earlier release you should be aware of this. Also, you may meet programs which do some strange things to avoid using these features because they were not available when they were written. The following OS COBOL features were missing in VS COBOL II 1.0 and 1.1 but restored in 2.0:

• Floating-Point numbers (COMP-1 and COMP-2)
• Exponentiation (X ** Y)
• TALLY special register
• SORT special registers
• Nested Occurs-Depending-On
• Abbreviated relational conditions (see below)

19.7.1   Abbreviated Relational Conditions

In Releases 1.0 and 1.1, the use of parentheses to alter the order of evaluation of abbreviated conditions was no longer allowed. This meant that certain complicated expressions had to be recoded more explicitly for the COBOL II compiler. The implicit term in the relational conditions must be reinserted. Listing 19-7 gives some examples of conditions that were not supported and their suggested replacements.

Certain features introduced with COBOL II changed since the early releases also. In Release 1.0, the EVALUATE statement did

Abbreviated condition not supported:

```
TAX-AMT MINIMUM-TAXABLE OR (AMT-EARNED AND AMT-UNEARNED)
```

Replace this with:

```
TAX-AMT  MINIMUM-TAXABLE
OR (TAX-AMT  AMT-EARNED AND AMT-UNEARNED)
```

Abbreviated condition not supported:

```
TAX-BRACKET  (MINIMUM-TAXABLE OR SPECIAL-LIMIT)
AND AMT-EARNED
```

Replace this with:

```
(TAX-BRACKET MINIMUM-TAXABLE OR SPECIAL-LIMIT)
AND TAX-BRACKET  AMT-EARNED
```

Abbreviated condition not supported:

```
TAX-BRACKET (= SPECIAL-LIMIT OR  MINIMUM-TAXABLE)
```

Replace this with:

```
TAX-BRACKET = SPECIAL-LIMIT
OR TAX-BRACKET  MINIMUM-TAXABLE
```

Abbreviated condition not supported:

```
TAX-BRACKET = SPECIAL-LIMIT AND ( MIN-TAX OR  MAX-TAX)
```

Replace this with:

```
TAX-BRACKET = SPECIAL-LIMIT AND
(TAX-BRACKET  MIN-TAX OR  MAX-TAX)
```

Listing 19-7   Unsupported Relational Conditions in COBOL II Early Releases.

not have an ALSO clause. DBCS support has changed over different releases. The compiler option GRAPHIC, which specified alternate shift-in and shift-out characters for the Double Byte Character Set, has been dropped in Release 2. Earlier references to this character set as EGCS have been largely deleted also, except on the Initialize statement. For a look at further changes which are coming, see Chapter 20.

19.8 MIGRATION AIDS

IBM makes available some products which help to convert programs from OS COBOL to COBOL II. The VS COBOL II Migration Guide is a publication which will assist in converting COBOL programs. The COBOL and CICS/VS Command Level Conversion Aid (5785-ABJ) converts CICS BLLs and SERVICE RELOADS to valid COBOL II. The COBOL Conversion Aid (5785-AAT) is a set of programs which run under ISPF to convert individual COBOL language elements. The Report Writer precompiler, which was mentioned previously, will convert programs which use the Report Writer feature into standard COBOL II. These products are not expensive; none is over ten thousand dollars. This is a trivial cost compared to the cost of programming and testing the conversion, much of which cannot be automated, and retraining.

The MIGR option of the OS COBOL compiler (Release 2.4) will flag statements that will be problems under COBOL II, although this option will not find every syntax problem. That is something you can do prior to the installation of COBOL II.

COBOL/SF (program 5668-786) is a restructuring tool. You may want to consider this if you have a lot of old, unstructured code in your installation. It only works on VS COBOL II, so you will have to make the conversion first by other means. There are versions of this type of product available from other vendors which also support OS/VS COBOL.

19.9 ASSESSING THE CONVERSION

Conversion to COBOL II is best done on an application system basis. In this way, you can maintain a family resemblence between programs which share files and other resources and are probably worked on by the same group of people. In this way, problems caused by differences in data and file types can be avoided. Examples of these problems are pointers in files and nested copy statements. It is possible to convert individual programs in a system, or to leave a few unconverted, if special requirements dictate. It is quite possible to combine OS COBOL and COBOL II programs, even to link them together. Chapters 8, 10, and 13 explain the call statement, CICS, and MVS/XA issues in this. Some of the deleted COBOL features are support for obsolete hardware and system software. Examples are ISAM files, printer channels, console displays, and multireel tape files. Applications which use these features will need review to determine their role in a more modern environment.

A conversion should consider the new COBOL II features to be included. These are covered throughout the book. The new features are not mandatory, and can be inserted at leisure, although they may be the reason for the conversion. Deleted OS COBOL features to be replaced were covered in this chapter; the bulk of the conversion effort will deal with these.

19.9.1 Programming Standards

It will be worthwhile to review the programming standards of the installation. Some rules will have been established because of limitations in COBOL which have now been eliminated. Examples might be blanket prohibitions on nested IFs or requiring each I/O statement to be in separate paragraphs. New features should be positively encouraged in the standards, too.

19.9.2 The Benefits of Conversion

Compared with OS COBOL, there are some unique features of COBOL II that may make its adoption a foregone conclusion for you. Some installations took it up immediately to solve their virtual storage constraints. If you need to write programs to manipulate Japanese or Korean language strings, the choice is simple. Some sites may have planned new applications which will rely on the increased compiler limits.

Most COBOL shops will not find the decision so simple. There are benefits, but they must be weighed against the costs of conversion. The structured programming features make the language easier to use, particularly for today's computer science students, trained in languages like Pascal and C. A third to half of the COBOL programs written for IBM mainframes today run under CICS. These will be substantially easier to code in COBOL II, because they are more like normal COBOL. This will eventually reduce training costs.

Several COBOL II changes offer features that were previously obtained from third-party vendors at additional cost. Among these are the improved compiler output, symbolic debugging, symbolic dump, and optimization.

OS COBOL has been functionally stabilized. New features will not be added, but we can expect it to be supported for many years. There is no pressing need to convert applications which are stabilized themselves. On the other hand, you will not want to write a large new application today in a language that has no future. The decision must be made on a case-by-case basis.

Some installations waited for the new release of COBOL II, which fully supports the ANSI 1985 standard and SAA. The next chapter explains the features that are available in Release 3.0.

20

Release 3 Features

In Chapter 1, I mentioned the ANSI standard and IBM's Systems Application Architecture as driving forces behind the introduction of VS COBOL II. The VS COBOL II compiler does not support either of these standards fully in Release 2, but Release 3 does. It incorporates all required modules for the high level of the ANSI 1985 standard. It is a superset of the Systems Application Architecture (SAA) standard, but by using the new FLAGSAA option you can identify elements which are not portable under SAA.

With the complete introduction of the SAA and ANSI 1985 features to VS COBOL II, program portability is greatly enhanced. Some users will take advantage of this to move programs to and from different machinery, including the IBM AS/400 and PS/2 and other mini- and microcomputers. Tandem and DEC have ANSI 1985 compilers, for instance.

There are some changes in Release 3 which can affect the run-time operation of programs. There are two compiler options which can be used to assist you in recognizing these changes. The COMPR2 option causes programs to behave as if compiled under Release 2. The FLAGMIG option generates warning messages for the situations which cause problems. The NOCMPR2 guarantees full ANSI compatibility.

The examples in the first 19 chapters of this book compile and execute correctly under Release 2, or under Release 3 with the

COMPR2 option. Examples in this chapter require Release 3 with the NOCMPR2 to compile and execute correctly.

20.1 PROGRAM APPEARANCE

Two changes introduced in Release 3 have a dramatic effect on the appearance of programs. The results are perhaps off-putting at first to the experienced programmer. However, when you examine them, neither change is of great significance.

First, programs can now be written in a mixture of upper- and lowercase. The compiler accepts both and ignores case. It is the trend with modern languages to allow mixed-case text, and it seems reasonable because research shows that people find it easier to read mixed-case or lowercase text than uppercase. It is, of course, an optional feature.

Secondly, division headers are now optional. The ID DIVISION is required, but the other three do not have to be coded if there is nothing in the division. Most serious programs will still have all four divisions, with the exception that CICS programs generally do not need an Environment Division. Listing 20-1 shows minimal programs in COBOL II Release 2 and Release 3.

20.2 DATA HANDLING

20.2.1 Class Conditions

In VS COBOL II Release 2, the class test ALPHABETIC is only satisfied by uppercase alphabetic characters and spaces. In Release 3, both upper- and lowercase characters and spaces will satisfy an alphabetic test. New class conditions Alphabetic-Upper and Alphabetic-Lower are introduced. The available class conditions in COBOL II Release 3 are:

```
NUMERIC
ALPHABETIC
ALPHABETIC-LOWER
ALPHABETIC-UPPER
user-defined-class

DBCS
KANJI
```

```
IDENTIFICATION DIVISION.
PROGRAM-ID. COBOLII.
ENVIRONMENT DIVISION.
DATA DIVISION.
PROCEDURE DIVISION.
    DISPLAY 'I AM COBOL II RELEASE 2'.

Identification Division.
Program-Id. COBOL85.
Procedure Division.
    Display 'I am Cobol II Release 3'.
```

Listing 20-1   Simple Programs in COBOL II Release 2 and Release 3.

Release 3 allows user-defined class conditions. Such a class can be any combination of alphanumeric characters chosen by the programmer. The class is defined in the CLASS statement of the SPECIAL-NAMES paragraph. Listing 20-2 shows an example of a user-defined class condition. Notice that unlike a condition-name, it can be used on any display field without further definition.

20.2.2   Changes to INSPECT and MOVE

Release 3 supports a new format of the INSPECT statement which is similar to the old TRANSFORM statement. This is INSPECT . . . CONVERTING, as illustrated in Listing 20-3.

Release 3 also permits two new MOVE statement combinations. You can now move data from a floating-point field to an alphanumeric field, and from a numeric-edited field to a numeric field. The second case is very useful for accepting user input into programs.

20.2.3   Reference Modifications

Release 3 introduces the idea of reference modification. This enables data areas, which are substrings of existing data-names, to be defined. This can be done at run-time and without any additional code in the Data Division.

The format of a reference modification is:

```
Data-name(start:length)
```

```
ENVIRONMENT DIVISION.
SPECIAL-NAMES.
    CLASS VOWEL IS 'A' 'E' 'I' 'O' 'U'.

DATA DIVISION.
01  FIELD-A      PIC X(12).
01  FIELD-B      PIC X.

PROCEDURE DIVISION.
    IF FIELD-A VOWEL OR FIELD-B VOWEL
        . . .
```

Listing 20-2   User-Defined Class.

Data-name can be any defined alphanumeric or display numeric data-name, including subscripts if appropriate. Start and length can be integer literals, variables, or arithmetic expressions. Start should be between 1 and the length of the data-item. Length plus start should not go beyond the end of the data-item. Listing 20-4 gives examples of reference modification. This feature brings a tremendous advance in sophistication to COBOL string-handling.

20.2.4   Accept from Day-Of-Week

A new form of the ACCEPT statement is available in Release 3. This is "ACCEPT FROM DAY-OF-WEEK." Day-of-Week acts like a field with usage PIC 9. It contains a value from 1 (Monday) to 7 (Sunday). This should remove much of the need for routines to calculate the day of the week from the date.

```
*  -- CONVERT INPUT-STRING FROM LOWER-CASE TO UPPER-CASE
INSPECT INPUT-STRING CONVERTING 'abcdefghijklmnopqrstuvwxyz'
                          TO 'ABCDEFGHIJKLMNOPQRSTUVWXYZ'
```

Listing 20-3   INSPECT CONVERTING.

```
DATA DIVISION.
01  IN-DATE  PIC X(08) VALUE '53/08/17'.
01  OUT-DATE PIC X(08).

PROCEDURE DIVISION.

    MOVE IN-DATE(4:2) TO OUT-DATE(1:2)
    MOVE '/'          TO OUT-DATE(3:1)
    MOVE IN-DATE(7:2) TO OUT-DATE(4:2)
    MOVE '/'          TO OUT-DATE(6:1)
    MOVE IN-DATE(1:2) TO OUT-DATE(7:2)

    DISPLAY OUT-DATE
```

Listing 20-4   Reference Modification.

20.2.5 The REPLACE Statement

Release 3 introduces the REPLACE statement. This operates similarly to the REPLACING option on the copy statement, but over the
whole program. This enables a programmer to code constant values,
then use a REPLACE statement to change them. Listing 20-5, which
is a COBOL translation of a well-known C program, is an example of
this.

20.3   CONTROL STRUCTURE CHANGES

20.3.1 Negated Conditional Statements

Negated forms of conditional statements such as AT END are available in COBOL II Release 3. These can improve program structure
by removing the need to set a switch. These negated conditional
statements are:

```
NOT AT END
NOT INVALID KEY
NOT ON OVERFLOW
NOT ON SIZE ERROR
NOT END-OF-PAGE
```

Listing 20-6 gives an example of the use of these.

```
Id Division.
Program-Id. REPLACE1.
REPLACE
     ==BOTTOM==    BY ==0==
     ==TOP==       BY ==300==
     ==INTERVAL== BY ==20==
Data Division.
01  FAHRENHEIT     PIC S9(08) BINARY.
01  CELSIUS        PIC S9(08) BINARY.

Procedure Division.
  PERFORM VARYING FAHRENHEIT FROM BOTTOM BY INTERVAL
  UNTIL FAHRENHEIT > TOP
      COMPUTE CELSIUS = (5.0 / 9.0) * (FAHRENHEIT - 32)
      DISPLAY FAHRENHEIT, ' ===> ' CELSIUS
  END-PERFORM.
```

Listing 20-5   Using REPLACE in COBOL II Release 3.

```
        PROCEDURE DIVISION.

            PERFORM UNTIL END-OF-FILE
                READ MASTER-FILE
                AT END
                    SET END-OF-FILE TO TRUE
                NOT AT END
                    PERFORM PROCESS-RECORD
                END-READ
            END-PERFORM
            ...
            WRITE VSAM-RECORD
            INVALID KEY
                PERFORM ERROR-ROUTINE
            NOT INVALID KEY
                ADD 1 TO RECORDS-WRITTEN
            END-WRITE
            ...
            WRITE PRINT-LINE
            END-OF-PAGE
                PERFORM HEADER-ROUTINE
                MOVE 5 TO LINE-COUNT
            NOT END-OF-PAGE
                ADD 1 TO LINE-COUNT
            END-WRITE
            ...
```

Listing 20-6   Negated Conditional Statements.

20.4   IMPROVEMENTS TO TABLE-HANDLING

Release 3 supports tables of up to seven dimensions. In other words, an element of a table can have up to seven subscripts or indexes. The previous limit was three.

Release 3 also supports relative references using subscripts. Relative references are expressions like (X + 1) or (X - 1). In previous versions, only indexes could be coded with relative references.

Finally, in Release 3 you can specify a VALUE clause on items in tables. Each occurrence of that item in the table will then have the same value.

20.5   CHANGES THAT ARE SYNONYMS

The new reserved words BINARY and PACKED-DECIMAL in Release 3 are synonyms for COMP (or COMP-0) and COMP-3, respectively.

The condition tests GREATER THAN OR EQUAL and LESS THAN OR EQUAL, or their abbreviations >= and <=, are allowed in Release 3. These are equivalent to NOT LESS THAN and NOT GREATER THAN, but some people find them easier to read.

The word FILLER is optional in Release 3. In other words, the two record layouts in Listing 20-7 are equivalent.

```
DATA DIVISION.
01   PAYROLL-RECORD.
     02   PAY-NUMBER       PIC X(08).
     02   FILLER           PIC X(10).
     02   PAY-NAME         PIC X(40).
     02   FILLER           PIC X(04).
     02   PAY-CLASS        PIC X.
     02   FILLER           PIC X(37).


01   PAYROLL-RECORD.
     02   PAY-NUMBER       PIC X(08).
     02                    PIC X(10).
     02   PAY-NAME         PIC X(40).
     02                    PIC X(04).
     02   PAY-CLASS        PIC X.
     02                    PIC X(37).
```

Listing 20-7   Filler Is Optional.

20.6 NESTED PROGRAMS

The nested program feature of Release 3 can lead to a substantial change in the manner of writing COBOL programs. Release 3 also introduces some major changes in the area of interprogram communication. While the COBOL CALL statement has long allowed programs to be split up into separate small units, most installations have in practice relied on the PERFORM statement to split programs up instead. While the PERFORM statement modularizes the Procedure Division, it leaves a single monolithic Data Division. This large Data Division is a characteristic of many production COBOL programs which makes them very difficult to understand and modify.

On the other hand, the CALL statement is difficult to use because it involves the management of separate source files. These files are joined together by the linkage editor, and there is no parameter checking performed. Errors caused by conflicting parameter values can be difficult to find. Also, while the CALL statement enforces a strict separation of data between program modules, it is too strict. There is no mechanism for defining global data or files which can be accessed by any module without parameter passing.

Release 3 allows programs to be nested inside each other. This nesting can be several levels deep. Listing 20-8 gives an example of nested programs in Release 3.

In Release 3, there are new ways to pass data between programs. Programs which are nested within others can access data items and files which are declared as GLOBAL in any of the programs in which they are contained. Data items and files can also be declared as EXTERNAL. This means that one copy is stored in the run unit external to any program module and accessible by all of then. A program in Release 3 can access and change data which has been passed by reference on a call statement, declared as GLOBAL in a containing program, or declared as EXTERNAL in any other program in the run unit. Listing 20-9 gives simple examples of passing data by means of EXTERNAL and GLOBAL variables. PROGRAM2 is internal to PROGRAM1 and shares a GLOBAL variable. PROGRAM3 is compiled separately and linked into the run unit, and shares an EXTERNAL variable.

A facility is provided in Release 3 to declare a program as a common sub-routine accessible from any module in the run-unit. Another facility lets you declare that a program should be placed in an initial state every time it is called. CALL BY CONTENT is extended to work on any variable, not just a constant or LENGTH OF.

```
ID DIVISION.
PROGRAM-ID. PROGRAM1.
ENVIRONMENT DIVISION.
DATA DIVISION.
WORKING-STORAGE SECTION.
01  AMOUNT          PIC 9(12)V99        VALUE 1000000.00.
01  INTEREST-RATE   PIC S99V9(06) COMP VALUE 11.5.
01  DAYS-AHEAD      PIC S9(08)    COMP VALUE 200.
01  DISCOUNT-AMOUNT PIC 9(12)V99.

PROCEDURE DIVISION.
    MOVE AMOUNT TO DISCOUNT-AMOUNT
    CALL 'DISCOUNT' USING  DISCOUNT-AMOUNT
                    BY CONTENT DAYS-AHEAD
                    BY CONTENT INTEREST-RATE
    DISPLAY AMOUNT,
            DISCOUNT-AMOUNT,
            INTEREST-RATE,
            DAYS-AHEAD
    GOBACK.


ID DIVISION.
PROGRAM-ID. PROGRAM2.
DATA DIVISION.
WORKING-STORAGE SECTION.
01  FLOAT-DAYS          COMP-2.
01  DISCOUNT-FACTOR     COMP-2.

LINKAGE SECTION.
01  DAYS               PIC S9(08) COMP.
01  RATE               PIC S9(04)V9(04) COMP.
01  AMOUNT             PIC 9(12)V99.

PROCEDURE DIVISION USING AMOUNT,
                         DAYS,
                         INTEREST.

    ADD 1 TO RATE
    MOVE DAYS TO FLOAT-DAYS
    DIVIDE FLOAT-DAYS BY 365
    COMPUTE DISCOUNT-FACTOR = RATE ** FLOAT-DAYS
    DIVIDE AMOUNT BY DISCOUNT-FACTOR
    GOBACK.
END PROGRAM PROGRAM2.

END PROGRAM PROGRAM1.
```

Listing 20-8   Nested Programs in COBOL II Release 3.

```
ID DIVISION.
PROGRAM-ID. PROGRAM1.
DATA DIVISION.
WORKING-STORAGE SECTION.
01   A1   PIC S9(9) BINARY GLOBAL.
01   A2   PIC S9(9) BINARY EXTERNAL.
PROCEDURE DIVISION.
        MOVE 20 TO A1
        CALL "PROGRAM2"
        MOVE A1 TO A2
        CALL "PROGRAM3"
        DISPLAY A1 A2
*****  PROGRAM WILL DISPLAY    120   620
        GOBACK

ID DIVISION.
PROGRAM-ID. PROGRAM2.
DATA DIVISION.
WORKING-STORAGE SECTION.
PROCEDURE DIVISION.
        ADD 100 TO A1.
END PROGRAM PROGRAM2.
END PROGRAM PROGRAM1.

ID DIVISION.
PROGRAM-ID. PROGRAM3.
DATA DIVISION.
WORKING-STORAGE SECTION.
01   A2   PIC S9(9) BINARY EXTERNAL.
PROCEDURE DIVISION.
        ADD 500 TO A2.
END PROGRAM PROGRAM3.
```

Listing 20-9   Passing Data Between Programs in COBOL II Release 3.

In Release 3, it is possible to pass parameters, which are not defined at the 01 or 77 levels, to a called program. This eliminates some unnecessary MOVE statements.

Like many of the other new features we have seen, these communication facilities were available in other languages. The form of nested programming adopted here is very similar to that in PL/I.

20.7 SUMMARY: RELEASE 3 AND SAA

The changes introduced in this chapter were introduced to VS COBOL II because they are part of the ANSI standard. Program portability will be greatly improved. The class condition enhancements and INSPECT . . . CONVERTING assist text string handling a little, and the reference modification is a tremendous improvement. The negated conditional statements and SET . . . TO FALSE clean up the structured features of the language. The facilities for interprogram communication will take a little time to learn, but they provide a clean mechanism for modular programming.

Syntax Reference

All the new statements and all the significant syntax changes introduced with COBOL II are to the Procedure Division. This appendix includes a complete syntax reference for the Procedure Division. All changes to the other divisions are included in Chapter 6.

NOTATION OF THE DIAGRAMS

The notation used is derived from that used by IBM in the latest DB2 and SAA manuals. The diagrams should be read from left to right, top to bottom, in accordance with the direction of the arrows. Each statement ends with a block marker. Required elements appear on the main path. Optional items appear below it.

Where there are several elements to choose from, they appear one above the other, in a stack. If you must choose at least one item, the stack begins on the main path. If choosing an element is optional, the stack appears below the main path.

An arrow looping back means that an element can be repeated. An arrow over a stack may also mean that several choices can be made from the stack.

COBOL key words appear in capital letters. User-supplied variable names appear in lowercase, and are described as one of:

```
identifier
literal
item
imperative-statement
arithmetic-expression
condition
condition-name
relation-condition
```

It is very important to understand how these terms are defined, as the meaning is not always clear from the word itself. For example, the term imperative-statement does not refer only to a single statement, but can refer to a group of statements, including conditional statements with scope terminators.

The syntax diagrams are complete for COBOL Release 2, except that certain synonym words (e.g., CORR = CORRESPONDING) and some "noise" words (optional words that have no semantic effect) have been omitted to improve clarity.

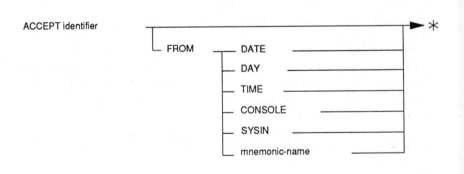

Figure A-1

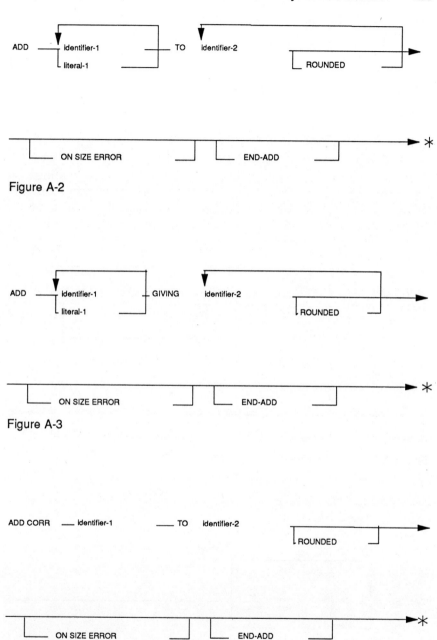

Figure A-2

Figure A-3

Figure A-4

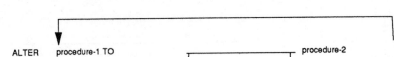

Figure A-5

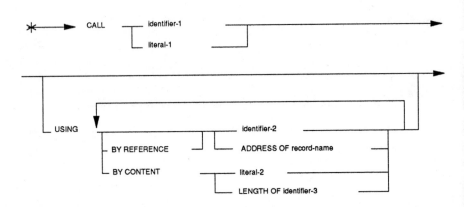

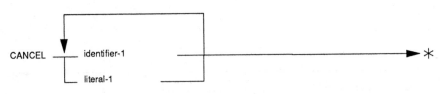

Figure A-6

Figure A-7

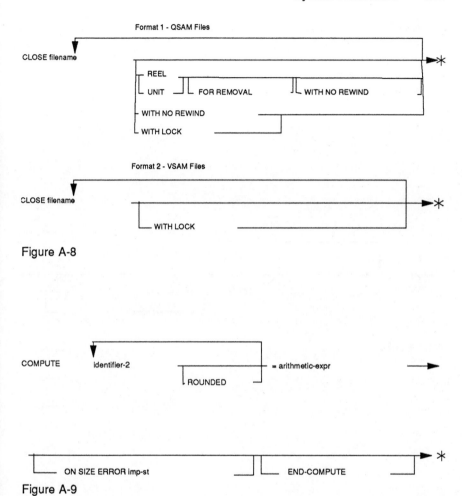

Format 1 - QSAM Files

CLOSE filename

REEL
UNIT — FOR REMOVAL — WITH NO REWIND
WITH NO REWIND
WITH LOCK

Format 2 - VSAM Files

CLOSE filename

WITH LOCK

Figure A-8

COMPUTE   identifier-2   ROUNDED   = arithmetic-expr

ON SIZE ERROR imp-st   END-COMPUTE

Figure A-9

CONTINUE

Figure A-10

Figure A-11

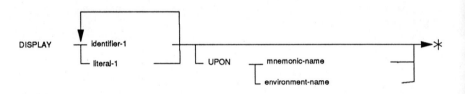

Figure A-12

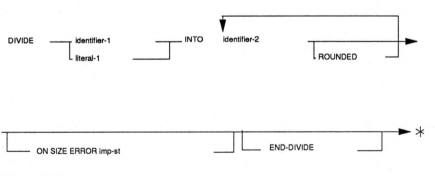

Figure A-13

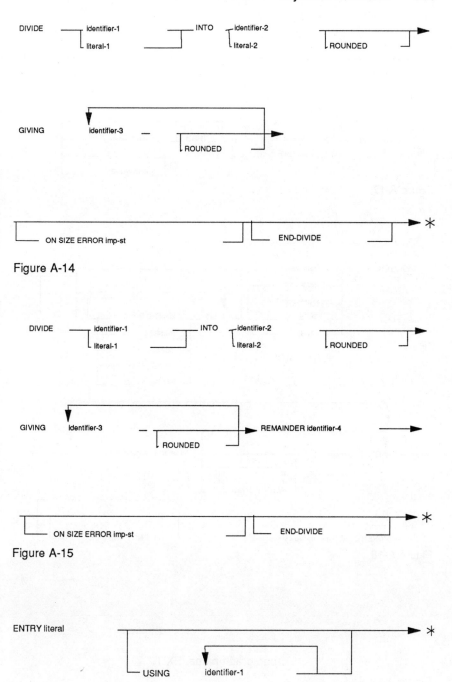

Figure A-14

Figure A-15

Figure A-16

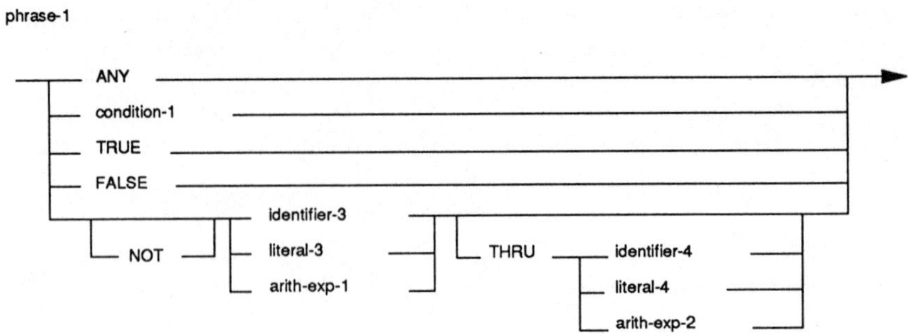

phrase-1

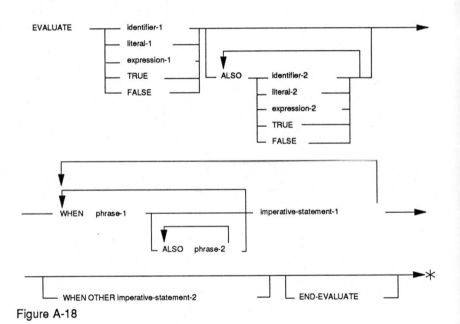

Figure A-17

Figure A-18

paragraph-name. EXIT.

Figure A-19

paragraph-name. EXIT PROGRAM.

Figure A-20

GOBACK ⟶ ✳

Figure A-21

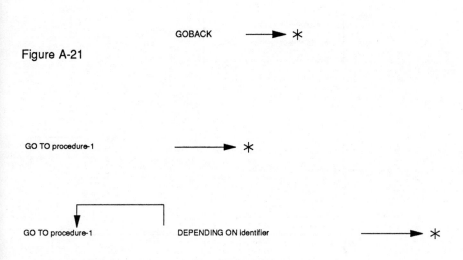

GO TO procedure-1 ⟶ ✳

GO TO procedure-1   DEPENDING ON identifier ⟶ ✳

GO TO ⟶ ✳

Figure A-22

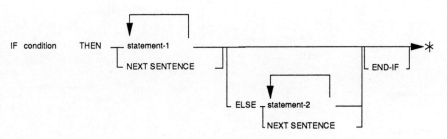

IF condition   THEN ⌐ statement-1 ⟶ ✳
                  └ NEXT SENTENCE ┘   └ END-IF ┘
                              └ ELSE ⌐ statement-2
                                      └ NEXT SENTENCE ┘

Figure A-23

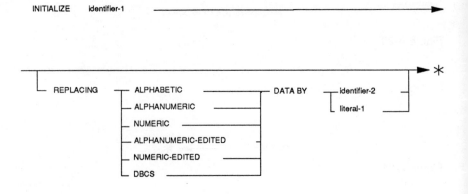

Figure A-24

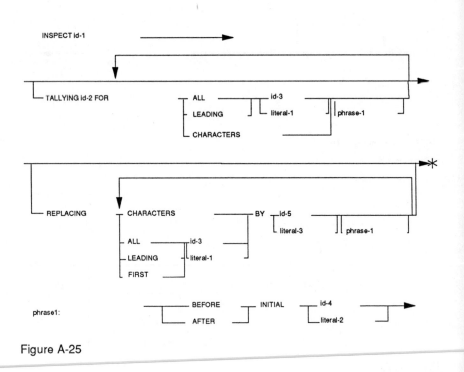

Figure A-25

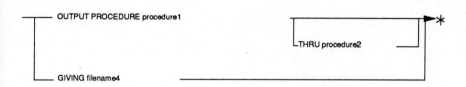

Figure A-26

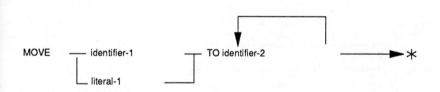

Figure A-27

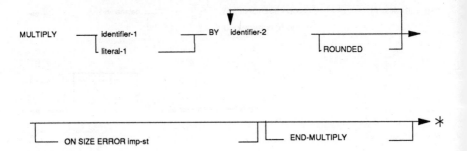

Figure A-28

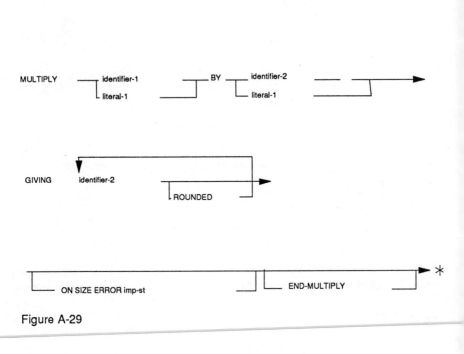

Figure A-29

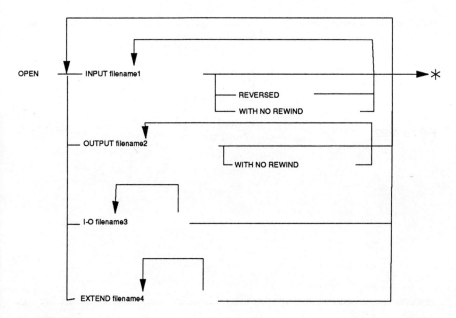

OPEN ─── INPUT filename1 ────────────────► *

REVERSED
WITH NO REWIND

OUTPUT filename2

WITH NO REWIND

I-O filename3

EXTEND filename4

Figure A-30

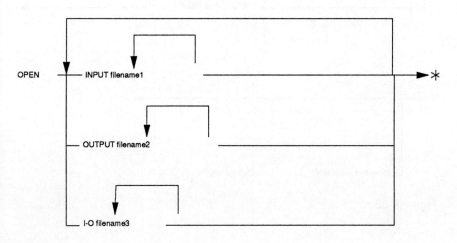

OPEN ─── INPUT filename1 ────────────────► *

OUTPUT filename2

I-O filename3

Figure A-31

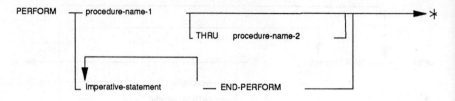

Figure A-32

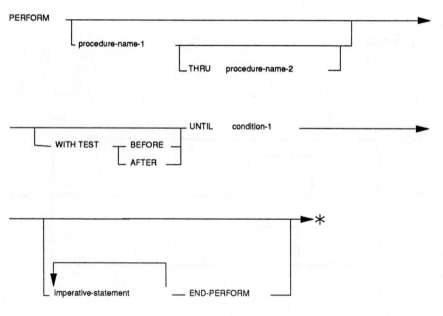

Figure A-33

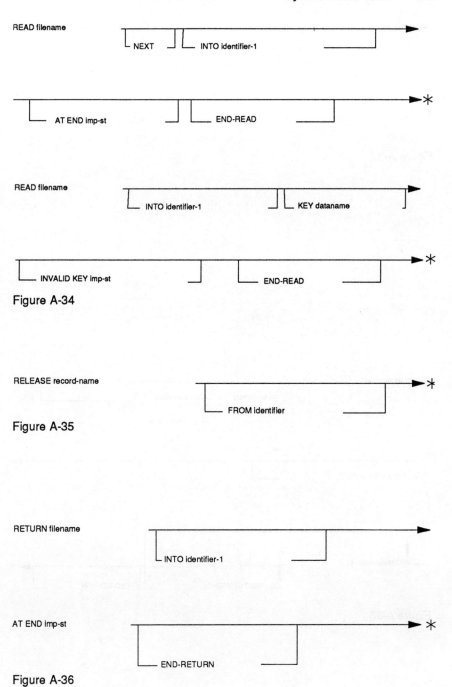

Figure A-34

Figure A-35

Figure A-36

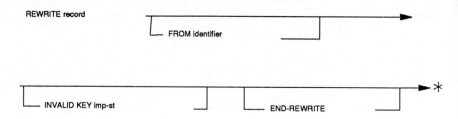

Figure A-37

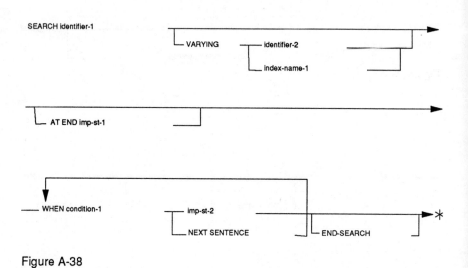

Figure A-38

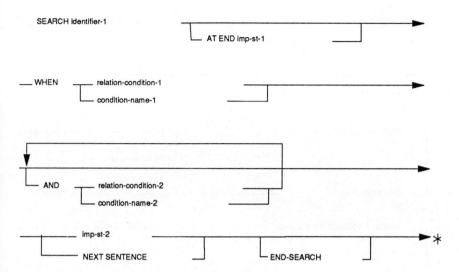

Figure A-39

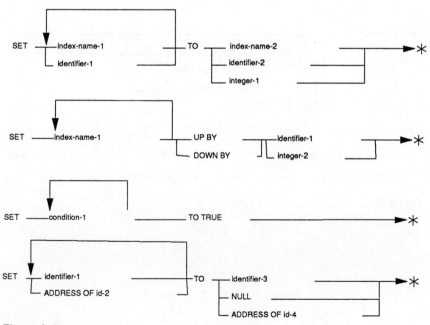

Figure A-40

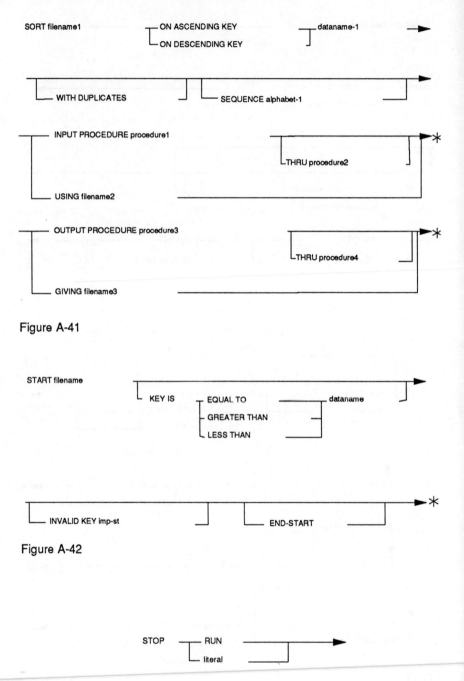

Figure A-41

Figure A-42

Figure A-43

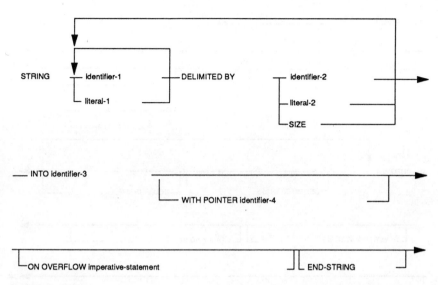

Figure A-44

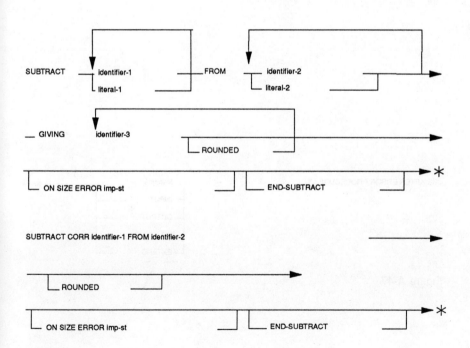

Figure A-45

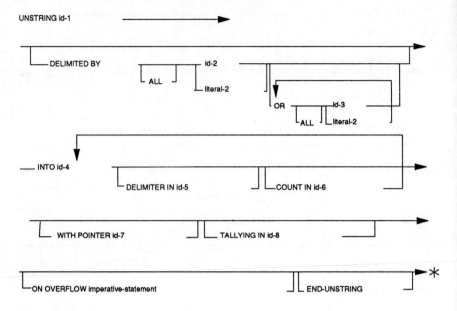

Figure A-46

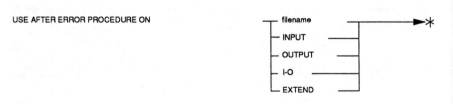

Figure A-47

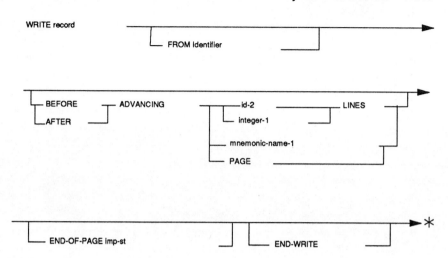

Figure A-48

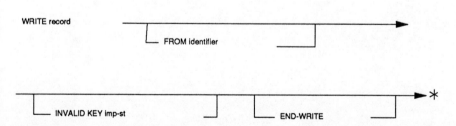

Figure A-49

B

Comparison to OS COBOL

The following tables compare the language elements of OS/VS
COBOL Release 2, Language Level 2, to those of VS COBOL II. Only
those elements which have changed in some way are listed.

The tables are divided by division and section. COBOL II does not
have a Communication Section or Report Section.

ID DIVISION

Language Element	OS COBOL	COBOL II	Comments
REMARKS	Y	N	

ENVIRONMENT DIVISION

Language Element	OS COBOL	COBOL II	Comments
(CONFIGURATION SECTION)			
SPECIAL-NAMES	Y	Y	Differences in names supported (see Ch. 5)

(INPUT-OUTPUT SECTION, FILE-CONTROL)

NOMINAL KEY	Y	N	ISAM not supported
FILE STATUS	Y	Y	New second field with extended status
RESERVE	Y	Y	COBOL II does not support ALTERNATE AREAS
TRACK-AREA	Y	N	ISAM not supported
FILE-LIMITS	Y	N	OS COBOL ignored

PROCESSING MODE	Y	N	OS COBOL ignored
(INPUT-OUTPUT SECTION, I-O-CONTROL)			
RERUN	Y	Y	COBOL II takes no checkpoint on the first record

DATA DIVISION

Language Element	OS COBOL	COBOL II	Comments
(FILE SECTION, FD Entry)			
LABEL RECORDS	Y	Y	TOTALING AREA and TOTALED AREA no longer supported
REPORT IS	Y	N	COBOL II does not support Report Writer
Report Writer FD entry	Y	N	COBOL II does not support Report Writer
(Data Description)			
OCCURS	Y	Y	COBOL II calculates length of ODO items differently
USAGE	Y	Y	POINTER, DISPLAY-1 are new. DISPLAY-ST is dropped.

PROCEDURE DIVISION

Language Element	OS COBOL	COBOL II	Comments
ACCEPT	Y	Y	COBOL II can ACCEPT from SYSIPT
ACCEPT MESSAGE COUNT	Y	N	COBOL II does not support ANSI Communication module
ADD	Y	Y	New END-ADD option
CALL	Y	Y	New BY REFERENCE, BY CONTENT: deleted USING procedure-name
CLOSE	Y	Y	FOR REMOVAL, POSITIONAL and DISP options are ignored
COMPUTE	Y	Y	New END-COMPUTE option
DELETE	Y	Y	New END-DELETE option
DISABLE	Y	N	No Communication module
DIVIDE	Y	Y	New END-DIVIDE option
ENABLE	Y	N	No Communication module

EVALUATE	N	Y	
EXAMINE	Y	N	Use INSPECT
EXHIBIT	Y	N	Use DISPLAY
GENERATE	Y	N	No Report Writer
IF	Y	Y	No OTHERWISE. New END-IF option.
INITIALIZE	N	Y	
INITIATE	Y	N	No Report Writer
MULTIPLY	Y	Y	New END-MULTIPLY option
NOTE	Y	N	
ON	Y	N	
OPEN	Y	Y	LEAVE, REREAD, DISP options not allowed
PERFORM	Y	Y	New in-line perform, new END-PERFORM option, new TEST BEFORE/AFTER options
READ	Y	Y	New END-READ option
READY TRACE	Y	N	Ignored by COBOL II
RECEIVE	Y	N	No Communication module
RESET TRACE	Y	N	Ignored
RETURN	Y	Y	New END-RETURN option
REWRITE	Y	Y	New END-REWRITE option
SEARCH	Y	Y	New END-SEARCH. Some restrictions on WHEN conditions (see Ch. 5).
SEEK	Y	N	OS COBOL ignored
SEND	Y	N	No Communication module
SET	Y	Y	New SET . . . TO TRUE. New SET pointer.
START	Y	Y	New END-START option. USING phrase dropped.
STRING	Y	Y	New option END-STRING
SUBTRACT	Y	Y	New option END-SUBTRACT
TERMINATE	Y	N	No Report Writer
TRANSFORM	Y	N	Use INSPECT
UNSTRING	Y	Y	New option END-UNSTRING. Cannot now unstring into numeric edited fields.
WRITE	Y	Y	No AFTER POSITIONING. New option END-WRITE. Cannot use on sequential files opened for I-O.

Compiler-Directing Statements

Language Element	OS COBOL	COBOL II	Comments
*CBL	N	Y	
*CONTROL	N	Y	
COPY	Y	Y	New nested copies. Some change in syntax. COBOL II block size file order limit.
SERVICE LABEL	N	Y	
TITLE	N	Y	

Declaratives

Language Element	OS COBOL	COBOL II	Comments
USE AFTER EXCEPTION/ERROR	Y	Y	GIVING option dropped: Use FILE STATUS.
USE BEFORE REPORTING	Y	N	No Report Writer
USE BEFORE STANDARD	Y	N	

Special Registers

Language Element	OS COBOL	COBOL II	Comments
ADDRESS	N	Y	
CURRENT-DATE	Y	N	Use ACCEPT . . . DATE
LENGTH	N	Y	
PAGE-COUNTER	Y	N	No Report Writer
SHIFT-IN	N	Y	
SHIFT-OUT	N	Y	
SORT-CONTROL	N	Y	
TIME-OF-DAY	Y	N	Use ACCEPT . . . TIME
WHEN-COMPILED	Y	Y	Format changed

COMPILER LIMITS

The following table compares the compiler limits of OS COBOL, Release 2, and COBOL II. Not all limits are given here; those which are unchanged from OS COBOL and rarely encountered, for instance, the limits on the SPECIAL-NAMES paragraph, are omitted for reasons of clarity. INF means infinite (no limit).

Limits on a particular system may be less because of operating system or resource limitations. For instance, there is no COBOL-imposed limit to the length of a record key but the only keyed file system available is VSAM, which has a 255-byte limit.

In COBOL II, the literal pool and Procedure Division together have a 4-Mb limit. These two elements previously had separate limits of 32K and 1Mb respectively.

Language Element	OS COBOL	COBOL II
Program size	1M lines	1M lines
Number of literals	16Kb	4Mb
Total length of literals	32Kb	4Mb
Items replaced in		
COPY REPLACING	150	INF
Select statements	64K	64K
RECORD KEY length	255	INF
BLOCK CONTAINS	32K	1Mb
RECORD CONTAINS	32K	1Mb
Item length	32K	1Mb
Working-storage section	1M	128Mb
77 datanames	1M	16Mb
01-49 datanames	1M	16Mb
88 condition names	INF	INF
VALUE	INF	INF
66 renames	INF	INF
PICTURE	30	30
Numeric item digits	18	18
Numeric-edited chars	127	249
PIC replication ()	99999	16M
PIC repl, editing	99999	32767
Group items	32/131K	16M
Elementary items	32K	16M
Total, all VALUEs	64K	16M
OCCURS	32K	16M
Number of ODOs	64K	4M
Table size	32K	16M
Table element	32K	8M
Number of keys	12	12
Total length of keys	256	256
Indexes on table	12	12

Total indexes	64K	64K
Linkage section	1M	128M
Total data items	255	INF
Procedure division	1M	4M (less literals)
USING identifier	INF	32K
Procedure-names	64K	1M
EVALUATE subjects		64
WHEN clauses		256
GO TO DEPENDING	2031	255
PERFORM	64K	4M
SORT/MERGE keys	12	INF
Total key length	256	4092
USING files	16	16
UNSTRING ids	15	255

C

Reserved Words

This appendix contains three tables. The first is a list of the reserved words deleted from OS COBOL. The second is a list of the new words introduced with COBOL II. The third is a list of all the reserved words in COBOL II.

The following table is a list of all reserved words in OS COBOL which are no longer supported in COBOL II. Some of these are flagged as an error, while others are simply no longer a reserved word.

Deleted OS COBOL Reserved Words

E = Error in COBOL II
N = No longer a reserved word in COBOL II

ACTUAL	E		EXAMINE	E
BASIS	E		EXHIBIT	E
CONSOLE	N		FILE-LIMIT	E
CORE-INDEX	E		FILE-LIMITS	E
CSP	N		INSERT	E
CURRENT-DATE	E		LEAVE	E
C01 . . . C12		N	NOMINAL	E
DEBUG	E		NOTE	E
DISP	E		OTHERWISE	E
DISPLAY-ST	E		POSITIONING	E

PROCESS	N	S01	N
RECORD-OVERFLOW	E	S02	N
REMARKS	E	TIME-OF-DAY	E
REORG-CRITERIA	E	TOTALED	E
REREAD	E	TOTALING	E
SEEK	E	TRACK-AREA	E
SELECTIVE	E	TRACK-LIMIT	E
SYSIN	N	TRACKS	E
SYSOUT	N	TRANSFORM	E
SYSPUNCH	N	UPSI-0 . . . UPSI-7	N

The following table contains all the new reserved words introduced with COBOL II.

New Reserved Words in COBOL II

ALPHABETIC	END-SEARCH
ALPHANUMERIC	END-START
ALPHANUMERIC-EDITED	END-STRING
ANY	END-SUBTRACT
BINARY	END-UNSTRING
CLASS	END-WRITE
COBOL	EVALUATE
COMMON	EXTERNAL
COM-REG	FALSE
CONTENT	GLOBAL
CONTINUE	INITIALIZE
CONVERTING	KANJI
DAY-OF-WEEK	NULL
DBCS	NULLS
EGCS	NUMERIC-EDITED
END-ADD	ORDER
END-CALL	OTHER
END-COMPUTE	PACKED-DECIMAL
END-DELETE	PADDING
END-DIVIDE	REFERENCE
END-EVALUATE	REPLACE
END-IF	SHIFT-IN
END-MULTIPLY	SHIFT-OUT
END-PERFORM	SORT-CONTROL
END-READ	TEST
END-RETURN	TITLE
END-REWRITE	TRUE

The following table contains all reserved words in COBOL II. Some words have no real function in this implementation, but are reserved for compatibility with other systems. These are flagged C, E, or N. New words are marked with an asterisk.

Reserved Words in COBOL II

C	=	Codasyl standard reserved word not implemented
E	=	OS COBOL reserved word, flagged as error
N	=	ANSI 85 COBOL reserved word not implemented
*	=	Reserved word introduced with COBOL II

ACCEPT			BEGINNING	
ACCESS			B-EXOR	C
ACTUAL	E		BINARY	*
ADD			BIT	*
ADDRESS			BITS	*
ADVANCING			BLANK	
AFTER			BLOCK	
ALL			B-NOT	C
ALPHABET	*		B-OR	C
ALPHABETIC			BOOLEAN	*
ALPHABETIC-LOWER	*		BOTTOM	
ALPHABETIC-UPPER	*		BY	
ALPHANUMERIC	*		CALL	
ALPHANUMERIC-EDITED	*		CANCEL	
ALSO			CBL	
ALTER			CD	N
ALTERNATE			CF	N
AND			CH	N
ANY	*		CHANGED	
APPLY			CHARACTER	
ARE			CHARACTERS	
AREA			CLASS	*
AREAS			CLOCK-UNITS	N
ARITHMETIC	*		CLOSE	
ASCENDING			COBOL	*
ASSIGN			CODE	
AT			CODE-SET	
AUTHOR			COLLATING	
B-AND	C		COLUMN	N
BASIS	E		COMMA	
BEFORE			COMMIT	C

COMMON	*	DATE-COMPILED	
COMMUNICATION	N	DATE-WRITTEN	
COMP		DAY	
COMP-1		DAY-OF-WEEK	*
COMP-2		DB	C
COMP-3		DB-ACCESS-CONTROL-KEY	C
COMP-4		DBCS	C
COMP-5	N	DB-DATA-NAME	C
COMP-6	N	DB-EXCEPTION	C
COMP-7	N	DB-RECORD-NAME	C
COMP-8	N	DB-SET-NAME	C
COMP-9	N	DB-STATUS	C
COMPUTATIONAL		DE	N
COMPUTATIONAL-1		DEBUG	E
COMPUTATIONAL-2		DEBUG-CONTENTS	
COMPUTATIONAL-3		DEBUGGING	
COMPUTATIONAL-4		DEBUG-ITEM	
COMPUTATIONAL-5	N	DEBUG-LINE	
COMPUTATIONAL-6	N	DEBUG-NAME	
COMPUTATIONAL-7	N	DEBUG-SUB-1	
COMPUTATIONAL-8	N	DEBUG-SUB-2	
COMPUTATIONAL-9	N	DEBUG-SUB-3	
COMPUTE		DECIMAL-POINT	
COM-REG	*	DECLARATIVES	
CONFIGURATION		DEFAULT	C
CONNECT	N	DELETE	
CONTAINED	N	DELIMITED	
CONTAINS		DELIMITER	
CONTENT	*	DEPENDING	
CONTINUE	*	DESCENDING	
CONTROL	N	DESTINATION	N
CONTROLS	N	DETAIL	N
CONVERTING	*	DISABLE	N
COPY		DISCONNECT	C
CORE-INDEX	E	DISP	E
CORR		DISPLAY	
CORRESPONDING		DISPLAY-ST	E
COUNT		DISPLAY-1	
CURRENCY		DISPLAY-2	N
CURRENT	C	DISPLAY-3	N
CURRENT-DATE	E	DISPLAY-4	N
DATA		DISPLAY-5	N
DATE		DISPLAY-6	N

DISPLAY-7	N	ENVIRONMENT	
DISPLAY-8	N	EOP	
DISPLAY-9	N	EQUAL	
DIVIDE		EQUALS	C
DIVISION		ERASE	C
DOWN		ERROR	
DUPLICATE	C	ESI	N
DUPLICATES		EVALUATE	*
DYNAMIC		EVERY	
EGCS	*	EXACT	C
EGI	N	EXAMINE	E
EJECT		EXCEEDS	C
ELSE		EXCEPTION	
EMI	N	EXCLUSIVE	C
EMPTY	C	EXHIBIT	E
ENABLE	N	EXIT	
END		EXOR	N
END-ADD	*	EXTEND	
END-CALL	*	EXTERNAL	*
END-COMPUTE	*	FALSE	*
END-DELETE	*	FD	
END-DISABLE	C	FETCH	C
END-DIVIDE	*	FILE	
END-ENABLE	C	FILE-CONTROL	
END-EVALUATE	*	FILE-LIMIT	E
END-IF	*	FILE-LIMITS	E
ENDING		FILES	C
END-MULTIPLY	*	FILLER	
END-OF-PAGE		FINAL	
END-PERFORM	*	FIND	C
END-READ	*	FINISH	C
END-RECEIVE	N	FIRST	
END-RETURN	*	FOOTING	
END-REWRITE	*	FOR	
END-SEARCH	*	FORMAT	C
END-START	*	FREE	C
END-STRING	*	FROM	
END-SUBTRACT	*	FUNCTION	C
END-TRANSCEIVE	C	GENERATE	
END-UNSTRING	*	GET	N
END-WRITE	*	GIVING	
ENTER		GLOBAL	
ENTRY		GO	

GOBACK			LEADING	
GREATER			LEAVE	E
GROUP	N		LEFT	
HEADING	N		LENGTH	
HIGH-VALUE			LESS	N
HIGH-VALUES			LIMIT	N
ID			LIMITS	
IDENTIFICATION			LINAGE	
IF			LINAGE-COUNTER	
IN			LINE	
INDEX			LINE-COUNTER	N
INDEXED			LINES	
INDEX-1	C		LINKAGE	
INDEX-2	C		LOCALLY	C
INDEX-3	C		LOCK	
INDEX-4	C		LOW-VALUE	
INDEX-5	C		LOW-VALUES	
INDEX-6	C		MEMBER	C
INDEX-7	C		MEMORY	
INDEX-8	C		MERGE	
INDEX-9	C		MESSAGE	N
INDICATE			MODE	
INITIAL	N		MODIFY	C
INITIALIZE	*		MODULES	
INITIATE	N		MORE-LABELS	
INPUT			MOVE	
INPUT-OUTPUT			MULTIPLE	
INSERT	E		MULTIPLY	
INSPECT			NAMED	
INSTALLATION			NATIVE	
INTO			NEGATIVE	
INVALID			NEXT	
I-O			NO	
I-O-CONTROL			NOMINAL	E
IS			NONE	C
JUST			NOT	
JUSTIFIED			NOTE	E
KANJI	*		NULL	*
KEEP	C		NULLS	*
KEY			NUMBER	N
LABEL			NUMERIC	
LAST	N		NUMERIC-EDITED	*
LD	C		OBJECT-COMPUTER	

OCCURS			QUEUE	N
OF			QUOTE	
OFF			QUOTES	
OMITTED			RANDOM	
ON			RD	N
ONLY	C		READ	
OPEN			READY	
OPTIONAL			REALM	C
OR			RECEIVE	
ORDER	*		RECONNECT	C
ORGANIZATION			RECORD	N
OTHER	*		RECORDING	
OTHERWISE	E		RECORD-NAME	C
OUTPUT			RECORD-OVERFLOW	E
OVERFLOW			RECORDS	
OWNER	C		REDEFINES	
PACKED-DECIMAL	*		REEL	
PADDING	*		REFERENCE	*
PAGE			REFERENCES	
PAGE-COUNTER	N		RELATION	C
PARAGRAPH	C		RELATIVE	
PASSWORD			RELEASE	
PERFORM			RELOAD	
PF	N		REMAINDER	
PH	N		REMARKS	E
PIC			REMOVAL	
PICTURE			RENAMES	
PLUS	N		REORG-CRITERIA	E
POINTER			REPEATED	C
POSITION			REPLACE	*
POSITIONING	E		REPLACING	
POSITIVE			REPORT	N
PRESENT	C		REPORTING	N
PRINTING	N		REPORTS	N
PRIOR	C		REREAD	E
PROCEDURE			RERUN	
PROCEDURES			RESERVE	
PROCEED			RESET	
PROCESSING			RETAINING	C
PROGRAM			RETRIEVAL	C
PROGRAM-ID			RETURN	
PROTECTED	C		RETURN-CODE	
PURGE	N		REVERSED	

REWIND		SOURCE-COMPUTER	
REWRITE		SPACE	
RF	N	SPACES	
RH	N	SPECIAL-NAMES	
RIGHT		STANDARD	
ROLLBACK	C	STANDARD-1	
ROUNDED		STANDARD-2	*
RUN		STANDARD-3	C
SAME		STANDARD-4	C
SD		START	
SEARCH		STATUS	
SECTION		STOP	
SECURITY		STORE	C
SEEK	E	STRING	
SEGMENT	N	SUB-QUEUE-1	N
SEGMENT-LIMIT		SUB-QUEUE-2	N
SELECT		SUB-QUEUE-3	N
SELECTIVE	E	SUB-SCHEMA	C
SEND	N	SUBTRACT	
SENTENCE		SUM	N
SEPARATE		SUPPRESS	
SEQUENCE		SYMBOLIC	
SEQUENTIAL		SYNC	
SERVICE		SYNCHRONIZED	
SESSION-ID	C	TABLE	N
SET		TALLY	
SHARED	C	TALLYING	
SHIFT-IN	*	TAPE	
SHIFT-OUT	*	TENANT	C
SIGN		TERMINAL	N
SIZE		TERMINATE	N
SKIP1		TEST	*
SKIP2		TEXT	N
SKIP3		THAN	
SORT		THEN	
SORT-CONTROL	*	THROUGH	
SORT-CORE-SIZE		THRU	
SORT-FILE-SIZE		TIME	
SORT-MERGE		TIME-OF-DAY	E
SORT-MESSAGE		TIMES	
SORT-MODE-SIZE		TITLE	N
SORT-RETURN		TO	
SOURCE	N	TOP	

TOTALED	E	USE	
TOTALING	E	USING	
TRACE		VALID	C
TRACK-AREA	E	VALIDATE	C
TRACK-LIMIT	E	VALUE	
TRACKS	E	VALUES	
TRAILING		VARYING	
TRANSCEIVE	C	WAIT	C
TRANSFORM	E	WHEN	
TRUE	*	WHEN-COMPILED	
TYPE	N	WITH	
UNEQUAL	C	WITHIN	C
UNIT		WORDS	
UNSTRING		WORKING-STORAGE	
UNTIL		WRITE	
UP		WRITE-ONLY	
UPDATE	A	ZERO	
UPON		ZEROES	
USAGE		ZEROS	
USAGE-MODE	C		

D

Alphabetic Reference of Compiler Options

In the entries that follow, the permitted abbreviation is capitalized. The IBM default is underlined.

ADV

ADV   Adds one byte to the record length of files which use WRITE AFTER ADVANCING, to contain the printer control character

NOADV   Assumes that a printer control character is included in the record layout of files which use AFTER ADVANCING

APOST

APOST   This option, which is the opposite of QUOTE, informs the compile that the single quote character (') will be used for literals

BUFSIZE

BUF(nnnnn | nnnK)   Allocates the amount of buffer storage for compiler work data sets

BUF(4096)

BUF(4096)

COMPILE

Compile   Full compilation, regardless of errors

NOCompile   Syntax check only

NOCompile(W | E | S)   Full compilation, unless an error of the given severity is detected, when only syntax checking occurs from that point

NOC(S)

DATA

DATA(24)   Ensures that data areas such as working storage are acquired from below the line, so that parameters can be passed to 24-bit programs

DATA(31)   Allows data areas to be acquired from any available storage, usually above the line

DECK

Deck   Produce object code on SYSPUNCH

NODeck   Do not produce object code on SYSPUNCH

DUMP

DUmp   Produces a system dump at compile time. Do not use this option.

NODUmp   Does not produce a system dump. Use this.

DYNAM

DYNam   Causes CALL literal statements in the program to be resolved dynamically

NODYNam   Causes CALL literal statements to be resolved statically

FASTSRT

FaStsoRT   Allows DFSORT to perform the I/O for certain sort statements. This is more efficient than COBOL I/O.

NOFaStsoRT   Does not allow faster sorting

FDUMP

FDUmp   This option causes the compiler to generate a formatted dump when an abend occurs.

NOFDUmp   This option causes a normal, unformatted dump to be generated when an abend occurs.

FLAG

Flag(x, [y])   The FLAG option determines the printing of error messages. The first option (x) determines which messages are printed at the end of the listing. The second option (y) determines which messages are printed embedded in the source listing. Both x and y can have the values I, W, E, S, or U.

NOFlag   Suppress the printing of error messages

FLAG(I)

LIB

LIB   The LIB option specifies that the program will use COPY or BASIS statements, which will refer to libraries in SYSLIB.

NOLIB   This means the program will not use COPY or BASIS statements.

LINECOUNT

LineCount   Specifies number of lines on each page of the compiler listing

LC(60)

LIST

LIST   The LIST option causes the compiler to generate an Assembly language listing of the Procedure Division. This also includes global tables, literal pools, working-storage information, and program statistics.

NOLIST   No assembly listing

MAP

MAP   The MAP option causes the compiler to produce a Data Division listing and map. This also includes global tables, literal pools, and program statistics.

NOMAP   No Data Division listing

NUMBER

NUMber   Number directs the compiler to use the numbers in columns 1–6 of the source code in error message and MAP, LIST, and XREF listings.

NONUMber   NONUMBER directs the compiler to generate line numbers for the source code and use these in its messages and listings.

OBJECT

OBJect   Produce object code on SYSLIN

NOOBJect   Does not produce object code on SYSLIN.

OFFSET

OFFset   The OFFSET option causes the compiler to generate a condensed listing (similar to OS COBOL CLIST). This option suppresses LIST. Using this option, the Procedure Division source listing will include line numbers and the location of the first assembly instruction of each statement.

NOOFFset   Does not generate a condensed listing.

OPTIMIZE

OPTimize   Reduces the run time of the generated program, but increases compile time

NOOPTimize   Faster compile, slower program

OUTDD

OUTdd(ddname)   Redirects display from SYSOUT

OUTDD(SYSOUT)

PFDSGN

PFDsgn   Tells the compiler to assume that all numeric fields have the correct sign, X"C" or X"D" for signed fields and X"F" for unsigned. This improves processing speed slightly. If this option is used, care must be taken to ensure that this is true. Use of redefinitions or group moves may generate the wrong sign.

NOPFDsgn   Does not assume correct signs

QUOTE

Quote   This option informs the compiler that the double quote (") will be used for literals. This conforms to the ANSI standard. The alternative to QUOTE is APOST.

RENT

RENT   Generates reentrant code

NORENT   Does not generate reentrant code

RESIDENT

RESident   Requests the Cobol Library Management Feature

NORESident   Does not request this feature

SEQUENCE

SEQuence   Causes compiler to check the sequence of the numbers in columns 1–6 of the source, and issues a warning message if they are out of sequence. This option uses an alphanumeric collating sequence if NONUM is set, or a numeric collating sequence if NUM is set.

NOSEQuence   Does not check sequence numbers

SIZE

SiZe(nnnnn | nnnK | MAX)   Specifies the amount of memory to be used by the compiler. The minimum is 512K. MAX will use all available storage

SZ(MAX)

SOURCE

Source   Causes the compiler to print a source listing

NOSource   Suppresses source listing

SPACE

SPACE(1 | 2 | 3)   Selects single, double, or triple spacing of the source code listing

SPACE(1)

SSRANGE

SSRange   Generates code which tests all array references to ensure that they are within bounds (discussed in Chapter 16)

NOSSRange   Does not generate array-bounds checking code

TERMINAL

TERMinal   Causes compiler to send messages to SYSTERM. This option is used with TSO foreground compilations.

NOTERMinal   Does not use SYSTERM

TEST

TESt   The TEST option causes object code to be generated which can be used with the COBTEST debugger. This option implies NOFDUMP, OBJECT, NOOPTIMIZE, and RES.

NOTESt   Causes object code to be generated without support for COBTEST.

TRUNC

TRUnc   Truncates binary (COMP) fields to conform to their PIC during arithmetic and MOVE statements. Conforms to ANSI standard.

NOTRUnc   Treats binary fields as halfword or fullword binary, without truncation. Recommended for CICS programs.

VBREF

VBREF   This option cross-references all verb types and the line numbers where they are used, and counts how many times each verb was used.

NOVBREF   No verb reference

WORD

WorD   The option WORD(xxxx) specifies that a user-supplied reserved word table will be used in compilation. This table must have the name IGYCxxxx.

NOWorD   Specifies that no user-supplied reserved word table is in use

XREF

Xref   The XREF option produces a sorted cross-reference listing (similar to OS COBOL SXREF)

NOXref   No cross reference

ZWB

ZWB   Ignores the sign when comparing PIC 9 and PIC X items, as when testing a numeric field for spaces. Conforms to ANSI standard.

NOZWB   Does not ignore signs in this way

Index